D1012943

pages from
HOPI
HISTORY

pages from

Harry C. James

HOPI
HISTORY

The University of Arizona Press
Tucson, Arizona

About the Author . . .

HARRY C. JAMES has for half a century been known both for his devotion to the conservation of the natural environment and for his interest in the welfare of the American Indian. A founder of the Indian Welfare League and the National Association to Help the Indian, James has used his perceptivity to foster productive relationships between the Indians and others involved in activities relating to the increasingly important cause of conservation. He was involved in several of the dramatic events reported in this book, including the sheep-dip bathing incident on June 10, 1920. James has written several books about Indians: *Treasure of the Hopitu*, 1927; *Haliksai! Hopi Legends of Grand Canyon Country*, 1940; *The Hopi Indians*, 1956; *Red Man, White Man*, 1958; *The Cahuilla Indians*, 1960; and in 1973, *Western Campfires.*

THE UNIVERSITY OF ARIZONA PRESS

Copyright © 1974
The Arizona Board of Regents
All Rights Reserved
Manufactured in the U.S.A.

I.S.B.N. 0–8165–0325–7 Cloth
I.S.B.N. 0–8165–0500–4 Paper
L.C. No. 73–86451

As always,
this must be for Grace

Acknowledgments

MUCH OF THE INFORMATION which I have included in this book came from old Hopi friends as we sat around countless campfires in Tusayan or on the edge of the Oraibi mesa at sunset time with the wide sweep of the Painted Desert below and the purple-black silhouette of the Mountains of the Kachinas against the far western horizon. Not until night was almost upon us and the skimming nighthawks pierced the silence with their shrill cries would our silence be broken. Then the stories would start and continue on and on until the wide arch of the sky would be powdered with stars.

Still more of their traditional history I learned while on walks with Tewaquaptewa of Old Oraibi into the Grand Canyon, and when we visited the Pacific Ocean, that "mother of rains," where we scattered cornmeal and pollen upon the waves breaking over the wet sands.

More stories came from Hopi friends as we climbed together in the San Jacinto Mountains of California to gain views of and make prayers to that same "mother of rains" for good rains *for all people*. After dinner these friends would pull our big cottonwood log drum before the fireplace and our log cabin would echo with one Hopi song after another before our long talks began.

It was nearly always the desire of these Hopi friends that their names should not be used if I ever wrote and published the things they told me. To be singled out from the Hopi community is contrary to the Hopi way of life. With reluctance I have deferred to their wishes, but I am deeply indebted to all of them.

Among the many Hopi of a later generation to whom I am indebted are Hubert Honanie, Fred Kabotie, Jim Kewanytewa, Pierce Kewanytewa, Anthony and Poli Numkema, Peter Nuvamsa, Myron Polequaptewa, Willard Sakiestewa, and Don Talayestewa.

I have also profited very richly from long friendship with the late Frederick Webb Hodge, who knew and understood the American Indian as few, if any other, authorities have. He knew the Hopi well and was particularly devoted to them.

Charles Fletcher Lummis, Edward S. Curtis, Jesse Walter Fewkes, and more recently, Walter V. Woehlke — all deceased — were generous in sharing with me the benefit of their extensive knowledge of the Hopi.

Even with all the information I have obtained from these many friends and from the innumerable published sources mentioned in the text and the bibliography, this book would have been impossible without the encouragement and assistance of the Museum of Northern Arizona — the late Harold S. Colton, its Founder and longtime President, Edward B. Danson, Director, Barton Wright, Curator, Katharine Bartlett, Curator of History and Librarian.

John G. Babbitt, Lynn R. Bailey, William Brandon, Glen Dawson, Charles Di Peso, Martha Dyck (daughter of H. R. Voth), Michael Harrison, Byron Harvey III, Barclay Kamb, Edwin McKee, Don Perceval, Carl Sharsmith, Edward H. Spicer, and Mischa Titiev — all have been most considerate in answering my many inquiries.

Various officials of the Bureau of Indian Affairs in both Phoenix and Washington also have been most helpful. I must thank particularly T. W. Taylor, and William B. Benge of the Washington office, and David M. Brugge, Curator, Hubbell Trading Post, National Historic Site.

The following organizations have my gratitude for their prompt replies to my queries for information within their sphere of interest: The staff of the Banning, California, Public Library; Bethel College Historical Library (Mennonite), Board on Geographic Names, Department of the Interior; University of California Libraries at both Berkeley and Riverside; the Field Museum, Department of Anthropology; the Huntington Library; the National Archives–General Services Administration; the Riverside, California, City and County Library; the Smithsonian Institution Archives; the Southwest Museum; Ganado Presbyterian Mission; and the Presbyterian Historical Society.

Finally my deep appreciation for the patience and the excellent work of Director Marshall Townsend and the editorial staff of the University of Arizona Press. To them a sincere "Kwa Kwa!"

HARRY C. JAMES
(*Honauwayma*; Walking Bear)

Contents

ILLUSTRATIONS

A Word From the Author

THE HOPI INDIANS are so different in so many ways from most of the Indian tribes of the Americas that the question often arises, even among the Hopi themselves, as to who these "peaceful people" are. Where did they come from? How did their unique way of life come about?

However, those who have come to know the Hopi well understand why so many people — including this author — have been impelled to write about them.

Government reports, scientific journals, journals kept by explorers and missionaries, magazine articles, newspaper stories, television reports and even movies, and personal reminiscences about experiences in the Hopi country are so massive in quantity as to bewilder and confuse and to seem totally out of all proportion to the size of the Hopi community of villages.

Most of this material is to be found only in the specialized collections of a limited number of libraries scattered throughout the country, and is not available to the general reader. For this reason several Hopi friends requested that we attempt to set down an account of some of the more significant events in the history of their people. They felt that such an account would be of interest to the general reader, and of particular value to their own young people, who in today's rapidly changing world have scant opportunity to learn their historic background from the stories of their "uncles" and other wise old Hopi as they would have learned it in the past.

The Hopi are the westernmost of the Pueblo Indians whose villages are a conspicuous and interesting part of the Southwestern scene. In search of peace and security from aggressive, warlike neighbors, ancestors of the present Hopi built their villages on high, precipitous mesa tops in the colorful part of northern Arizona called the Painted Desert.

Because it is both euphonious and convenient we frequently use the term "Tusayan" in referring to the Hopi country, although we do so with misgivings. The word apparently is derived from "Tuçano" which Coronado understood to be the name of one of the Hopi villages. Tusayan was commonly used by early Spanish explorers, gold-seekers, and Franciscan priests, and later by American anthropologists.

In nearly all the older published accounts of the Hopi we find them referred to as the "Moqui." This is most unfortunate, as the word is a term of derision never used by the Hopi themselves. The origin of the term is somewhat obscure, but it was widely used by the first white people to come in contact with the Hopi — the Spaniards — and was perpetuated by writers from that time until the modern period.

Among the many unique aspects of the Hopi is their name for themselves, *Hopitu-Shinumu*. It can best be translated as "all people peaceful" or "little people of peace," which is quite unlike the aggressive names by which many peoples designate themselves. At this point it might not be amiss to state that the Hopi have developed many behavior patterns which militate against their aggressions and have many traditional ways of meeting aggression.

The spoken language of the Hopi belongs to the great Uto-Aztecan linguistic family. The complexities and richness of the Hopi language demonstrate the high intelligence of the people who speak it. Intelligence tests given Hopi children have shown them to rate well above the average of white children in the United States.

People who have always pictured the Indian as a tall, haughty, uncommunicative, war-bonneted horseman are often surprised when they meet the Hopi, for they are a short, mild-mannered, simply dressed people. Many of their children and young people are decidedly handsome, and the older people are usually very dignified, striking personalities. They are friendly, but inclined to reticence with strangers. Although they are a "peaceful people," they are by no means timid, as their history certainly proves.

To most people, both Indian and white, the Hopi are best known for their highly dramatic and picturesque religious observances, such as those performed by the Snake and Antelope priests and the various kachina rites. To call these ceremonials "dances" gives a most misleading impression of their true nature, for they are in fact rich in symbolism and in poetic and colorful interpretation of ancient Hopi tradition. They reflect the tenacity with which the Hopi hold to their traditional way of life.

The depth of Hopi feeling for their own religious beliefs and observances proved baffling and exasperating to early Spanish explorers and missionaries. Their determination to keep their own way of life made the work of missionaries futile and was one of the reasons why much of that period was such an unpeaceful one. A very few Hopi became converts to Christianity, but they were dubbed "Kahopi," *not* Hopi, a very opprobious term in their language, which is singularly lacking in such terms. Why indeed should a people of peace be expected to change and become followers of a "Prince of Peace" who had no meaning for them, especially when their basic tenets were much the same? It is a question which still awaits an answer.

Like all peoples of the world, the Hopi have their own myths, legends and theories of the creation of the universe and their place in history following that creation. Most societies, however, have had written languages with which to perpetuate standardized concepts of their traditional beliefs. The Hopi have not. Small wonder then that the legends bearing on certain Hopi traditions are so many and so varied as to detail. The greater wonder is that they are recognizably similar!

Although not a secretive people, most leaders of Hopi ceremonial life have become increasingly reluctant to impart to the white man the legendary stories so basic to an understanding of the beginnings of their history. Only too often when they shared their knowledge with white visitors they later found, to their deep chagrin, that the resulting versions were sadly garbled or even purposely distorted.

Furthermore, few scientists have gone into the Hopi country who were fluent in the Hopi language. Many Hopi interpreters were far from adept in English. This language barrier has made it difficult to find in the published record accounts which meet with general approval among Hopi leaders of today.

Even respected authorities who have published stories of the Hopi clan system have not been in complete accord regarding them. Talks with Hopi friends on all three mesas have served only too well to underline the fact that there is disagreement among the Hopi on this subject.

It is impossible within the scope of this work to give more than a single variation of Hopi traditional stories of the creation of the universe, the emergence of the people from the "Underworld," and the migrations of the many clans. The versions set forth herein are a synthesis of the most reliable published accounts of scholars who worked among the Hopi and were trusted by them. An effort has been made to glean essential elements from the various accounts and to weave them into a generally valid tale which may be as acceptable as possible to the Hopi.

Only a relatively few of the more important clans and clan societies in Hopi history are dealt with in the book. The reader should keep in mind that never did all clans exist in any one Hopi village, and that many of the earlier clans are now extinct; in fact, in some cases the Hopi have resorted to widespread adoption practices in order to help preserve valuable ceremonies possessed by clans in danger of dying out.

By necessity all Hopi words are spelled phonetically, so no uniformity of spelling has ever been achieved. The results are confusing. However, under date of December 3, 1952, the Board on Geographic

Names, Department of the Interior, recommended the following spellings for the names of various Hopi villages:

Bacobi	Mishongnovi	Oraibi	Shipolovi	Sichimovi
Hotevila	Moencopi	Polacca	Shongopovi	Walpi

For an appreciation of the extent of the problem, be advised that in his *Handbook of American Indians,* Hodge lists more than two dozen spellings for Oraibi.

H. C. J.

Haliksai!
This Is How It Was

THE LEGENDARY WORLD of Hopi origins lay deep below the surface of today's earth. This may seem strange to people brought up with the concept that the world below is not by any means a place of heavenly bliss but one of hellish damnation. When one stops to realize that the dominant features of the vast region of the Hopi world are the magnificent and mysterious landscapes of the Grand Canyon of the Colorado River it is not surprising that the Hopi concept of heaven should be an ideal nether world.

In the beginning the wide Underworld beneath the present world was one vast sea, the Hopi have told their descendants down through the ages. Far to the east and to the west lived two female deities — the owners of such precious things as seashells, coral, and turquoise. Each of these Hurung Whuti, as the Hopi called them, lived in a house similar to a kiva in the Hopi village of today. The Hurung Whuti of the East had one gray and one yellow fox skin tied to the top of the high ladder which led down into her kiva-like house, while that of the deity of the West had a large turtle-shell rattle.

Every day Sun dressed for the early morning in the gray fox skin, and for the full day he donned the skin of the yellow fox. He rose from the north end of the kiva of the Hurung Whuti of the East, slowly passed over the waters of the Underworld, and, after touching the turtle-shell rattle on her ladder, he descended into the kiva of the Hurung Whuti of the West.

Eventually the two Hurung Whuti decided there should be some dry land in the Underworld, and parted the waters so that land appeared. But Sun could discover no sign of life upon it and he reported this to the Hurung Whuti of the East, who journeyed over a great rainbow to confer with her sister of the West. After a long council they decided that they would create life. They took clay and fashioned a small wren. Placing a piece of cloth over the wren, they sang certain songs which imparted life to it.

[1]

Then they instructed Wren to fly here, there, and everywhere over their newly created land to see if it could find any signs of other life. Wren failed to see Spider Woman, the deity of the earth, who lived in her kiva home away to the southwest — so he reported that the whole land was barren.

Thereupon, the Hurung Whuti of the West created many birds and animals in the same way as the wren had been created. She sent them out to inhabit the earth. As her sister had created the birds and the animals, the Hurung Whuti of the East created a man and woman out of the same kind of clay and covered them with the same cloth. Again the Hurung Whuti sang their special songs, and the man and the woman were endowed with life. The two Hurung Whuti taught the man and the woman a language, and the deity of the East led them back over the rainbow to her home. There they lived for a short time before they and their children wandered out over the eastern land to make homes of their own.

While the Hurung Whuti were busy creating the birds, the animals, and the first man and woman, Spider Woman decided that she, too, would create men and women. Thereupon she gave life to all kinds of people, and with the help of Mockingbird (Yaupa) taught each group its own language before sending it off to live throughout the Underworld.

After a council with her sister, the Hurung Whuti of the West decided that she must create more people to inhabit the lands of the West. These were the ancestors of the Hopi. After this was accomplished the Hurung Whuti parted and went to live for all time in their homes under the waters far to the East and far to the West.

The Hopi still remember the Hurung Whuti and make many prayer offerings to them. Turquoise, seashells, and coral still serve the Hopi as sacred reminders of those beneficent deities of creation.

Emergence of the People From the Underground

Although it would seem that Hopi history rightly begins with the story of creation, many Hopi commence their accounts with the emergence of mankind from the Underworld.

Long after the first animals and the first people were created they lived together in peace, friendship, and happiness in their Underworld. There were gentle rains — corn, beans, melons, squash, and other useful plants grew bountifully; there were flowers everywhere, and all the people were content.

However, as the years went by, many of the people whom Spider Woman had created began to quarrel; first with each other, and later with the people who had been created by the two Hurung Whuti. Thus was engendered the dissension that has plagued humanity from that day to this. Many of the quarrelsome people became brutal and corrupt. The good rains stopped. The crops began to fail. There were no flowers to gladden the heart.

Conditions became so bad that finally the chief of all the people living in the Underworld called a meeting of his wisest councillors. For three days they met around their small council fire to ponder what they could do to protect all the people of good will from the wicked ones.

On the fourth day the wise men came slowly to the council fire, their steps heavy with worry and sadness over the plight of the people. They took their places silently around the fire, while the chief filled his pipe, blowing the smoke to the four world directions, and up and down, while he made his prayers for guidance and power. As he finished smoking he passed the pipe to the wise one next to him saying, "I pray that the gods, our fathers, and our uncles, may have mercy on us and grant us their aid. We must find a way to get out of this sinful place. We must find a new place either above us or below us where we can lead our good people to live in peace."

The councillors all sat in silence as their chief spoke, their arms folded, their heads bent. When he finished they assured him, "We stand with you. We pray with all our hearts that we may achieve success."

Slowly the pipe made the circle of the wise ones. When it was smoked out each lit his own pipe, which in turn made the circle of the council, as once more they all prayed for guidance and power.

As no answer came to their prayers, the old chief once more stood and addressed them, "Now we must call for help from someone more powerful than we are. We must sing a special calling song to summon Mockingbird."

When Mockingbird came, he asked, "Why have you called me? What may I do to help you?"

The chief then explained to Mockingbird why they were in such need of advice and help: "You are much wiser than we are. You know all the songs of the gods. We must be certain that we make no mistake in our efforts to help the people among us who are not corrupt."

With this he handed Mockingbird a tray of prayersticks (*pahos*). Mockingbird thanked the chief and his council for the prayersticks, but told them, "Yes, I am wise and I know all the ceremonial songs, but there is someone more powerful than I am — Yellow Bird (Sikya-chi). You must call upon him for help. While you are doing this I shall hide, because he might be jealous if he knew you had called upon me first. But remember that if he comes and agrees to help you, and wants me to work with him, I will be happy to do so; for I see that you are of good heart and are sincere in your desire to help your worthy people."

Again the chief and his councillors made their calling song. Soon Yellow Bird came flying toward them and fluttered to rest on a nearby bush.

"Welcome," said the chief.

Yellow Bird flew down and sat before them. "What do you wish of me?" he asked.

The chief explained their great concern and need for help, adding, "You are the wisest of all. We pray to you to help us."

"I know about your troubles," said Yellow Bird. "My feathers are in many of your prayer offerings; I have long wondered why you waited so very long before calling upon me to help you."

The chief explained to him, "Our minds are so full of troubles that we can no longer think straight. Please forgive us. We did not mean to be neglectful of you."

"I understand this," Yellow Bird assured them, "but I alone cannot do everything that will be needed to help you. I cannot perform my ceremonies without the proper sacred songs. We must have Mockingbird with us. Please call him at once."

Mockingbird joined them almost as soon as they began their calling songs, and they all welcomed him gladly. He agreed at once to help Yellow Bird. The two birds disappeared behind a great rock and, when they emerged, the chief and his councillors were astonished to see that they had changed into two fine-looking, tall men with long, straight black hair.

Under the direction of the two Bird Men the chiefs began to build an altar. They smoothed sand into a level square, in the center of which they placed a small ceremonial water bowl. Then a perfect ear of yellow corn was placed to the north of the bowl, a blue ear to the west of it, a red ear to the south of it, and a white ear to the east of it.

When this was properly finished a great discussion took place as to whom they would call upon to search for the place whence the good people could go out from the Underworld and where they could live in security and peace. It would require someone of great strength and courage.

The Bird Men suggested that they first call upon Golden Eagle (Kaw-hu). At the end of each of the eagle-calling songs they sprinkled a few drops of water to each of the world directions. Even as they were singing Golden Eagle lighted inside their circle.

"Why have you called upon me?" he asked.

"Welcome," said the chief. "We are in great trouble. As you are strong of wing, we are sure that you can help us find an entrance to a place where our good people may go and live in peace."

"I will try to do this," Golden Eagle assured them, "but, although I have strong wings, this will be very difficult even for me. You must pray with all your hearts to give me the power to come back alive."

As Golden Eagle prepared for his flight, prayer feathers were tied around his neck and to each of his feet. Whereupon he circled higher and higher above them until he was lost to sight.

All that day the chief and his helpers smoked and prayed for the success and safe return of Golden Eagle. Finally in the early dusk they could see him far, far above them. He was flying as if exhausted; and, to their great concern, he dropped unconscious to the ground before them. They rushed forward to help him. They rubbed him and prayed over him until he regained consciousness and was ready to talk to them.

"My news is discouraging. When I flew higher and higher above the clouds I found nothing, not a living thing. I began to worry about ever finding a place to rest. I flew higher and yet higher. I became very tired. Finally when I knew I could fly no higher, I looked up and there seemed to be an opening still much higher above me. But I was exhausted and could fly no higher. I knew that if I did not start back I might never return to you alive."

The chiefs were deeply disappointed, but they rewarded Golden Eagle with proper prayer offerings, and asked him to stay with them as they continued their efforts to find a way of escape.

Time after time all the next day they sang their calling songs. Bird after bird responded; among them, Sparrow Hawk (Kee-sa), Cliff Swallow (Pavaki-yutu), and Mourning Dove (He-awi). Each of these birds in turn flew up to try to find the opening Golden Eagle had seen, but not one of them was successful.

On the morning of the sixth day Yellow Bird stood before them and said, "We must make one last try by calling our brother Shrike (Si-katai)." Shrike came at once in answer to their songs and agreed to help them. He flew off swiftly.

Again the day seemed long indeed to the waiting council, but late in the evening Shrike returned with good news: "I flew and flew even higher and at last I could clearly see an opening above me, but it looked very small; like the opening into a kiva. As I flew closer to it, it appeared somewhat larger, and I discovered a jagged rock to one side of it; there I rested to regain my strength. Soon I was able to fly on up through the opening into the sunshine of the Upper World."

Shrike then told them that seated on a rock close to the entrance was a fearsome-looking man who called out to him, "Sit down. I know you have come for some purpose, what is it?" Shrike explained the unfortunate condition of the good people living back in the Underworld, and the man replied, "I am Masau-u, the god of Fire and Death.* I live here in poverty, but in peace. Tell those good people of the Underworld that, if they wish to share such a life, they are welcome."

"This is indeed good news," said the chief, "but let us all again make prayers in the hope that we may find some way for our people to reach that distant entrance to the world so high above us."

There was a long period of silence which was broken at last by a deferential voice which came from a small boy whom none had noticed sitting far back among the rocks: "I am Ko-choi-laftiyo, one of the five grandsons of Spider Woman. As you know, I am not an important person, but my brothers and I live to help people of ill fortune."

"If you wish to help us, you are welcome to our council," said the chief. "Come and sit here on my left. What do you suggest?"

In a soft voice the boy answered, "I know a small animal, Chipmunk (Koonah), who knows how to make plants, and even trees, grow fast and tall. If he would plant one of his trees it might grow high enough to reach through the opening to the world above."

"Good!" the chief said, "Mockingbird, please call Chipmunk."

Mockingbird took his rattle and began to sing. After a few moments, in darted Chipmunk — slowly waving his tail — and ran right up to the altar.

"What can I do to help you?" he asked.

"You are wise," the chief replied, "You know how to plant seeds so that they grow rapidly. We hope that you will plant a tree for us that will grow tall enough to reach to the Upper World."

"I will do what I can," Chipmunk assured them. "But as I work you must smoke your pipes and make your strongest prayers for me."

Chipmunk reached into a small bag and selected the seed of a spruce tree. He sang four magic planting songs as he carefully placed it in the earth. Then, taking his rattle made of small seashells, he began his sacred growing songs. Soon the spruce tree began to grow. While Chipmunk sang, he pulled it higher and higher, but it failed to grow tall enough to reach the opening.

---

*Masau-u, the god of Fire and Death, is a complex deity, including among his many attributes, power over the germination of seeds and the growth of all plants.

This spot is thought by some to be Sipapu, entrance to the Hopi Underworld. It is a sacred place of pilgrimage for the Hopi, at the bottom of the Canyon of the Little Colorado above its junction with the Colorado River.

Chipmunk was not discouraged. He tried seeds of different kinds of pine trees and even one of a giant sunflower, but none of them would reach the opening to the Upper World.

"Do not despair," Chipmunk said, "I have still another idea."

He disappeared, but soon returned with a root cutting from a tall reed. With great care he also carried the shell of a pinyon nut filled with water.

He placed these on the altar in a small basket plaque, smoked his pipe, and made his prayers over them. Everyone in the council followed his example. When this part of the ceremony was finished, Chipmunk dug deep into the ground and placed there the tiny shell of water. On top of this he carefully planted the reed. He then took sacred cornmeal in his right hand and, standing over the planting, he made many silent prayers. When he had finished his prayers he threw the cornmeal upward, praying that the reed would grow quickly right up through the opening. One by one all the others followed his example. Then the Bird Men sang their sacred songs, calling to everyone in the council to join them.

The reed began to grow with great rapidity. From time to time Chipmunk would run lightly up to its top to pull it, and urge it to grow higher and higher toward the entrance to the Upper World. As the reed was growing, Golden Eagle, Sparrow Hawk, Cliff Swallow, Mourning Dove, and Shrike kept flying up to see how close it was to the opening. The reed finally had grown so high that only Shrike could reach its top, and he perched there until it grew right through the opening. With great speed he flew back to report the wonderful news.

The chief and all his helpers were jubilant, but even as they looked upward, the tall trunk of the reed seemed to disappear completely from view.

"How can our people ever climb so high up that smooth trunk?" one of the wise men asked.

"Again, I can help you," Chipmunk assured him, and he began gnawing a hole at the base of the reed. "You see, the trunk is hollow, and it will be easy for everyone to climb up inside it."

Although they were all eager to climb up inside the reed at once, to see for themselves the world above, they knew that they must make full preparation for it. Once more they smoked their pipes and sang their sacred songs and made their prayers around the altar.

When morning came the chief appointed Eagle and Swallow to stand guard to make certain that no evil people would be able to join them in the world above. Prayer offerings were made as further protection and to give support to the reed. At long last, they could sing out for the good people to assemble.

After the chief had explained what the people were to do, he led the way up the hollow reed. When he stepped out into the Upper World, Shrike joined him in singing prayers of thanksgiving. As more and more people climbed up the reed they, too, joined in the songs.

Mockingbird took his position beside the opening to the world above; he assigned everyone their places in the Upper World and taught them the languages they were to speak.

When Mockingbird's songs were finished, no more people were permitted to enter the Upper World through Sipapu — as the entrance-way was, and still is, called. Those still inside the giant reed were imprisoned there, and they form the joints that can be seen in this kind of reed even today.

The Promised Land

YOUKEOMA, who early in this century founded the village of Hotevila, once related how ancestors of the Hopi searched for the permanent homeland promised them by Mockingbird.

In brief, his story, told to H. R. Voth, was as follows:

Each group leaving Sipapu was accompanied by an old woman (*sowuhti*) whose great wisdom could be counted on during the long days of wandering; from that time forward Hopi women have played an important part in both the religious and the secular lives of their people.

At first all the people headed eastward. White Brother (Bahana), following instructions, led his people so far to the East that he could touch his forehead to the Sun itself. There they halted and planted their fields and built their villages. The groups of Hopi people scattered far and wide. From time to time they halted at certain places for several seasons before continuing their search for the "promised land."

There they knew they would find security from warlike enemies, soil suited to the plants of their limited agriculture, an adequate supply of game and, most important, a dependable supply of water. These they found in the mesa country east of the Little Colorado River in northern Arizona, and it was here that they built their permanent villages.

The major villages of the Hopi are situated on the tips of three precipitous, finger-like projections at the southern end of Black Mesa. Black Mesa is an extensive high plateau, ranging in altitude from 6,000 to over 8,000 feet at Lolomai Point. Early travelers to Tusayan usually entered the Hopi country from the east, so these three promontories came to be referred to as First Mesa, Second Mesa, and Third Mesa. We shall consider them in that order.

There are three villages on First Mesa and one below to the east of the mesa: Walpi, Sichimovi, Hano, and Polacca.

Walpi, sitting tall — like a fortress castle upon its high cliffs — was built, according to tree-ring records, about 1700. The name Walpi comes from the combination of two Hopi words: "Walla," a gap or cleft in the cliffs, and "ovi," a place; so it means the "Place of the Gap." It is so named because of the great break in the mesa just north of the Tewa village of Hano.

At the beginning of the Christian era an earlier people dug primitive dwellings, "pit houses," around the base of the mesa. Evidence of these can still be seen. The ruins of a small chapel built by the Franciscans during the Spanish mission period are on a terrace below the south end of the mesa.

Sichimovi means the "Place of the Mound Where Wild Currants Grow." It lies between Walpi to the south and Hano to the north. It was established about the middle of the eighteenth century by a group of people from Walpi. According to A. M. Stephen, these were people of the Patki, the Lizard, the Wild Mustard, and the Badger clans. At one time, smallpox devastated the village and many of the survivors left the mesa to live at Tsegi Canyon in the Monument Valley area and at Zuñi. These people eventually returned and rebuilt the present village.

Hano is not a Hopi village. It was established late in the seventeenth century by Tewa people who emigrated from the Rio Grande country following the Pueblo Rebellion of 1680 and the reconquest of New Mexico by Vargas. Before granting these strangers sanctuary, the Hopi of First Mesa, following Hopi tradition, asked what contribution the Tewa could make to the community. Soon the Tewa were able to prove their worth.

Wehe, of the Kachina Clan of Hano, told Stephen of an important incident which may well have prompted the Hopi to allow the Tewa to build their homes permanently on First Mesa on condition that they become the guardians of the trail up "the Gap."

According to Wehe, when the Tewa first came to Tusayan they lived near Coyote Spring (Isba) close by certain yellow rocks. The Utes had made a raid on Walpi, killing eight persons and driving off many Walpi horses. The leaders of Walpi appealed to the Tewa for help.

Armed with bows and arrows, the Tewa crossed the Gap and pursued the Utes up the Wepo wash, west of Walpi. The Utes retreated a mile or so up the valley to a high ledge where they had cached a store of dried venison and elk and antelope meat. There they made a breastwork of the packages of dried meat and leveled a heavy fire from their bows and arrows at the approaching Tewa. Finding that they could not dislodge the Utes by a direct charge, the Tewa climbed to a higher ledge overlooking the Ute position. When the Utes discovered the Tewa ready to shoot down on them, they abandoned their store of meat and fled up the valley. The Tewa pursued them and slew all except one man, who pled for mercy and whom the victorious Tewa allowed to go free upon his promise to tell his people that the warrior Tewa were now living in Tusayan.

Hano, also known as Tewa, is said to be a nickname given the village because its Tewa inhabitants seemed to say "Ha" between every word. For many years Hano was the home of Nampeyo, the famous potter. Down through the years the people of Hano have preserved their cultural integrity and their language. Even today the people of Hano consider themselves Tewa, not Hopi, although there has been sufficient intermarriage and cultural exchange so that they are often referred to as "Hopi-Tewa." They have been accepted by the Hopi as a proud "minority group."

Polacca was named for Tom Polaccaca, a Tewa of Hano who built the first store below the mesa. The spelling was later changed and shortened to Polacca. The village of Polacca grew up around the First Mesa day school in the last decade of the nineteenth century. The village has no political entity nor does it have any religious ceremonials. All of its Hopi and Tewa residents owe allegiance in these matters to the villages on top of the mesa.

Second Mesa is split at its end into two fingers. On one are the villages of Shipolovi and Mishongnovi, and on the other Shongopovi. Below Shipolovi and Mishongnovi to the southwest is Toreva Spring, one of the best in the Hopi country.

The name Shongopovi is derived from combining three Hopi words: "shong-o-hu," a tall jointed reed; "pa," a spring, and "ovi." The name thus means, the "Place by the Spring Where the Tall Reeds Grow." (The white man has spelled it at least fifty-seven different ways.) Shongopovi was established by members of the Bear Clan, and the village chief has always been from that clan. According to tradition, Shongopovi is the oldest of the Hopi villages. However, the original village was not built where the present one is located.

Another clan important at Shongopovi is the Water Clan. When its people petitioned for entrance to the village they were, as usual, asked to demonstrate what they could do for the pueblo's welfare. At that time there was only one spring, Shungopa, so the Cloud Clan planted a small olla of water as a "spring seed" and enacted their special ceremonial prayers. In a few moments, water began to flow out of the ground around the olla. This fine, new spring was named Gray Spring (Masipa). It has been neatly walled in and is still in use by the villagers. The older spring dried up in 1870 when the ledge above slumped down in a local earthquake.

For hundreds of years Shongopovi was located about two hundred yards north of Gray Spring. From the extent of the ruin it is estimated that several hundred people once lived there. Pieces of broken pottery found in the refuse dumps of the ancient village, led to an estimation by the late Harold S. Colton that it was established before 1250 and was occupied until the early part of the fifteenth century. The village was then moved down by the spring where it existed during the Spanish mission period.

The Franciscan mission of San Bartolomé was built on the top of a level ridge about 500 yards above the spring. From the ruins that remain it has been established that the nave of this church was approximately 44 x 18 feet and the apse about 10 x 10 feet. Of the badly crumbled ruins, a part of the north end and the northern part of the west wall currently serve as part of a Hopi sheep corral.

From 1629 to 1680 Shongopovi, or at least a goodly portion of it, was near the mission. Following the Pueblo Rebellion, the present village was constructed. Some of the beams of the mission building were incorporated in the houses and in one kiva of the new village.

According to Stephen, Shipolovi is the name of a midge, the design of which was engraved on a stone brought to the village by a kachina and preserved in a shrine. Colton and several others believed that this midge was a mosquito and that Shipolovi really means "The Mosquitoes." There is a traditional account which states that the founders of Shipolovi once lived at Homolovi, near Winslow, and were driven out by the hordes of mosquitoes which infested the area.

However, the presence of beams from the old mission at Shongopovi gives support to a theory that Shipolovi was settled by people from old Shongopovi. According to the latter story, there was a schism among the people of Shongopovi when they abandoned their village around the mission. Although most of the people went to live in the new pueblo on top of the mesa, several went to the other arm of Second Mesa, near Mishongnovi, and established Shipolovi.

Stephen claims that Mishongnovi was named after four pillars of rock which stand in a row about three hundred yards distant from the village and that it was founded largely by female survivors of Awatobi, a pueblo destroyed in 1700 during a "religious war" with neighboring Hopi. However, the explanation of the name given by Colton is more likely correct — the "Place of the Black Man." This refers to a chief, Mishong, a member of the Crow Clan who led his people from the San Francisco Peaks region. They were refused admission to Shongopovi but later were permitted to establish a village below the shrine at Corn Rock, which is a prominent feature at the end of Second Mesa. This permission was granted by the chiefs of Shongopovi on condition that the people of Mishongnovi would for all time protect the Corn Rock shrine from desecration.

Scientists think that early Mishongnovi was occupied from the thirteenth century to the beginning of the eighteenth. A Franciscan chapel was established in 1629 and was serviced until 1680 by a priest from Shongopovi. The move to the present site occurred during the 1700s.

Third Mesa has Old Oraibi at its tip; Hotevila, some eight miles northwest; and Bacobi, eight miles north. At the foot of Third Mesa is New Oraibi.

The name Oraibi refers to a rock called by the Hopi "orai." This village is now largely in ruins. In their day several blocks of these crumbling houses had been built over the ruins of still older houses. Lyndon L. Hargrave describes it thus: "Oraibi is old. Beneath the present town are the remains of houses, room upon room. Through the centuries, these houses have fallen into decay upon the mounds of which successive generations have reared their homes. At every point where a hole is dug, mute evidence of the antiquity of the pueblo is upturned. Some years ago the edge of the village road was cut through a huge trash mound at the bottom of which were found buried remains of even older and better built houses."

When Victor Mindeleff was at Oraibi in 1882–83, obtaining material for his study of architecture in Tusayan, he found that Oraibi was then the largest of all the Hopi pueblos and contained half the entire Hopi population. In 1968, a scant 167 were living in what scientists are confident is the oldest continuously inhabited town in the United States. It is generally agreed that Old Oraibi dates back at least to A.D. 1150. Traditions of the Bear Clan in the next chapter give in detail the story of the founding of Old Oraibi.

Although devastating plagues and an occasional earthquake have had tragic effects upon Old Oraibi, internal dissension — long brewing between the Bear and the Spider Clan people and their associates — was the basic cause for the dissolution of this once important Hopi community in 1906. Dissension eventually reached such a point that Tewaquaptewa, then village chief, ordered all those who had, or intended to, become Christians to leave Old Oraibi. This initiated a small but steady flow of emigrants from the mesa to a settlement they called Kiakochomovi, the "Place of the Hills of Ruins." Commonly spoken of as Lower Oraibi, or New Oraibi, it has grown to be one of the larger Hopi villages and is headquarters for the Hopi Tribal Council.

Not all who moved to New Oraibi were Christian converts. Several families went there because of its proximity to schools, the store, the post office, and a good water supply. When Oraibi High School was built nearby it also served as an incentive for still more families to desert the mesa top.

Hotevila is eight miles northwest of Oraibi on the same mesa. Its name resulted from the joining of two Hopi words, "hota," a back, and "veli," to skin off or peel. This refers to the main spring of the village which used to be in such a low cave that on entering or leaving one usually scraped his back against the rough rocks of the cave roof.

Hotevila was founded by Youkeoma and his followers after the disturbances in Oraibi. Youkeoma was steadfast in his refusal to agree to many of the things demanded of him by the officials of the Bureau of Indian Affairs. An almost constant atmosphere of tension and hostility

The old trail up to Walpi.

H. R. Voth photo; Field Museum of Natural History

Old Oraibi in the late 1890s.

developed and persisted as long as Youkeoma lived. To this day Hotevila is one of the most conservative of the Hopi villages and a faction there continues to maintain a hostile attitude toward Indian Bureau officials and policies.

Bacobi, the "Place of the Jointed Reed," is located a half mile east of Hotevila. It was founded in 1907 by a splinter group from Hotevila.

Moencopi's name means the "Place of the Flowing Stream." Although not on Third Mesa, but some forty miles to the north, Moencopi is in a very real sense a colony of Old Oraibi. The people there who live according to the Hopi traditional way of life recognize the authority of the village chief of Oraibi. It is built on and around sites which had been occupied by migrating Hopi clans in the ancient past. The present community was established in the 1870s by an Oraibi chief by the name of Tuba.

Today Moencopi is virtually two communities. Upper Moencopi, the more modern town, is built around the day school in the old village. Lower Moencopi remains more of a traditional Hopi village. In one of its streets there are the ancient fossil tracks of a chirotherium, a dinosaur-like creature.

It seems fantastic that the same ancient muds in which those "dinosaurs" made their tracks so many aeons ago now serve as a rocky pavement for the feet of Hopi kachina dancers and of tourists from all over the world who come to the Painted Desert country.

It is interesting to compare recent population figures of the Hopi villages with those given by Thomas Donaldson in his Extra Census Bulletin, *The Moqui Indians of Arizona,* for 1890–91:

	1968	1890–91
FIRST MESA		
Walpi	80	232
Hano	241	161
Sichimovi	364	103
SECOND MESA		
Shongopovi	475	225
Shipolovi	142	126
Mishongnovi	530	244
THIRD MESA		
Oraibi	167	903

No mention is made of Moencopi, and of course Hotevila and Bacobi were not in existence when the 1890–91 census was reported. In 1968 Upper Moencopi had 432 inhabitants; Lower Moencopi, 278. New Oraibi at the foot of Third Mesa had 401.

Clan Migrations

WOVEN INTO THE VERY WARP AND WOOF of the fabric of Hopi secular and religious life are the traditions relative to their wanderings after leaving the Underworld. It was during these wanderings that the complex system of Hopi clans and clan societies came into being. These clans and clan societies, called "phratries" by many scientists, eventually coalesced into the Hopitu-Shinumu.

Involved in every Hopi religious ceremonial of today is a multitude of references and symbols pertaining to these clan migrations. Details that may seem inconsequential to the reader may symbolize something of great importance in Hopi religion and/or history.

It is generally accepted that the people of the Bear Clan were the first to arrive in the Hopi Tusqua, or land of the Hopi.

Bear Clan

According to tradition, a wandering party of Hopi whose chief was named Matcito came upon the body of a dead bear near the Little Colorado River. Considering this an important omen, Matcito announced that from then on they would call themselves the Bear Clan (Honau-wungwa). They removed the paws from the dead bear, then skinned and stuffed them with dry grass to serve as symbols·of their clan.

Some time later a second band of Hopi found the body of the bear. Since they were having difficulty carrying their possessions, they cut long straps from the bear's hide to better tie up their great bundles. This party became the Strap Clan.

Many days later a third group came upon the carcass of the bear, by now little more than a skeleton. As they approached it they were surprised to find several bluebirds perched on top of the bones, where-upon they named themselves the Bluebird Clan.

Soon after the Bluebird Clan had left, a fourth group came by. When they examined the skeleton of the bear they discovered a spider web with a large spider sitting in the center of it. They took the name Spider Clan.

Still another party came. It found around the skeleton many earth castings which had been made by moles. Thus the Mole Clan came into being.

Many months passed before a final group came upon what was left of the dead bear — merely bones scattered widely over the ground. When they examined the skull they found a strange, greasy substance in the eye cavities, so they gave themselves the curious name of The Greasy Eye Cavities Clan.

While the Bear Clan was encamped at a place called Kuiwanva — about a mile northwest of where Old Oraibi stands today — the death god, Masau-u, also patron of the earth and all food plants, came to visit. The people of the Bear Clan asked if he would give them some of his land and allow them to build their permanent village there. Matcito urged Masau-u to take his place and become chief of the Bear Clan. This Masau-u refused to do, saying that Matcito was their right and proper chief. However, he readily agreed to show them a place where they could build their village and plant their fields. He designated a site east of the Oraibi bluff. Ruins still mark the place where those early Bear Clan people built their houses.

The Bear Clan brought with them the Soyal, an important winter solstice ceremony, the Soyal Kachina, and Eototo, chief of all the kachinas. After the Bear Clan had become established at Oraibi, the Strap, the Bluebird, the Spider, and other clans also sought homes there. Whenever the chiefs of these clans applied for sites, Matcito would inquire if they had any helpful ceremonies that would contribute to the general welfare of the village. If they had, they were welcomed and lands were assigned to them in accordance with Masau-u's instructions.

Snake Clan

One group of Hopi settled for a time at a place called Tokoonavi, which was northeast of Grand Canyon near Navajo Mountain and close to the Colorado River. Tiyo, son of the village chief of Tokoonavi, often sat on a high rock near the rushing water and wondered where all the water flowed. His curiosity became so great that one day he went to his father and gained his permission to journey down the river.

Tiyo worked hard to construct a boat by burning and scraping out a large cottonwood log which he made as watertight as possible. He made a large *paho* to serve as a paddle. When the day came for him to start on his journey, his father and other ceremonial leaders of the village furnished him with a supply of food and many *pahos*. As they pushed Tiyo and his boat out into the swiftly flowing water they made him promise to bring back shells and corals from the abode of the Hurung Whuti of the West. Soon Tiyo was lost to sight far down the river.

After a long journey he came to the far-off western ocean where he drifted against a small island. He found it to be the home of Spider Woman, who invited him to enter. The entrance was so small that he could not possibly get in. Spider Woman directed him how to enlarge it so that he could enter. He then told Spider Woman the story of his journey and presented her with a *paho*. He explained that one of the objectives of his journey was to collect shells and beads. Spider Woman pointed out another kiva, which loomed out of the waters in the far distance, and instructed him on how to get there, at the same time giving him powerful medicine.

Perching behind his right ear, she said she would accompany him. Prompted by Spider Woman, Tiyo sprayed the medicine over the waters toward the distant kiva entrance. Instantly, a pathway like a rainbow formed straight from Spider Woman's kiva to the kiva across the waters.

As they came closer to the kiva a large mountain lion stopped them. Again following Spider Woman's directions, Tiyo sprayed some of his medicine on the mountain lion and gave him a *paho*. The mountain lion accepted the *paho* and allowed them to proceed. Then, in turn, they encountered a bear, a wildcat, a gray wolf, and a gigantic rattlesnake — all of which they appeased in the same manner as they had the mountain lion.

Fastened across the entrance door to the kiva was an *aouta natsi* — a long hunting bow decorated with eagle feathers, weasel and skunk skins, and red tassels. A bow, similarly decorated, is always fastened near the top of the ladder leading into the kiva used during the Snake Cere-mony. Tiyo, with Spider Woman still riding behind his ear, descended the ladder into the kiva where they found many men and women assem-bled. The men's faces were painted with a metallic-looking black paint and they were dressed in blue kilts. Around their necks they wore many strings of shell and coral beads. Tiyo noted that the walls of the kiva were covered with ceremonial costumes made of the skins of enormous snakes.

No one spoke as Tiyo took a seat near the kiva fireplace. As he looked about he saw several young girls, one of whom he thought was particularly beautiful. The men looked at Tiyo for a long time in complete silence. Finally, their chief picked up a bag of tobacco and his pipe, which he filled and smoked four times. Then he handed it to Tiyo, telling him to smoke and to inhale the smoke.

Knowing that this was a test, Spider Woman whispered to Tiyo to do the chief's bidding and she would keep him from getting dizzy by sucking out the smoke just as soon as he had inhaled it. The fact that Tiyo did not become dizzy from inhaling the smoke made the people in the kiva realize that he had power and was a person of importance. Now they welcomed him, and Tiyo in turn presented their chief with a special green *paho* and several prayer feathers (*nakwakwosis*).

The chief was pleased with Tiyo's gift and determined to reward him for it and for his courage in making the long, dangerous journey. Tiyo was told to face the wall of the kiva, and in a few minutes was ordered to turn around. To his astonishment he found that all of the men and women, except the chief, had donned the snakeskin costumes and, more than this, that in doing so they had actually turned themselves into snakes of every description: large and small — racers, bull snakes, rattlesnakes — all writhing over the kiva floor, hissing and rattling.

Spider Woman whispered that this was another test for Tiyo, but that with her help, he now had power to touch and handle the snakes without danger. The chief told Tiyo to select one of the reptiles. At this, snakes began to hiss and rattle even more savagely than before. Spider Woman told Tiyo not to be afraid and to choose the large, yellow rattlesnake, for it was in truth the handsome girl he had admired when they first entered the kiva. The rattlesnake seemed particularly vicious; but, when he sprinkled it with the medicine Spider Woman had given him, it became very docile. He picked it up and stroked it upward four times.

The chief, pleased to note that the young man again demonstrated great power, once more instructed him to face the kiva wall for a moment. When he turned around this time all the snakes had resumed their human forms. They gathered around to congratulate him on his courage and to announce that he was now one of them.

Food was brought down into the kiva, and all ate together. Tiyo gave the young woman he admired some of the food he had brought with him. She shared it with obvious pleasure. While they were all eating, he explained that one of his reasons for making his long journey was to obtain shell and coral beads such as they were wearing.

The snake people urged Tiyo to stay with them, but Spider Woman wanted to return to her own home. It was decided that Tiyo should take her there and then come back to the kiva. Throughout the night, after his return, the chief of the snake people instructed him in every detail of their religion and its ceremonies.

When dawn came Tiyo left the kiva of his snake brothers and sisters and again visited Spider Woman. Now she made another rainbow path across the waters, but this time it led to the home of the Hurung Whuti of the West. Tiyo found her to be an old withered hag. On the walls of her kiva home hung long strings of coral and shell beads, and large piles of different kinds of shell and corals lay stacked in the corners of the room. The old woman said nothing in greeting, but when Tiyo presented her with a *paho,* she thanked him in a very faint, cracked voice.

At sunset the old woman disappeared into a side chamber of the kiva. To his amazement, when she returned she had been transformed into a beautiful young woman — clothed in fine wildcat and buffalo robes. She told him that he must spend the night with her. Spider Woman, who again was perched behind his ear, whispered that he should do as this young woman requested.

In the morning when he awoke he found by his side, snoring loudly, not the beautiful young woman of the evening before, but the withered old hag of the preceding day.

For four days and nights he remained with the Hurung Whuti. Every evening at sunset the same change occurred in the old hag, only to be reversed when morning came.

On the morning of the fifth day Tiyo decided that it was time for him to start back to his own people. He went into a small chamber on the north side of the Hurung Whuti's kiva and took from it one turquoise bead; from a similar room on the west side, he took another turquoise bead; from a room on the south, a red coral bead; and from an east room, a white shell bead. The Hurung Whuti then gave him a small sack containing all kinds of beads, but she cautioned him that he must not open the sack until he returned to his own people or all the beads would disappear. Again she instructed him to visit the snake people, who would give him clothes and food for his journey home.

He spent four days and nights in the kiva of the snake people. The chief gave him the young woman he so admired to be his wife, and supplied them with what they would need for the long trip ahead of them. Before they set off, the chief told Tiyo that when he got back to his people he was to teach them the ceremonies in which they had instructed him, and that his wife would bear many children to help him in these ceremonies.

Spider Woman warned him that he must not touch his wife on his return journey or both she and his precious sack of beads would disappear. Every morning the sack of beads grew heavier and heavier. When they had traveled for four days Tiyo became so impatient that he disregarded the original warning of the Hurung Whuti and opened the sack. Before they went to sleep that night he decked himself in long strings of beautiful beads and spread the others over the ground to admire them. When morning came he was bitterly disappointed to find that all the beads had disappeared except for the four he had taken from chambers in the Hurung Whuti's kiva.

After returning to his people, Tiyo's wife bore many children, but all of them were snakes. These snakes went to live in the surrounding sandhills and fields, where the Hopi children often played with them. Sometimes a Hopi child would be bitten and Tiyo's people would become angry. Finally, Tiyo gathered all his snake children into a blanket to take them back to his wife's people. Before he left, his father gave him many *pahos* which he put on top of the snakes. Tiyo made the journey, explained to the snake people why he had to bring them his snake children, and presented the *pahos*.

Eventually Tiyo and his wife decided to seek a new home farther to the southeast. They stopped at various places but none satisfied them. One morning they saw smoke rising from the village of Walpi, high on its mesa. They climbed up close to the base of the cliffs below the village and announced their presence.

When the chief of Walpi came down to them, Tiyo explained that if they might be permitted to live at Walpi they would help the people there with their ceremonies, and he told of the powerful ceremonies taught to him by the snake people. Finally the Walpi chief gave permission for them to enter.

Tiyo's wife later gave birth to human children instead of snake children, and these became the founders of the Snake Clan at Walpi. According to Lomavantiwa of Shipolovi, it was at Walpi, therefore, that the first Hopi Snake Ceremony was conducted — with a snake fetish, a snake altar, and costumes all made in accordance with the instructions given Tiyo by the snake people. He also claimed that this ceremony spread from Walpi to Shongopovi, then to Mishongnovi, and finally to Oraibi.

Various incidents of Tiyo's adventures are reenacted in the Hopi Snake Ceremony, such as when the snake priests gather up the snakes at the conclusion of the ceremony and liberate them at the proper shrines on the desert below the mesa. At this time *pahos* similar to those given Tiyo by his father are deposited with the freed snakes.

Water Clans

The clans associated with the Patki or Water Clan were the Young Corn, the Cloud, the Tadpole and Frog, the Snow, and the Rabbitbrush clans. Some of these are now extinct. According to their traditional history, they migrated to the Hopi country from a region of red rocks to the south which is referred to as Palotquopi and sometimes as Palatkwabi.

Studies being brought into focus by Charles Di Peso and his associates of the Amerind Foundation offer some basis for that when the great pueblo of Casas Grandes in northern Chihuahua, Mexico, was destroyed by the Opata Indians in A.D. 1340, ancestors of the Hopi Patki or Water Clan people and some related clans such as Tobacco, Kachina, and Parrot (or Macaw) may have been among the survivors. Di Peso informs us that to the immediate west of Casa Grandes there is a valley in red-rock country very similar to Oak Creek Canyon in northern Arizona.

In their migration north in search of a permanent home they likely lived for some time at Háwikuh (one of the villages of the Zuñi of that period) before resuming their journey north into the Hopi country.

Saquistiwa of Walpi related to Edward S. Curtis that while the Cloud Clan of the Water Clan Society was living at Palatkwabi many of its people became evil. When they went rabbit hunting they quarreled about the game and sometimes cut rabbits in two, which was considered a very bad omen. The young people had no respect for the elderly or for the virtue of women and girls. When the village chief became desperate, he decided on a plan to teach his people a lesson.

One night they descried a strange moving light in the far-off distance. As they watched, it came closer and closer until it came right into the village, where it ran about the streets. From time to time the light stopped. Then there could be heard the curious sounds of corn-grinding stones and of singing. After a while the mysterious light disappeared in the direction from which it had come. The older people of the village believed that the light was caused by a sorcerer and that it would bring them disaster.

After dark the men of the village stationed themselves along the trail by which the light had entered their village the night before, but when it again appeared they lost their courage. One very poor, small boy named Ko-choiplaftiyo — following the advice of his grandmother, Spider Woman — remained steadfast, and when the light came toward him he seized it and cried for help.

Many men came running and they discovered that the light was made by the fiery breath of the "sorcerer" coming from its rabbit-skin mask, similar to one worn by Masau-u. Underneath this mask were three different kachina masks, one over the other. When they stripped away the last mask, the men were astonished to find behind it the son of their village chief.

He assured them that there was no evil in his thought toward them — that he was acting thus only to teach them a lesson. He insisted that they bury him alive in the center of the village with four fingers of one hand showing above the ground. Each day they were to bend down one of his outstretched fingers.

Nothing happened until the night of the fourth day. All the village was sleeping when a violent earthquake shook the village. Water began streaming into the corners of all the houses and through the fireplaces. The able-bodied people put the old and feeble on high shelves, hoping that the water would not reach them, and then they fled to higher ground. The village was soon flooded.

In the morning a little boy and his sister, who had been left behind accidentally, awoke and looked out over the water. They made their way over the housetops to the edge of the plaza where they were amazed to see the Great Horned Water Serpent (Palulukon) floating on the water.

He told the children to come to him. When he saw that they were afraid to enter the water, he caused it to flow back and he advised them to follow the trail of their people by noting where the ground had been trampled. The Horned Water Serpent, who also was really the village chief's son, then insisted that the boy cut off a piece of flesh from his side. When the boy did this, the Horned Water Serpent explained that he and his people must use this portion of serpent's flesh for magic purposes and that they were to sing certain songs to produce rain for their crops.

Since the flood had destroyed their village, the Water Clan people started their search for a new home. Each morning they stood a cornstalk upright and then set off in the direction indicated when it fell to earth. It is said that they lived for a time on the Little Colorado River (near Winslow, Arizona) and later at Pakatcomo in the Walpi valley.

When they finally arrived at Walpi, they were met by the Snake Chief, who asked them where they came from and if they wanted to live at Walpi. The leader of the Water people told him their story and asked to be admitted to his village. The Snake Chief inquired if they had brought food and water. In reassuring him, the chief of the Water Clan told him that they not only had food and water with them, but also they had power to bring rain and food. Then the Snake Chief, to show that he too had power to bring rain, began to sing. As he sang, black clouds came up from the north and a misty rain began to fall.

The Water Clan Chief then demonstrated his power to bring rain, as given to his people by the Horned Water Serpent. He had the women of his clan open their mantas and from them he took out beautiful baskets decorated around the edges with feathers. As the women sang four different songs, heavy white rain clouds came rolling in from the south until they hung heavy over the entire valley. Then snow began to fall. By nightfall, it was knee deep. The next day a heavy rainstorm of enormous drops deluged the valleys. So heavy was the rain that, according to tradition, many of the deep arroyos still seen in Tusayan were cut out by that cloudburst.

Realizing the great power possessed by the Water people, the Snake Chief welcomed them to Walpi and assigned them fields on the south side of the mesa.

Today in the women's Lakon Ceremony, much of this traditional history is reenacted.

In his *Truth of A Hopi,* published by the Museum of Northern Arizona, Edmund Nequatewa gives a long account of this same tradition. Still another version was given by Sikanakpu of Mishongnovi to the Mennonite missionary, Heinrich R. Voth, and published by the Field Museum in Voth's *Traditions of the Hopi.*

Like the Water Clan Society, the Kachina and the Parrot (or Macaw) clans associated with them also came to Tusayan from far to the south. There is some reason to believe that many, or even all, of them may have come north from Casas Grandes. However, Fewkes writes in his 1898 report, "Tusayan Migration Traditions," that the only ruins connected with the Kachina Clan and its associates were their early homes at Kiou and Winaba (also called Kacinaba) situated about three miles east of Sikyatki on the lower levels of that same mesa.

The fact that trips to gather salt at Zuñi Salt Lake have always been associated with the people of the Parrot (or Macaw) Clan would seem to indicate that at least some of the clans in this society may have lived for some time with the Zuñi either at ancient Háwikuh or at one of the other Zuñi villages.

The Kokop Clan

The society of the Firewood — or Kokop Clan, as it is usually called — includes the Coyote, the Masau-u, the Cedar, the Yucca, and the Pinyon clans. It is one of the ancient societies among the Hopi villages.

Katci, chief of the Kokop Clan at Walpi at the time Fewkes was working there toward the close of the nineteenth century, claimed that his people originally had come from Jémez Pueblo in New Mexico or from related villages on the Jémez plateau.

After living for different periods of time at a variety of locations, including Keams Canyon and Eighteen-Mile Spring, they settled permanently at Sikyatki during the fourteenth century. The ruins of Sikyatki can still be seen about two miles north of Polacca.

We assume that by "his people" Katci meant all the clans associated in the Kokop Society at Sikyatki. If this is correct, then the destruction of Sikyatki played an important part in their history.

Sikahpiki of Shipolovi gave Voth one account of its demolition.

According to him, some kachinas from Walpi went to Sikyatki to have a race. While this was in progress, one of the Walpi men, instead of snipping off just a small bit of hair from one of the Sikyatki Runner Kachinas — as is often done — cut off all his hair in a very brutal manner. This made the Sikyatki kachina very angry, and when he returned to his own village he practiced running day after day, to make himself so strong that he could take revenge upon the man from Walpi.

One day when men from Walpi came to Sikyatki to have a race, his chance came. Dressed and masked as a Homsona Kachina, he participated in the races and the clowning antics practiced by the Runner Kachinas. He spotted the young sister of his enemy, standing with another girl on a rooftop watching the performances; whereupon, he dashed up the ladder after her. She tried to hide in one of the houses, but he soon found her and — jerking from his belt a long sharp knife — he sliced off her head. Brandishing his gory trophy, he raced through the village waving the severed head so that everyone could see him. The men of Sikyatki gave chase, but he soon outdistanced them and fled back to his home in Walpi. Although Sikahpiki did not say so, this seems to have been the beginning of bad blood between Walpi and Sikyatki.

Some time later the village chief of Sikyatki became bitterly disappointed with his own people, who were, he felt, not living according to the proper Hopi way of life. Meeting with the chief of Walpi, he arranged that when his people were out in their fields planting the people of Walpi should smear the houses of Sikyatki with quantities of pinyon pitch, set fire to it, and destroy the village. This was done, and while the village was burning fiercely the Walpi men attacked the Sikyatki people, widely separated in their various fields.

Sikahpiki claimed that the Sikyatki people were all killed. If this were so, of course it would have been impossible for representatives of the Kokop clans to migrate to Walpi. It is possible that, through marriage or otherwise, representatives of these clans may have migrated to Walpi long before Sikyatki was so tragically destroyed.

It seems much more likely, however, that the story of the destruction of all the Sikyatki people, like a similar story about the later destruction of Awatobi, was considerably exaggerated; and that, again as in the case of Awatobi, certain people judged friendly and useful were spared, becoming the ancestors of the Kokop clans of Walpi and of other Hopi villages.

Several informants have told the author that when the Kokop Clan people came to Oraibi and asked for admission to that village, Matcito, then village chief and the legendary founder of Oraibi, refused to admit them. It was not until Oraibi was besieged by enemy forces that Matcito invited them to live in Oraibi with the condition that they serve the village as warriors.

The Kokop Clan people were the founders of the Warrior Society, Momtcit, the control of which they shared with the Spider Clan, one of the early clans to join the Bear Clan people at Oraibi. The Kokop Clan and many of the clans associated with it have a variety of observances connected with war and are often known as "the redheads" by their fellow Hopi. The Aztecs represented their enemies as redheads. This may well be another of the many tenuous links betwen the Hopi and the people of Montezuma.

Sun, Eagle, Wild Mustard, and Warrior Kachina Woman Clans

The Sun, the Moon, the Stars, the Sun's Forehead, and the Eagle clans, two different Hawk clans, and the Turkey Clan also came from the region of the New Mexico pueblos, according to Pautiwa of Walpi.

Nequatewa writes that, when the Sun's Forehead Clan arrived in Tusayan and asked for admission to Shongopovi, they were refused because they were considered inferior, having no important religious ceremonies that would benefit the village. Their spokesmen protested that they had no time for religious ceremonials, that they were nothing but warriors who had had to fight their way to Shongopovi, as the country was full of tribes who were their enemies. The village chief of Shongopovi agreed to their admittance with the understanding that they would act as his warriors. He then persuaded the people of the Parrot Clan to grant the Sun's Forehead people some of their lands.

Later on, the Sun Clan people arrived at Shongopovi and met with the same reception as had the Sun's Forehead Clan. Whereupon, the latter shared with the newcomers the lands they had already been allotted.

The Wild Mustard Clan, often called the Tansy Mustard, and its related Warrior Kachina Woman Clan also came to Tusayan from New Mexico. They were probably among the latest groups to join the Hopi. According to their story, their ancestors lived first near where Santa Fe is today and later moved to near Abiquiu. The present town of Abiquiu is built over the ruins of an ancient Indian village which may well have been one of their ancestral homes.

Shortly after they left on the long journey that eventually brought them to Tusayan, a child on its mother's back began to cry. Some of the people pulled up some wild mustard weeds and gave them to the child to play with. The child stopped crying. Thus, they decided that the wild mustard (*asa*) must be the name of their clan. Later, they met a Warrior Kachina Woman (Chakwaina) whom they also included in their party.

On their westward migration they stayed for certain periods at Santo Domingo, at Laguna, at Acoma, and finally at Zuñi. Then they migrated north and built a village on Antelope Mesa near Awatobi. Again they moved on, this time to a place near Walpi. While there, they aided their kinsmen — the Tewa people of Hano — in a fight against the Utes. Later a long period of drought forced them to move once more. (These could very well be the Hopi mentioned by Juan Bautista de Anza, governor of New Mexico, in the account of his visit to the Hopi in 1780; these Hopi told him of being driven to the Navajo country by prolonged drought.)

This time they built houses and planted crops in Canyon de Chelly, where the crumbling ruins of their village can still be seen. While living there many of them intermarried with the Navajo. Eventually, when the period of drought ended, they returned to the Walpi mesa. There the village chief assigned them a site for a new village, at the head of the trail leading up from the valley, provided that they would defend it.

Near the end of the eighteenth century most of the women of the Wild Mustard Society moved to another point on the Walpi mesa and founded the pueblo of Sichimovi. Although they eventually spread to the villages of Second Mesa, they seemed never to have become established at Oraibi, or at any of the other villages on Third Mesa.

Badger Clan

After their emergence from the Underworld the Badger Clan people and their associates wandered about the earth for a long time before settling at a spring, Kisiu-va, high in the Mountains of the Kachinas (the San Francisco Peaks near Flagstaff) where, according to an informant of Edward S. Curtis, they lived for a time with members of the Kachina Clan.

Early in their wanderings they established a village at Tuwanacabi; its ruins can be seen north of the Hopi villages. From there they wandered to Oraibi Wash where they built a village, the ruins of which are called Siu-va, after the spring close by. It was while they were there that they became so interested in a badger which they frequently saw coming out of his hole that they began calling themselves the Badger people.

About that time they also encountered a porcupine, but they did not accept him as their *natuila,* or clan relative. Porcupine felt badly about this and decided that he would do something so that the Badger Clan people would be glad to accept him, too, as their *natuila.* He ate a great quantity of pinyon gum and defecated a magical blue paint; he ate berries of the skunk bush and vomited a red paint; he ate flowers of the rabbit bush and defecated a yellow paint. This so amazed the people that some of them did accept the porcupine as their particular *natuila*.

Some time later a few of the people made friends with a butterfly. They told the butterfly that some day they hoped to find a better place to live. Butterfly told them that he would fly all around the country until he found a good place for them to settle.

As the butterfly flew farther and farther away he came one day to the village of Oraibi. When he reported his discovery to the Badger and the Porcupine people they decided to move toward Oraibi mesa, but the people living there would not let them enter their village. As a result they lived for a short time directly below the mesa and later moved about three miles farther down the valley.

During one winter the son of the Crier Chief at Oraibi was hunting rabbits far down the valley. He was chasing one fine, fat rabbit when it disappeared into some low bushes. He was unable to find its tracks and was about to give up the search when he heard a voice, "I am here."

In the middle of a clump of tall grass from which the voice had come he discovered a round hole. As he bent over it the same voice invited him, "Come in." He hesitated, but the invitation was repeated, "There will be no harm — come in."

As the young man descended into the hole he was surprised to find himself in a large kiva full of people. He discovered that the rabbit he had been following was really one of the girls who was now sitting in the kiva, and that the people were the same Badger Clan people whom the Oraibi chiefs had not allowed to enter their village a few years before.

He was given food and invited to smoke with the men. Later on he was told to watch carefully what the women and girls were doing. They were weaving kachina sashes with the conventionalized design which represents the mask of Wiyakote, an uncle of the kachinas.

That night, after the men in the kiva performed certain kachina dances, they told the young man from Oraibi, "In the morning you must return to your own people and show them how they too can perform the dances we have shown you, and also how they can make the proper sashes to be worn while performing these dances."

When the young man returned to Oraibi he found that his father, the Crier Chief, was out on the desert searching for him. That evening when the old man returned he and his son smoked together. The young man then told of his adventures with the Badger people and how kind they had been to him, in spite of the fact that they had been treated with contempt by the chiefs of Oraibi.

His father then called the village chief and had his son repeat his story. He ended by giving the two chiefs a full description of the beautiful kachina dances he had been taught. The chiefs were so impressed that they sent the young man back to the Badger people at once to invite them all to come and join the people of Oraibi.

The Badger people came to Oraibi with quantities of food so that everyone in the village could join them in a great feast. The young man was told by the chiefs of the Badger people that he must marry the girl who had led him to them and that he then would be chief of the new Kachina Clan.

Many years after the Badger people came to Oraibi one of their women married a Hopi of Walpi, and in that way the Badger Clan was established at Walpi. (This account is based in part on the version given by Curtis in the Hopi volume of *The North American Indian* and in part on accounts related by several Hopi.)

The traditions of the Badger Clan also tell of some kachinas who came to a field below Oraibi. After lining up in a hollow square around the field they began their particular kachina dance and its songs. Soon many of the people of Oraibi ran down to watch them. When the dance and the songs were finished, the earth in the center of the kachina-surrounded field began to heave and break. Finally Badger (Honani) came up from below (*at-kyaa*). On his back was a great bundle containing all kinds of medicines and in his left hand were the downy wing feathers of a buzzard.

Badger introduced himself and told the kachinas and the Oraibi people that he knew the charms for curing all kinds of sickness.

"Anchai (thanks)," the kachinas replied, "Now we shall all change ourselves into Badger Clan people and you, Badger, shall be our clan chief."

The Badger who came up through the earth at Oraibi was the first of the old Hopi healing society (Poboshwimkya), the members of which were celibate and not allowed even to touch a woman in an affectionate way.

When Awatobi was destroyed, some of the captive Badger Clan women were taken to villages on Second Mesa, and thus the Badger Clan was also established there.

Horn and Flute Clans

Tokoonavi, north of the Colorado River, was not only the village of young Tiyo, founder of the Snake Clan, but also that of the ancestral founders of the Horn Clan. According to the account by Jesse Walter Fewkes, after leaving Tokoonavi the founders of the Horn Clan searched widely for a permanent village site which would grant them both security and productive fields. Eventually, they came to a pueblo called Lenyanobi which was inhabited by people of the Flute clans. There they were made welcome, and soon the Horn and the Flute Clan people became very closely related and even joined forces in the performance of religious ceremonies.

According to their tradition, the Flute Clan people originated when their clan ancestor returned to the Underworld. His flute playing so charmed a beautiful girl there that they fell in love and were married. On their return to the Upper World she became the mother of the Flute Clan.

The Horn and the Flute clans remained at Lenyanobi for quite some time, but eventually they moved on in their long search for the homeland they felt was destined to be theirs. Finally, they entered Tusayan and, at a spring called Kwactapahu near Walpi, they built a village.

In time, they came to realize that this was not the place of their destiny. Tired from their long search, their religious leaders supplicated Alosaka, the deity of reproduction, to aid them. Alosaka took pity on them and explored all the surrounding country for them. Finally he returned and told them of Walpi, where the Snake people had established a secure village, and of the many fertile fields surrounding it. When Alosaka informed them that the Snake Clan people, who had once lived with them years ago at Tokoonavi, were now living at Walpi, the Horn Clan members were certain that they and their Flute Clan friends would be welcomed.

The two clans soon journeyed forth again. As they approached Walpi from the north they came to a line of cornmeal drawn across the trail — a symbol that Walpi was closed to them. Standing back of the line were the chiefs of the Bear and the Snake clans who challenged their right to enter Walpi. The leaders of the Horn and the Flute clans reminded the Bear and the Snake chiefs that they were all of the same Hopi blood, and that the Horn and the Flute people possessed ceremonies which had great power to bring clouds and rain that would be of benefit to everyone. This challenge and its response were repeated four times, after which the Bear and the Snake chiefs wiped out the line of cornmeal and bade them welcome.

Down through the years there have been dramatic reenactments of this coming of the Horn and the Flute clans to Walpi. Leaders of the ceremony make pilgrimages to various springs in the surrounding country where the Flute and the Horn clans had lived before becoming part of the population of Walpi. Various rites are performed in which rain-cloud symbols are drawn on the earth, accompanied by fervent prayers for rain and bountiful crops. As the ceremonial leaders return to Walpi they are again challenged by the chiefs of the Bear and the Snake clans, and then the ceremony of welcome is again performed. This historical pageant serves well as a significant prelude to the elaborate and beautiful ritual of the full Flute Ceremony which follows.

In the centuries following the arrival of the various clans and their establishment of the village communities in the region Mockingbird had assigned them on their emergence from Sipapu, the Hopi led a busy and increasingly involved life. What hours they did not spend in the fields or in the care and preparation of their food and other household tasks were devoted to their decidedly complex religious duties.

In spite of their isolation in the heart of a seemingly boundless desert there is much evidence that considerable trade was carried on by foot trail between the Hopi and other Southwestern tribes. It is more than likely that rumors had reached them of the strange, bearded white men who had come to Mexico from somewhere across the great ocean to the east. Even when the story of the arrival of some of these white men at Zuñi became known to the Hopi they were still a long and thirstful distance by trail from them. The Hopi undoubtedly felt safe in their fortress-like villages.

Encounter With Spain

NOT A SOUND had penetrated the thick stone walls of the old Hopi Indian pueblo of Kawaioukuh that night late in July, 1540. Secure in their village on the edge of Antelope Mesa, the people had slept as usual without fear or premonition of what the morrow would bring.

At dawn one of the men of the village wandered out close to the mesa's edge, and his startled cry woke several of the sleeping villagers. Soon all the men, women, and children of the community crowded along the edge of the cliff, looking down in dismay and unbelief. Even the wise old men of the village could offer the people no reassuring explanation.

During the night a forbidding-looking party of strangers had quietly made camp under the protection of the cliffs. The sharp eyes of the Hopi saw men with bearded faces that were white. But stranger still, these curious white-faced men had with them great animals such as no Hopi had ever seen or heard of. Were they some species of monstrous dog?

As they watched, these beasts occasionally pawed the ground and snorted, blowing puffs of smoke — or was it simply dust? — into the air. A few of these creatures were even more fearsome to behold — they seemed part man and part animal, for the upper part of a white man's body grew up from their backs. There were gasps of astonishment when one of these hybrid animals began to split in two, and the man-like part of it suddenly displayed legs and jumped to the ground where it walked about like any other man.

The people of Kawaioukuh were looking down on a Spanish expeditionary force consisting of seventeen cavalrymen, a few foot soldiers, and Zuñi Indian guides, accompanied by the warlike Franciscan priest, Juan Padilla, all under the command of Pedro de Tovar. These were the first white men and the first horses the Hopi had ever seen.

Why had they come to the Hopi country?

For an adequate answer we must go back more than a score of years.

[33]

In February, 1519, a party of Spanish adventurers, led by Hernando Cortés, set out to attempt the conquest of Mexico for the glory of King Charles the First of Spain (Emperor Charles V of the Holy Roman Empire) and their own personal enrichment. The expedition consisted of some five hundred soldiers, a few toy-like cannon, and sixteen horses.

The Indians along the coast where they landed were suspicious and hostile to these strange bearded white men and their awe-inspiring firearms and horses. They lost no time in dispatching runners to report the invasion to Montezuma, ruler of the Aztec empire, in his capital city 250 miles inland.

It seems incredible that within the space of a few years such a force could conquer the mighty Aztec empire, but three factors played into the hands of the Spaniards.

First: The arrogant power exercised by the Aztecs had alienated great numbers of other Mexican Indian tribes and they were ripe for rebellion.

Second: For centuries before the arrival of the Spaniards the concept of a plumed snake deity had been widespread in the Americas. The legends about this very complex deity are many and varied. He was commonly known as Quetzalcoatl, the name applied to him by the Aztecs, which literally means "quetzal-feathered serpent." The name, however, has many mystical inner meanings. Compared with some of the bloody Aztec deities dominant at the time of Cortés, Quetzalcoatl was a beneficent deity who had disappeared across the ocean to the east, leaving with his followers the feeling that he would return one day. It was this that led Montezuma and his people to think that Cortés and his men might well be descendants of that Quetzalcoatl whose return was anticipated. Therefore, the strangers must be welcomed and not opposed in any way. Nevertheless, Montezuma and his councillors were not altogether free from doubts.

Third: Shortly after a battle with one hostile tribe of Indians, the victorious Cortés and his men were appeased with gifts of "four diadems, some gold lizards and ducks, and two masks of gold," along with Malinche, an Indian girl who had been a slave of the conquered tribe. Baptized and renamed Marina, Malinche became the mistress of Cortés and also his chief interpreter, diplomat, and strategist.

A Spaniard once remarked to an Aztec chief, "The Spaniards have a disease of the heart for which gold is the specific remedy." As the conquest of Mexico proceeded this "disease of the heart" seems to have assumed epidemic proportions. Within less than a score of years the Spanish invaders had depleted even the vast gold reserves of central Mexico and had begun to search farther and farther afield for new sources of treasure.

Rumors had reached the Spaniards in Mexico that far, far to the north there were seven magnificent cities, rich in gold and turquoise — another Mexico to enrich the ruthless conquerors!

Under the leadership of Francisco Vásquez de Coronado an immense expedition was assembled at Compostela in the Mexican province of New Galicia. Coronado was only thirty years old at the time and many of the high-born soldiers of fortune who joined him were scarcely more than boys. The expedition consisted of a veritable army: 336 Spaniards, several hundred Indians, 559 horses, 150 cows, 5,000 sheep, several Franciscan˙priests, servants, slaves (some of whom were blacks), and even women and children. Coronado's own personal staff consisted of black slave-servants, a head groom and several lesser grooms, and a page, and he had a regular arsenal of arms. He even carried along a suit of armor with a feather-crested golden helmet.

Pedro de Tovar was appointed by Coronado as chief ensign, or standard bearer. He must have been one of the glamor boys of the expedition. According to H. E. Bolton, Tovar joined Coronado equipped "with thirteen horses, a coat of mail, some cuirasses and an assortment of native accouterments and weapons." He even took along several dogs.

When the vanguard of the Coronado expedition reached the fabled golden cities — the "Seven Cities of Cibola" — they turned out to be the then scattered pueblos of the Zuñi Indians. The disappointment of the Spaniards was overwhelming. This was no new El Dorado — not another Mexico weighted with gold. Instead of a great city sparkling with rare jewels they saw before them the small Zuñi mud-and-stone pueblo of Háwikuh.

The Spaniards were not welcomed by the Zuñi and hostilities soon broke out. Moreover, the Spaniards were greatly in need of food and they helped themselves to everything the Indians possessed that was of food value — corn, melons, turkeys, beans, and salt.

Eventually a short-lived peace of sorts was established with the heroic Indian defenders of Háwikuh. Again, the legend of Quetzalcoatl had preceded the Spanish. Were they, the Zuñi wondered, the white gods that would some day come to rule over the country with peace and justice?

The aggressive nature of the invaders soon dispelled any illusions the Indians may have had in this regard. Like ever-receding ripples from a paddle tossed into wide waters, the stories of Spanish brutality to the Indians spread far and wide by what is even today one of the most efficient means of human communication, the "moccasin telegraph" of the Southwest.

For several years the priest Bartolomé de Las Casas had been preaching against the brutality the Spaniards were exercising toward the Indians of Mexico. Like most Europeans of that day, the Spaniards whole-heartedly accepted the Aristotelian doctrine that one part of mankind is set aside by nature to be slaves in the service of masters born for a life of virtue free from manual labor. Largely because of de Las Casas, Coronado was ordered to treat the Pueblo Indians with considerate kindness. These orders were only too soon disregarded.

When Coronado found no gold among the Zuñi, he and his followers listened with eager ears to stories told them of another seven cities far to the north. Maybe these would prove to be the true golden Seven Cities of Cibola. To verify these accounts, he dispatched Tovar to lead a small party north into the province they named Tusayan, the Hopi country of today.

What happened on the July morning in 1540 when the Hopi discovered the Spaniards below their mesa cliffs is best told in the words of Castañeda's narrative of the Coronado expedition:

But in the morning they were discovered and drew up in regular order, while the natives came out to meet them, with bows, and shields, and wooden clubs, drawn up in lines without any confusion. The interpreter was given a chance to speak to them and give them due warning, for they were very intelligent people, but nevertheless they drew lines and insisted that our men should not go across those lines toward their village. While they were talking, some men acted as if they would cross the lines, and one of the natives lost control of himself and struck a horse a blow on the cheek of the bridle with his club. Friar Juan, fretted by the time that was being wasted in talking with them, said to the captain: "To tell the truth, I do not know why we came here." When the men heard this, they gave the Santiago [battlecry] so suddenly that they ran down many Indians and the others fled to the town in confusion. Some indeed did not have a chance to do this, so quickly did the people in the village come out with presents, asking for peace. The captain ordered his force to collect, and, as the natives did not do any harm, he and those who were with him found a place to establish their headquarters near the village. They had dismounted here when the natives came peace-fully, saying that they had come to give in the submission of the whole province and that they wanted him to be friends with them and to accept the presents which they gave him. This was some cotton cloth, although not much, because they do not make it in that district. They also gave him some dressed skins and cornmeal, and pine nuts and corn and birds of the country. Afterward they presented some turquoises, but not many. The people of the whole district came together that day and submitted themselves, and they allowed him to enter their villages freely to visit, buy, sell and barter with them.[1]

Castañeda's brief account of this first meeting of the Hopi with the white man certainly gives scant foundation for the stories, current in Zuñi just a few years later, to the effect that Tovar virtually demolished

Kawaioukuh and killed great numbers of its inhabitants. It is possible that he did. Castañeda was certainly in error regarding the cotton cloth, since, according to Hodge, the Hopi even then were the principal cotton-growers and weavers for that entire region.

Bitterly disappointed upon finding that the Hopi villages had nothing to satisfy the greedy Spanish appetite for gold and having not been commissioned to go beyond their villages, Tovar returned and reported to Coronado at Zuñi.

During his brief visit the Hopi had told Tovar of a great river many days' journey across the desert to the northwest, where strange giants lived. He retold the story to Coronado, who evidently was so intrigued by it that he quickly appointed his right-hand lieutenant, Don García López de Cárdenas, to lead a detachment of twenty-five horsemen and the usual retinue of servants and Indian guides back to Tusayan by the same route Tovar had taken.

Despite their bitter experience with Tovar, the Hopi received Cárdenas without hostility and even furnished him and his party with lodging and enabled him to recruit Hopi guides who were familiar with the long trail toward the "great river."

In all probability, the Hopi guides led Cárdenas' party along the well-known trail from Oraibi to their sacred shrines and salt deposit located near where the Little Colorado joins the main stream of the Colorado River as it enters Grand Canyon proper. One branch of this trail led over the plateau country and down into Cataract Canyon, the home of the Havasu Indians, friends of the Hopi. It was from some point close to this old trail that the Spaniards got their first view of the Grand Canyon.

Again, Castañeda's narrative describes the event:

After they had gone twenty days they came to the banks of the river, which seemed to be more than three or four leagues in an air line across to the other bank of the stream which flowed between them. This country was elevated and full of low twisted pines, very cold, and lying open toward the north, so that, this being the warm season, no one could live there on account of the cold. They spent three days on this bank looking for a passage down to the river, which looked from above as if the water was six feet across, although the Indians said it was half a league wide. It was impossible to descend, for after these three days Captain Melgosa and one Juan Galeras and another companion, who were the three lightest and most agile men, made an attempt to go down at the least difficult place, and went down until those who were above were unable to keep sight of them. They returned about four o'clock in the afternoon, not having succeeded in reaching the bottom on account of the great difficulties which they found, because what seemed to be easy from above was not so, but instead very hard and difficult. They said that they had been down about a third of the way and that the river seemed very large from the place which they reached, and that from what they saw they thought the Indians had given the width correctly. Those who stayed above had estimated that some huge rocks on the sides of the cliffs seemed to be about as tall as a man, but those who went down swore that when they reached these rocks they were bigger than the great tower of Seville. They did not go farther up the river, because they could not get water. Before this they had had to go a league or two inland every day late in the evening in order to find water, and the guides said that if they should go four days farther it would not be possible to go on, because there was no water within three or four days, for when they travel across this region themselves they take with them women loaded with water in gourds, and bury the gourds of water along the way, to use when they return, and besides this, they travel in one day over what it takes us two days to accomplish.[2]

These few words give us the basic account of how the first white men, thanks to the good offices of their Hopi guides, "discovered" the scenic grandeur of Grand Canyon.

Cárdenas and his party returned to the Hopi country travel-stained, weary, and badly frustrated in their fruitless search for the river of the giants. They seem to have entertained no concept of the importance of the river they had seen at the bottom of the great canyon. Castañeda makes no comment whatsoever that could lead us to conclude that they had any depth of appreciation of what they had experienced. They were not out to enjoy scenery! He concludes his account by stating simply, "They endured much thirst and hunger... and returned to Cibola [Zuñi] where they rejoined Coronado."[3]

Cárdenas' narrative concludes, "... the pueblos of that province were left in peace for they never again visited them, nor did they make attempts to find other settlements in that direction."[4]

With the departure of Cárdenas, the Hopi saw nothing of the Spaniards for forty-three years, but the memory of their aggressive inhumanity was not forgotten. During those years more and more stories of their brutality were carried to the Hopi from Indian settlements ravaged by Coronado. Undoubtedly the Hopi learned in gruesome detail of how the Spaniards had attacked some of the villages to the east of Zuñi. At one village, even after the Indians had surrendered, the Spaniards burned a hundred or more captives at the stake, according to the Castañeda narrative.

It is small wonder indeed that this introduction of the "little people of peace" to the white men who professed to be followers of the gentle founder of Christianity, served to sow deep and wide throughout the Indian Southwest bitter seeds of doubt, suspicion, and outright hatred.

The Hopi of the village of Awatobi, therefore, had no welcome for Antonio de Espejo when early in 1583 he and his party arrived below their mesa cliffs.

According to his own account, Espejo's journey up from Mexico into the Hopi country was a high-minded affair for the purpose of rescuing some missionary priests who had been working in New Mexico. As a matter of fact, this was only a subterfuge, for it was known in Mexico at the time that the priests were no longer alive.

Espejo himself was a fugitive from justice who hoped to become enriched by finding and conquering a new province. Just a year before this one of his companions, Gáspar de Luxán, had conducted a slave raid into the Indian country.

After journeying to the buffalo country of eastern New Mexico, Espejo's party turned westward and visited the pueblos of Zía and Acoma on their way to Zuñi. In Zuñi a dispute broke out among some members of the party and many of them left to return to Mexico. Espejo, however, lured by stories of a fabulous lake of gold — stories probably told him by the people of Zuñi in order to get rid of him — started northward with the remainder of his party and with about one hundred fifty Zuñi warriors he had been able to recruit; the Zuñi and Hopi were enemies at this particular time. Also in his party were a number of Indian slaves seized during the earlier part of the expedition.

The Hopi at Awatobi, remembering only too well Tovar's behavior at Kawaiokuh, sent warning to Espejo not to visit them, and to make a show of strength they managed to gain the support of neighboring Navajo. The Hopi women and children of the village, meanwhile, took their flocks and sought refuge in distant high country. Not deterred by the warning, Espejo and his party continued his march toward Awatobi (referred to in the chronicle of the expedition as "Aguato").

No doubt the people of Awatobi were greatly dismayed when they saw the size of the contingent of Zuñi warriors and Indian slaves of other tribes that Espejo had managed to assemble to support him. As the "people of peace," they decided that the odds were against them and that their best course was to make peace.

Espejo's own account of what occurred reads:

A league before we reached the province over two thousand Indians, loaded down with provisions, came forth to meet us. We gave them some presents of little value, which we carried, thereby assuring them that we would not harm them, but told them that the horses which we had with us might kill them because they were very bad, and that they should make a stockade where we could keep the animals, which they did. A great multitude of

Indians came out to receive us, accompanied by the chiefs of a pueblo of this province called Aguato. They gave us a great reception, throwing much maize flour where we were to pass, so that we might walk thereon. All being very happy, they begged us to go see the pueblo of Aguato. There I made presents to the chiefs, giving them some things that I carried for this purpose. The chiefs of this pueblo immediately sent word to the other pueblos of the province, from which the chiefs came with a great number of people, and begged that we go to see and visit their pueblos, because it would give them much pleasure. We did so, and the chiefs and *tequitatos* of the province, seeing the good treatment and the gifts that I gave, assembled between them more than four thousand cotton *mantas,* some colored and some white, towels with tassels at the ends, blue and green ores, which they use to color the *mantas* and many other things. In spite of all these gifts they thought that they were doing little for us, and asked if we were satisfied. Their food is similar to that of the other provinces mentioned, except that here we found no turkeys. A chief and some other Indians told us here that they had heard of the lake where the gold treasure is and declared that it was neither greater nor less than those of the preceding provinces had said. During the six days that we remained there we visited the pueblos of the province.[5]

From Awatobi, Espejo sent back to Zuñi five of his companions with much of the expedition's baggage, and he and four other companions, together with four Hopi guides and the usual retinue of Indian slaves, plodded westward in search of fabulous mines about which the Hopi had told him. When they came to the mines and Espejo discovered that they contained only copper, not gold or silver as he had envisioned, he returned with his party to Zuñi, disconsolate that once again no dreamed-of riches had materialized.

The failure of Coronado, Espejo, and their followers to find the golden "Seven Cities of Cibola" or the great lake of solid gold did not discourage other Spaniards from continuing to believe that somewhere in the vast expanse of country to the north an El Dorado of unimaginable riches awaited them. Petition after petition was made to the Spanish viceroy in Mexico City for authorization to organize expeditions for further exploration. However, it was more than ten years after Espejo's return before such authorization was granted. Finally in 1595 an agreement with Juan de Oñate for the conquest and Spanish settlement of what we now know as New Mexico and Arizona was given royal approval.

Oñate was a member of a family that had taken a prominent part in the conquest of Mexico. His wife was a granddaughter of Cortés and a great-granddaughter of Montezuma. His contract made him governor, *adelantado,* and captain-general of such provinces as he might conquer in the name of the King of Spain. He was also given a substantial government subsidy and extensive privileges. In addition, colonists who would accompany him were also given promises of important privileges and exemptions.

With great pomp and ceremony, lists were opened throughout Mexico for the recruitment of persons desiring to colonize the lands which they believed to offer such rich rewards. They were certain of conquest through subjugation of the Indians. The Spaniards undoubtedly felt that these conquered and cowed Indians would give them a bountiful supply of slave labor for the development of the region.

Changes in the viceroyalty, jealously, bickering — all came into focus against Oñate, with the result that it was not until February 7, 1598, that his party got under way. Notwithstanding the initial obstacles, no fewer than 400 men enlisted for the venture, and of these 130 took their families with them. Eighty-three carts of various kinds were needed to carry the baggage of the expedition, and a herd of more than three thousand head of cattle was driven on foot. Shortly after the cavalcade started it was joined by a large group of missionary priests under the leadership of Father Alonso Martínez.

A nephew of Oñate, Captain Vicente de Zaldívar, was able to lead the colonists on a new and more direct route to the Rio Grande than that taken by earlier expeditions, and the party arrived at the river on April 30, 1598. There, Oñate, with great pomp and circumstance, took possession of "all the kingdoms and provinces of New Mexico on the Rio del Norte [the Rio Grande] in the name of our Lord King Philip." One of the priests preached a sermon which was followed by both a religious and a secular celebration, much firing of guns, and very general rejoicing. During the afternoon, a comedy was performed, and the eventful day ended with the blessing of the royal standard.

As Oñate penetrated farther up into the valley of the Rio Grande he went through some sort of ceremonial at each village he encountered. Without any consideration of the Indians living in the area, he took possession of their lands in the name of the King of Spain and for the benefit of any of the Spanish colonists with him who might want to exploit them.

At the ford on the Rio Grande where El Paso stands today, Oñate took sixty men and pressed on ahead to "pacify the land" and to prepare it for settlement by the Spanish. But once more, the "moccasin telegraph" spread word ahead of him, and the Spanish found village after village deserted. By July 7 the party reached Santo Domingo Pueblo, and the record says that there Oñate received the submission of the chiefs of seven provinces.

By the eleventh of July he was at the village of Caypa, which he christened San Juan. He decided to make it his headquarters, and there the others of his party caught up with him.

He impressed fifteen hundred Indians to dig an irrigation ditch and start work on the establishment of what was to be a City of San

Francisco. By September 8, a small church had been completed. On the following day representatives from all the Indian villages' of the Rio Grande country so far explored were given rods of authority and the various pueblos were assigned to eight Franciscan missionaries.

A few weeks later, Oñate sent Zaldívar and sixty men east to hunt buffalo and to escort two priests to their assigned mission at the pueblo of Pecos. It was Oñate's hope that some buffalo could be caught alive and brought back to San Juan for breeding purposes.

On October 6, 1598, Oñate himself and a party started southeast to Zuñi. When he reached Acoma the people there supplied him liberally with corn and other foods. At Zuñi they stayed for several days. Among the tales told them there was that of the Zuñi Salt Lake, historically valuable to the Hopi as well.

Oñate sent Captain Marcos Farfán to see for himself. After three days Farfán returned to report, according to one narrator, that he was

convinced that it must be the best saline in the world, and truly, its salt would indicate this, for besides being exceedingly white and of marvelous grain, the saline was a league around, and in the center of it there was a spring from which the saline is engendered, and therefore is very salty; it has a depth of over a spear's length, and in all this depth the salt forms a hardened crust, so that in order to extract the salt it is necessary to use a bar or a pick-axe.[6]

In his sworn statement about the saline, Farfán said that he was "certain that neither in all Christendom nor outside of it, is there anything so grand, nor has the king anything to equal it."

It was November 8 when Oñate continued from Zuñi to the Hopi country. One of the historical chronicles says of the journey:

...we set out for the province of Mohoqui, or Mohoce, going four leagues without water. It snowed all the time, for it was midwinter. Next day, after travelling five leagues, we came across water near the road in a marsh. We camped for the night without water. Next day five leagues to some springs to get water, which was small in quantity. After travelling six leagues we camped for the night without water. On the following day we went five leagues to Mohoqui, and on the road only the men drank at a small spring which was underneath a rock. After going two leagues, at the first pueblo of Mohoqui or Mohoce they came out to receive us with tortillas, scattering fine flour upon us and upon our horses as a token of peace and friendship, and all of those provinces, which are four pueblos, rendered obedience to his Majesty and treated us very well.

We rested there one day. Next day we traveled three leagues to another small pueblo. On the following day we spent the night at the last pueblo. ...In all of them they received us as in the first. We rested for one day and on the following day we retraced the same ground, returning to the second pueblo of the said province. Next day we went to the first, where we rested three days.

From there on Friday, November 17, because of the reports of the rich mines, the governor sent Captain Marcos Farfán de los Godos with eight companions to make the exploration. Then, on Saturday, we set out on the return, by the same marches and places, to the province of Cuni, where we awaited the said explorers of the mines for seventeen days; and at the end of twenty-one days from their departure Captain Farfán and Captain Alonso de Quesada returned, having left the other seven companions in Mohoqui, as the animals were worn out. They brought flattering reports of the good mines discovered thirty leagues from the said province of Mohoqui, and they brought very good ores from which silver was later extracted by many and divers very rich assays, by means of mercury. This infused new life into over a hundred lifeless residents of this camp. They are ores which can be smelted.[7]

Oñate left the Hopi country on November 18, 1598, not to return until 1604, when he set out from his headquarters at San Juan Pueblo in search of the "South Sea" (Gulf of California), and again in 1605 on his way back. These visits were very brief and of no particular consequence as far as the Hopi were concerned. The Spaniards were too busy colonizing New Mexico, where better agricultural lands were available, to give much thought to the Hopi, distant so many arid miles to the west.

The only significant mention of the Hopi during the intervening years is an account of an incident at Santo Domingo Pueblo in 1599 when five or six hundred citizens of Acoma Pueblo were brought to trial there on charges of rebellion. Captured with them were two Hopi who had been visiting the great "pueblo of the rock." All were found guilty and each of the Acoma rebels was sentenced to have one foot cut off and to put in twenty years at hard labor for the benefit of the Spaniards. The two Hopi were only slightly more fortunate — each lost his right hand and was sent home as a warning to his people.

Hopi memories are long, and although it was thirty years before any Spaniards again played an important role in their history, it is not at all likely that this brutal maiming of the two visitors to Acoma had been forgotten.

Kachina or Christ?

THE TWENTIETH OF AUGUST, 1629, was to prove to be one of the most memorable days in Hopi history. From that date forward life on the Hopi mesas was never to be the same again.

Earlier in the year thirty Franciscan missionaries had left Mexico City to further the work of their church among the Indians of the Southwest. Three of these — Francisco Porras, Andreas Gutiérrez, and a lay brother, Cristobal de la Concepción, all known for their zealous dedication to the conversion of the Indians — arrived in New Mexico early in the summer and were assigned to set up a mission in the Hopi country. Porras, considered by fellow Spaniards to be a man of intelligence and character, as well as a missionary of genuine dedication to his church, was undoubtedly the inspiration and driving force behind the Franciscan attempt to convert the entire Hopi people to Christianity.

Accompanied by twelve soldiers, the three Franciscans — with crucifixes swaying against their grey-blue robes and tall staffs in hand — set out on foot on the long, rough, dry trail to Tusayan. It was August 20, the feast day of San Bernardo, when they arrived at Awatobi. Following the custom of their church, they dedicated the mission they planned to establish to this same San Bernardo.

The priests and their military escort did not meet with a friendly reception in Awatobi. They put this down as an attempt by the devil himself to impede and obstruct their plans for the conversion of the Hopi. The good fathers were sure that the Hopi were the willing tools of an apostate Indian from one of the pueblos on the Rio Grande.

According to an account written by Father Estévan de Perea, a leading missionary in New Mexico, the devil "took for his tool an Indian apostate from the Christian pueblos; he, preceding them, told the people of Moqui that some Spaniards, whom they would meet shortly, were coming to burn their pueblos, steal their property, and behead their children, and that the other Spaniards with the tonsures and vestments were nothing but imposters and that they should not allow them to sprinkle water on their heads because they would be certain to die of it."

In a short time the hostility of the Hopi mounted to such a pitch that the Spaniards had to post guard all night, every night. They must often have wondered if the fate of their newly established mission was not already sealed before they had made a single convert or were the recipients of a single friendly reassuring gesture.

Then an incident occurred that, to the friars — and to the people of Awatobi too — seemed nothing short of a miracle. This incident is briefly related in the Benavides *Memorial* of 1634:

After he [Fray Francisco de Porras] had converted nearly all the people by his preaching, always bearing one of the original crosses of Mother Luisa de Carrión, he inspired them to such devotion to the holy cross that the idolatrous priests in their anger incited many people to rebellion. They went to him, bringing a boy of twelve or thirteen who had been blind from birth; with great wrath their leader said to him, "You go about deceiving us and disturbing the people with what you call a cross. If what you say about it is true, place it on the eyes of this boy: if he regains his sight, we shall believe everything you tell us; but if not, we will kill you or cast you out in shame." The blessed father, with the spirit that the occasion demanded, went down on his knees with this very cross in his hands, raised his eyes to heaven, and beseeched the divine majesty to work a miracle, not only for the confusion of all these infidels but also for His own greater glory and that of His holy cross. Arising with great faith and courage, he placed it on the eyes of the blind boy, who instantly opened them and saw perfectly and began to shout, professing that he was now able to see. The Indians were so stunned and convinced that they venerated the father as a saint and promised to believe what he taught them. They took the boy in their arms and carried him through the streets and plazas, proclaiming that all should become Christians and do as the father taught them, for it was the truth and their own priests were deceiving imposters.[8]

This apparent miracle accomplished what the persuasion of the missionaries had so far failed to do. Large numbers of the Awatobi people were so impressed that they ceased their violent hostility and were eager for baptism. Thus the way was opened for the construction of the mission church of San Bernardo at Awatobi, and also hostility was lessened to such a degree that construction could be started on missions San Bartolemé at Shongopovi and San Francisco at Oraibi.

We know surprisingly little about these two missions and their branches, or *visitas,* in neighboring villages to which priests made regular visits in their missionary endeavors. Even the dates of their establishment are in doubt, and what records are now available are confusing as to the priests who served them.

In spite of the impression made upon the people of Awatobi by the

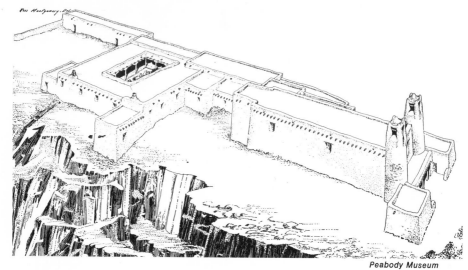

Peabody Museum

A conjectural reconstruction of San Bernardo de Aquatubi [Awatobi].

apparent miracle performed by Father Porras, the Hopi of the other villages proved to be much more unwilling converts.

The very zeal of Father Porras and his co-workers likely was their undoing. Ambitious plans were drawn up for the three major mission churches; the first, naturally, at Awatobi. Judging from the meager ruins, this was to have been a most impressive structure. However, work on the original plan was abandoned — why, we can only guess. Possibly the builder found that it would be difficult indeed to get timbers heavy enough and long enough to reach across the main part of the church. It is more likely that the excessive labor enforced upon the Indians was breeding dissent among them. Also, there is considerable evidence that the ceremonial leaders of the village remained steadfast in their determination to oppose the conversion of their people.

In June, 1633, just four years after he arrived in Tusayan, Porras died. His fellow Franciscan, Benavides, writing just a year later, states in his *Memorial*: "Not being able to kill the father openly, as they had often tried, they killed him secretly with poison, to the great sorrow of all the Christians and the friars but to his own great joy because he had attained the goal which he sought, namely, to give his life in the preaching of our Holy Catholic faith."

Hostile as the Indian religious leaders may have been to Porras, to students of the Hopi it seems decidedly unlikely that they would resort to poison to get rid of him. It seems much more probable that he died suddenly from natural causes.

It was about this time that construction work on the large church at Awatobi was abandoned in favor of a much smaller one at a different site. The Franciscans purposely chose a location where there was an important kiva. This they carefully filled with clean sand and over the top of it they built the main altar of their church, thus demonstrating the superimposition of Christianity over the religion of the Hopi.

This church of San Bernardo was an impressive structure with two imposing bell towers, quarters for the priests — including a walled garden — and work rooms, classrooms, crude sanitary facilities, pens for livestock, as well as quarters for the soldier guards. There is evidence that it served as headquarters for the entire missionary effort by the Franciscans in Tusayan.

Despite widespread and intense opposition by Hopi leaders and the majority of the Hopi people, the work of building the various mission establishments and the attempts to convert the Hopi went on year after year. The Franciscans in Tusayan were a long way from their fellows in the missions along the Rio Grande and still farther from church supervisory authorities in Mexico City. This isolation and the fanatical zeal of some priests led to many incidents that served to still further alienate the unconverted Hopi from the Spaniards and their Christian church.

In considering stories of mistreatment of Indians by Christian missionaries, we must remember that Spanish military and secular government authorities were very often at serious odds with Spanish religious authorities. Several charges of a serious nature were made against one Alonzo de Posadas who was at Awatobi from the spring of 1653 until sometime in 1655. One of these accusations was brought by the then governor of New Mexico, Don Diego de Peñalosa. In the latter's deposition, he states that when Posadas

was *guardian* in the pueblo of Aguatubi [Awatobi], being fearful that a leading Indian of the pueblo, whose name was Sixto, was making trouble with an Indian woman with whom Fray Alonzo had improper relations — the woman's name, according to the deponent's memory, being Isabel — Fray Alonzo ordered two *capitanes a guerro* to kill Sixto. When they had killed him, the friar feared that they would reveal the crime, and asked one Salazar, a *mestizo* who was *alcalde* mayor in the pueblo, to bring the two captains to swift and summary trial — in accordance with the practices of war — upon some pretext of disobedience and hang them, which he did.[9]

To the Hopi, at least to those who had not been converted, a rather amusing incident occurred during Posadas' time at Awatobi. According to the record:

During Father Posadas' absence from the pueblo [a Hopi named] Juan summoned the Indians to the church, where he put on the friar's vestments, took the incense burner and censed an altar, chanted the *Salve,* and then sprinkled holy water in the manner priests do it. For this offense, and because he was also guilty of grave sexual immorality, he was taken to Santa Fe and deposited in the convent. The prelate, Father Ibargaray, taking into account Juan's lack of understanding (*incapacidad*) of the seriousness of his acts, sentenced him to a period of service in the convent where he could be instructed in the faith.[10]

It can be presumed that Juan, knowing full well the great license allowed clowns in many Hopi ceremonials to poke ribald fun at the most respected citizens and revered religious characters, wondered at the severity of his punishment for staging what must have been quite a performance.

According to the records of a hearing before church authorities in Santa Fe during 1655 one of the most brutal acts inflicted upon the Hopi by a Franciscan missionary was perpetrated by Friar Salvador de Guerra. A man of Oraibi named Juan Cuna had been discovered in some act considered highly idolatrous by de Guerra. Before the people of the entire village, the Friar subjected the Hopi to such a severe beating that he was "bathed in blood." Not satisfied with this, de Guerra dragged Cuna into the church and thrashed him again. He then poured turpentine over the hapless Indian and set him on fire. Juan Cuna died as a result.

Was his act of idolatry merely the making of a kachina doll?

At the hearing in Santa Fe several Hopi testified that other Hopi had been whipped and doused with turpentine by de Guerra in the same way. As a result the friar was removed from the Hopi country but allowed to serve further in New Mexico.

In the report of a hearing held by the Inquisition in Mexico City on May 11, 1663, occurs the story of a soldier, Nicolás de Aguilar, who was charged with contempt of the church and using insulting language to priests while on duty in Tusayan. In his defense Aguilar declared that about eight years before, when Fray Francisco de Velasco was *guardian* of what he thought was the pueblo of Zuñi, and Fray Salvador de Guerra was *guardian* of the pueblo of Jongopabi,

> they took from the Indians a great amount of cloth and [other] tribute. The Indians went to the custodian to complain, or else to the governor. When the Indians returned . . . Fray Salvador had them brought to him and he went into their homes to search them. He found some feathers, or idols, and consequently seized [the people] and ordered turpentine brought so as to set fire to them.[11]

Aguilar said that he did not know how badly they were mistreated but that he knew a few of them who were marked by burns and that one of them was sent home to his pueblo. "The Indian," he went on, "was about to die of his burns and could not walk. Fray Salvador provided him with a horse, the Indian dying soon after, in spite of this. Whereupon the custodian immediately removed the two friars to the villa of Santa Fe, where they remained for a long time . . . saying no mass on account of this crime. Finally, they are still there; they say mass, and are *guardianes*. . . ."[12]

Aguilar had also heard that "these religious of Saint Francis caused some Indians in Moqui to dress as very penitent hermits; they walked about praying in penitence, carrying a cross and some large beads, and wearing haircloth shirts. They cooked [only] some pots of herbs for them to eat, so that the Indians were about to die, and complained. The religious punished the Indians and were themselves removed."[13]

This is one of the few references in the documentary history of the Hopi Spanish missions where there is a record of discipline being meted out to a missionary for conduct unbecoming a representative of the Christian religion.

That there are so few historical references to misconduct by Franciscan missionaries to the Hopi cannot be interpreted to mean that such incidents were rare during the fifty-year period of mission activity. Documents relative to the period that exist in archives in Spain, in Mexico, and in our own country are woefully inadequate. The existence of the accounts we have quoted, and a few others of similar content, certainly gives the impression that an unbecoming number of Spanish missionaries — in their fanatic dedication to winning converts — condoned such methods of discipline, just as their lonely isolation led some of them to violate their Church's regulations pertaining to chastity and general priestly conduct. Surely there were saints among them, but it should be remembered that the Franciscan friars led a hard life among largely hostile people. Men must be judged in relationship to their time, and those were harsh and cruel times.

The harsh labor enforced upon the Hopi in building the missions and in supplying food to the missionaries and their soldier guards, the brutal punishments inflicted upon apostates and those who rebelled, the failure of some priests to live up to the vows which the Hopi had learned were expected of them, the determination of the Franciscans to obliterate every aspect of Hopi religious belief and practice — all of these sowed the wind only too well for the whirlwind of the Pueblo Rebellion which swept the entire Southwest in 1680.

Pueblo Rebellion

LIKE THE HOPI, the Indians of the other pueblos chafed under Spanish oppression. Time after time the military and civilian authorities had to take ruthless measures to subjugate revolt in the many villages all the way from Taos to Zuñi. One of the most serious revolts, from the standpoint of the Spaniards, was that of the Zuñi in 1632 when two of the Spanish priests there were killed. As a result of this a punitive expedition was sent against the Zuñi, but they deserted their villages and found refuge on the top of Taaiyalone (their sacred Corn Mountain), where they remained for more than two years before they felt it was safe to return to their homes.

Close ties had always existed between the Hopi and the people of the New Mexican pueblos, especially Zuñi, and the Hopi were well aware of the various abortive attempts that had been made by them to throw off the Spanish yoke. During this troublous period a runner was dispatched to the Hopi from one of the Rio Grande pueblos, bearing pictures painted on buckskin to complement his message which was a plea to the Hopi to join in an uprising against the Spaniards. The Hopi, however, did not feel they were ready to participate in such an uprising. It was not until 1680 that a concerted effort was made by the majority of the pueblos to rid themselves of the Franciscans and all other Spaniards in the Southwest. The leader of this secretly planned and well-organized rebellion was an Indian religious leader of San Juan Pueblo, Popé. Considered by the Spaniards as a dangerous rebel leader in league with the devil himself, Popé well knew the punishment that would be meted out to him and to all those associated with him who were discovered fomenting an uprising against the Spaniards. He was determined that this time the Indians should not fail.

Popé and his allies spent many years in recruiting and perfecting their organization. As a religious leader he was granted admission to one of the large kivas at Taos. This great double pueblo became his headquarters. In this kiva he was said to communicate frequently regarding the rebellion with his special spiritual advisers — spirits, according to old Spanish records, named Caudi, Tilini and Tleume.

Among Popé's trusted lieutenants — again according to Spanish records — were Jaca of Taos, Catiti of Santo Domingo, and Tupatú of Picurís. Unfortunately, these records make no mention of Popé's lieutenant among the Hopi. He may well have been a young Hopi of Awatobi, known to the Spaniards as Francisco de Espeleta. This supposition is borne out by his background and the part he played in encouraging Hopi hostility toward the Spaniards in the years following the rebellion. If he was not Popé's chief Hopi lieutenant, he was at least one of his most valuable associates.

As a small boy in Awatobi, Francisco had been taken as a house servant by Father Joseph de Espeleta. According to church history, Father Espeleta reared the boy and taught him to read, write, and speak Spanish. Undoubtedly the name Francisco de Espeleta was given to him upon his being baptized into the Christian faith. Whatever Father Espeleta's motives may have been in virtually adopting this Hopi boy, in later years he must often have felt that the child had turned out to be the proverbial snake in the grass, for young Francisco developed a searing hatred of the Spaniards that flamed throughout his life.

Popé and his associates brought their plan for a concerted rebellion against the Spaniards to all the Pueblo and Hopi villages except those of the Piros far to the south — near where Socorro, New Mexico, is today. A knotted cord was carried by runners to all the villages which had agreed to join the rebellion. This set the date for a general uprising to take place apparently on August 13, 1680.

In spite of the great precautions that Popé and his leaders had taken to keep the date secret from the Spaniards — no woman, we are told, was entrusted with the secret — there were leaks. Popé accused his own son-in-law, Nicolás Bua, governor of San Juan Pueblo, of treachery and killed him. A few converted Indians confessed the plot to their priests. When word reached Governor Antonio de Otermín at Santa Fe, he attempted to send warnings to outlying missions.

When Popé realized that the cat was out of the bag, he knew that the only hope they had for success lay in immediate action. By his orders the people of the northern pueblos struck early on the morning of August 10. The rebellion spread like wildfire. The purpose of the Indians was to absolutely wipe the Spaniards and everything Spanish from the Southwest, and the bloodbath that ensued almost achieved its purpose within a few days.

The few hundred Spaniards who escaped took refuge with Governor

Otermín in his headquarters in Santa Fe. Others found refuge and defended themselves for a few days in the mission at Isleta Pueblo before fleeing the country. The account which follows was distilled from several sources, notably the works of Charles Wilson Hackett, Earle Forrest, Hubert Howe Bancroft, Hodge, and Lummis; Otermín's report also was helpful, as were tales remembered by a few old Hopi friends.

The siege of Santa Fe began on the morning of August 15, when the Spaniards discovered a large band of Indians south of the town burning the deserted houses, singing their victory songs, and jeering at the Spaniards as they advanced toward the thick-walled headquarters of the governor. Otermín sent out a small troop of soldiers to reconnoiter. They at once spotted an Indian known to them as Juan leading the advanced Indians. He was on horseback — armed with harquebus, sword, dagger, and other Spanish military equipment — and wearing a wide sash of red taffeta, which the Spaniards recognized as being from the convent at Galisteo. The soldiers managed to persuade him to enter the plaza to confer with the governor.

Otermín began the interview by accusing him of having betrayed the confidence of the Spaniards. Juan paid little attention to this accusation. The rebellion, he said, was sweeping the entire province and the Indians who had come with him were fully determined to destroy Santa Fe and to kill all the Spaniards there unless they were willing to leave the country forever. He then displayed to the governor two crosses, one red and the other white. If the Spaniards were determined to resist the Indians they should choose the red one. If they agreed to leave the country they should choose the white cross. Otermín, not yet realizing the extent of the rebellion, refused even to consider such alternatives, and the Indian leader rode back to join his forces.

When the Indians heard of Otermín's decision, they raised a great shout and began ringing all the church bells in the parts of the town they controlled. As a further sign of their defiance, they set fire to the chapel of San Miguel.

Every day more and more Indians from distant pueblos joined in the siege. They cut off the water supply, and the plight of the Spaniards became desperate. The cattle and horses they had brought with them into the patio of the governor's headquarters began to die. After five days Otermín realized that their position was hopeless and, making the best preparations possible, he decided to make a break for it.

At daybreak the Spanish soldiers and all other men able to bear arms led a surprise attack on the Indian besiegers. They succeeded in breaking through and in capturing forty-seven Indians, whom they shot. As the Spaniards fled to the south, they were taunted by victorious

Indians singing their victory songs and calling out to the Spaniards, "God, your Father, and Santa María, your mother, are dead. Our own gods whom we have obeyed have never died!"

In the vast orgy of the successful rebellion, from Taos to Zuñi, everything Spanish that the victorious Indians could find was destroyed. The old story of violence breeding violence was reenacted with a thoroughness bred of desperate frustration.

In the far distant Hopi country the same bitter frustration, stemming from years of Spanish domination and religious intolerance, aroused even the "people of peace" to violence.

Unfortunately, from the historian's point of view, the destruction that occurred everywhere in the Spanish provinces—their New Mexico—included all church and government records. We are told that in the Hopi country no Spaniards were left alive to record the uprising. What information we have is sparse indeed. We do not even know the exact date when the rebellion began on the Hopi mesas. Even in Hackett's definitive account of the great uprising we find only a few scattered details of what occurred in Tusayan. He does inform us that at Oraibi Father Joseph de Espeleta and Father Agustín de Santa María of San Miguel Mission were killed, as were Father Joseph de Figueroa of San Bernardo Mission at Awatobi and Father Joseph de Trujillo of San Bartolomé Mission at Shongopovi, and that the mission churches were all destroyed.

Apparently several of the Hopi at Awatobi remained steadfast to their conversion to Christianity, but the Hopi who remained loyal to their own religion succeeded in destroying the church there and they converted the quarters of the priests into part of the native village. The Christian altar, which had been erected in "superimposition" over the Hopi kiva, was torn down. Even the bells of the mission were broken. The churchyard was put to use as a sheep corral.

The great squared, lightly carved *vigas* of the mission churches were regarded as too valuable for firewood. Many of them eventually were used in various Hopi buildings and some, very appropriately, became roof beams for kivas in Oraibi and Shongopovi.

In even relatively recent years two of these great beams lay in the street before Tewaquaptewa's house in Old Oraibi, and the old village chief took very evident delight in telling white visitors about them. He would always take any visiting group a few hundred feet along the eastern edge of the mesa back of the village to show the deep ruts there. These, he would explain, had been worn by the butt ends of the logs which Hopi had been forced to drag many long miles from Black Mesa into Oraibi to help in the building of the Spanish mission church there. To

Ruts in the hard rock at Oraibi Mesa, made — according to legend — when the Hopi were forced to drag in logs from great distances for the building of the Franciscan mission.

help out his little English, Tewaquaptewa would pantomime the back-breaking work impressed upon the Oraibi people by the Spaniards. On the way back to the village he would delight in going through the motions of a Hopi dancer and singing a kachina song.

Although the great rebellion drove the Spaniards from Tusayan most effectively, Spanish influence on Hopi life was indelible. The myth that the white-faced Spaniards were descendants of Quetzalcoatl returning to help the Indians was dispelled forever. There developed a distrust, even a hatred, of everything Spanish which has permeated Hopi thinking down through the centuries. A deep and painful schism developed between the small minority of Hopi converted to Catholicism and the great majority who remained true to the Hopi religion.

The years following the rebellion brought many refugees into the Hopi country from the ravaged pueblos of New Mexico. For the most part these in time were absorbed into the Hopi way of life.

Introduced into the Southwest by the Spaniards, sheep, cows, and chickens from that time on would add protein to the Hopi diet. Horses and burros would prove useful in transporting Hopi over the wide reaches

of their deserts. Indeed, what would a Hopi village be without a burro
or two chewing on corn husks and flapping long ears in the dry sun-
drenched air?

The only Franciscan contribution to the religious life of the Hopi
was not exactly an intentional one. In certain present-day Hopi ceremonials, a curious participant can be observed. At first glance its costume
is much the usual kachina one, but it wears a mask with horns and a
cow-like snout and ears. Thus, thanks to the hated Spaniards, to the richly
varied pantheon of Hopi supernatural characters has been added the
Cow Kachina.

Following the destruction of the mission churches a period of
relative calm and reflection settled over Tusayan, but the stories that came
to the Hopi villages from the pueblos of the Rio Grande told only too
vividly that the ignominious retreat of the Spaniards from Santa Fe was
not followed by an era of freedom and a restoration of tranquility. Like
the after-shocks of a terrific earthquake — often almost as devastating
as the original convulsion — the chaotic conditions which followed the
great rebellion were often as unpleasant for the Indians concerned as
were the oppressive measures of the Spaniards.

Popé and his chief officers, like the leaders of many a revolution,
apparently became drunk with success and power. Knowing very well
the rules of personal conduct expected of a ceremonial leader, the Hopi
must have found it difficult to believe the tales that came so constantly
over the long trails from Santa Fe. Time and time again came the rumors
that Popé and his captains were taking the most beautiful women in all the
pueblos for themselves, and that men who opposed them often were killed.
Excessive tribute was being exacted by them from all the villages which
had participated in the rebellion. Soon the entire region in New Mexico
that had united so successfully to drive the Spaniards out was torn with
civil strife and war.

To make matters worse, a bitter drought descended upon the
area, and raiding parties of Utes and Apaches took full advantage of
the situation to plunder the disorganized pueblos.

The period of peace enjoyed by the Hopi after the rebellion did not
last long. The Spanish priest Juan Amando Niel, whose *Apuntamientos*
have been quoted by Bancroft, related how during this period half the
Tano people — four thousand men, women and children — left their
pueblos in New Mexico and "went away with their Spanish plunder to
preserve themselves and let their cattle increase. They went via Zuñi
to Moqui, and having induced that people to give them a home, gradually
gained possession of the country and towns, reducing the original Moquis

to complete subjection, extending their conquests far to the S. W., and seating their young king, Trasquillo, on the throne at Oraibi."[14]

It is difficult to believe that four thousand Tanoan people could "dispossess" the Hopi without leaving a trace of their culture or their language. In many an ancient document we find decided exaggerations as to numbers, especially when such distortion of fact might in some way favor the Spanish historical image. The fact remains that the Tanoan villages were abandoned and as a people they disappeared.

Escalante, a Franciscan missionary who naturally saw things from the Spanish viewpoint, wrote:

> The rebel pueblos began to quarrel and wage bitter war. The Queres, Taos, and Pecos fought against the Tehuas and Tanos; and the latter deposed Popé — on account of his despotism, etc. — electing Luis Tupatú in his place. He ruled the Tehuas and Tanos till 1688, when Popé was again elected; but died soon, and Tupatú was again chosen. Alonso Catiti died earlier; entering an estufa to sacrifice, he suddenly burst, all his intestines coming out in sight of many Indians. Later each pueblo of the Queres governed itself. The Apaches were at peace with some of the pueblos, but in others did all the damage they could. The Yutas, as soon as they learned the misfortunes of the Spanish waged ceaseless war on the Jémez, Taos, and Picuries, and especially the Tehuas on whom they committed great ravages. Not only thus and with civil wars were the apostates afflicted, but also with hunger and pestilence . . . of the Tiguas only a few families escaped and retired to the province of Aloqui (Moqui); of the Piros none escaped.[15]

It was during this turbulent period that large numbers of the Tewa people left their villages along the Rio Grande, especially Santa Clara, and sought refuge elsewhere — some with the Hopi and some with the Navajo. Tewas from a village known as Tsawarii, so Hodge was convinced, at this time established the village of Hano on First Mesa. The Hopi's long tradition of offering asylum to other Indians who also sought a peaceful life made sanctuary possible for great numbers of these refugees. Some of these people became, to all intent, Hopi and remained Hopi all their lives. From time to time other groups returned to their former pueblos, once they felt that they would be secure there.

Stories continued to reach the Hopi that the Spaniards were planning to return and reconquer the entire province from which they had been driven so ignominiously. During the years following, therefore, the Hopi wisely decided to move their villages of Walpi, Mishongnovi, and Shongopovi to higher locations on their mesa tops which would offer them a strategic advantage, not only against the Spaniards should they indeed return, but also against bands of Utes, Navajos, and Apaches from whose raids the Hopi were suffering.

The Hopi of Oraibi, already perched high on the edge of its mesa and commanding a sweeping view over the surrounding desert, felt secure in their ancient location. They took no added precautions other than to roll and carry quantities of rock to the edges of the mesa overlooking the few steep trails that were the only means of access to the old village from the desert below.

In the closing years of the seventeenth century word came to the Hopi that the Spaniards were indeed bent on reconquest. Stories from Isleta, Zía, Santo Domingo, and other New Mexican villages told of bloody attempts at reconquest. Otermín with a force of 146 soldiers, 112 Indian allies, 975 horses, and a supply train of oxcarts and pack mules left Paso del Norte and on December 6, 1681, recaptured Isleta. His lieutenants brought reports of the hostility of Cochití, Santo Domingo, and certain other pueblo villages. They had learned that the villages had already sent runners to gain the support of the Hopi in once more driving Otermín and his forces back where they had come from. This news prompted Otermín to retreat once more and on January 1, 1682, he did so, taking with him 385 people from Isleta.

Everywhere Otermín or his lieutenants had gone they had followed a ruthless scorched-earth policy, burning or otherwise destroying everything in their path that they considered would be of value to the Indians.

Although Otermín retreated, he left behind him nothing to give the Hopi the impression that the Spaniards had achieved any change of heart regarding their long-held concept that Indians were destined to be slaves.

Attempts at Reconquest

RUMOR UPON RUMOR CONTINUED to reach the Hopi that the Spaniards were determined to regain what they considered to be their lost provinces and to resubjugate the Indians. Undoubtedly these rumors prompted long discussions among wise old Hopi as they smoked and counseled together in their kivas. No true unanimity resulted from these councils as to exactly what policy should be followed if and when Spanish soldiers should come again to Tusayan.

Francisco de Espeleta, Father José de Espeleta's protégé, now a bitter enemy of the Spaniards, was a leader of those opposing any policy of moderation or compromise. There is indication in the Spanish records that Francisco had become village chief of Oraibi. It seems likely, however, that the majority of the Hopi leaders decided that the only effective way they could possibly cope with the armed might of Spain was to follow as much as possible a policy of nonresistance and noncooperation.

According to *The Mercurio Volante* by the Mexican scholar Don Carlos de Sigüenza y Góngora (published in 1693), Governor and Captain General Don Diego de Vargas Zapata y Lujan Ponce de León entered Tusayan by way of Zuñi to retake it for the glory of the King of Spain and for what enrichment Spanish settlers might wrest from it. With the Captain General were sixty-three Spanish soldiers and a still larger band of Pueblo Indians under the leadership of Don Luis Tupatú who had been one of Popé's lieutenants in the Pueblo Rebellion. Oxcarts and pack mules carried the baggage.

Of their journey up from Zuñi we learn that

From the 15th to 19th of November, 1692, this stretch was covered with indescribable hardship which was [hardly] lessened by the fact that almost unexpectedly the General found himself in the midst of 800 Moqui Indians, all armed, while the horses of our men were coming up very slowly and almost in a state of exhaustion on account of the lack of water. So literally true was this situation that there were scarcely 25 men up with the General. It is

[59]

obvious that, of the whole campaign, this was the day most fraught with peril, for the Moqui imitated the Hemes in throwing dust, and with even more raucous shouting and din, went so far as to take away the weapons from some of our men. No resistance was made to this because the General, by the severest injunction, forbade them to do so. The chief of this pueblo (Awatobi), Miguel by name, who had come out at the head of his men, rode at the General's side.[16]

Vargas made an unsuccessful attempt to convince an assembly of Hopi at Awatobi that his was a peaceful mission. Although the Awatobi chief known to the Spaniards as Miguel made friendly overtures to Vargas, the crowd continued its hostility. Realizing that he was making no impression, Vargas changed his tactics and threatened violence. The Hopi then decided to try nonresistance. The chronicle continues:

. . . they laid down their arms and knelt on the ground. After this the Spaniards went on to the pueblo and entered what served as a public square, whose gateway permitted only one person to go in at a time, and that by turning sideways, and there they took possession of the town in the name of the King and our Lord. When he had told the natives that he would return the following day for their reconsecration, the General, accompanied by many Indian troops, left the town and went to a nearby waterhole [probably Tallahogan spring]. He ordered them to bring some firewood, because it was very cold, and, noting that they appeared sullen, he threatened that the fire would be built with their own weapons and even their own bodies . . . they brought him a great deal of wood. . . . On the morning of the following day, November 20th, an entry was made and the reconsecration of the church and the baptism of infants was performed. When the chief, Miguel, asked the General to act as godfather to his grandchildren and had received this favor, which he prized highly, he begged the Spanish governor to honor him again by being his guest.[17]

The next day Vargas disregarded the dire warnings of Miguel and insisted upon visiting Walpi and the villages of Second Mesa. With Miguel riding by his side Vargas ignored hostile "howlings and whoop-ings" and received the leaders of Walpi.

In accordance with their decision not to resist the Spaniards these Walpi leaders set up a cross and permitted the people of Walpi to be consecrated to the Catholic faith as loyal subjects of the King of Spain. Spokesman for these Hopi, Vargas relates in a letter to his King, was an old man accompanied by Ute, Apache, and Havasupai allies.

Considering how few Hopi had even the most meager knowledge of Spanish, this Christian ceremonial must have had little meaning for them, except that it was saving them from Spanish harquebuses, muskets, stone-throwing mortars, and slavery.

From Walpi Vargas journeyed on to Mishongnovi and Shongopovi, where the same ceremonial procedure was carried out. He did not travel on to Oraibi but claimed that in response to a message sent there demanding their allegiance "a submissive answer was given."

Vargas and his entourage left Awatobi on November 24 to return to Zuñi, assured, at least according to his statements in the records, that the province of Tusayan had indeed been reconquered for the glory of Spain and its people consecrated to the Catholic faith.

In only a short time, however, he realized how mistaken he had been. In 1693 and again in 1696 serious rebellions against the Spaniards broke out in many of the New Mexican pueblos, and these had important effects upon the Hopi. Again freedom-loving Indians sought sanctuary in that Switzerland of the New World, Tusayan. So serious was the rebellion of 1696 in New Mexico that a large band of Tewa Indians founded a village of their own close to the Hopi mesas, possibly at a site known as "Five Houses" on the road from Winslow to Polacca.

In 1697 Vargas was replaced as governor by Pedro Rodríguez Cubero. Two years later, according to Bancroft, the Oraibi chieftain Espeleta, disturbed by the submission to the Spaniards of many Indian nations in the Southwest, led a delegation of twenty of his followers to Santa Fe to meet with Cubero. He proposed to the governor that they agree each of their nations, Spain and the Hopitu-Shinumu, should live in peace with the understanding that each would recognize the other's right to its own religion! Cubero would not accept these terms and Espeleta and his delegation returned to Tusayan.

Bitter hostility continued in Tusayan between the minority group of Hopi — who remained constant to their baptism into Christianity and friendly to the Spaniards — and the majority who never deviated from the Hopi way of life.

Of that situation Father José Valverde wrote:

In the . . . year 1700, carried away by . . . [apostolic] zeal, Fathers Fray Juan de Garicochea and Fray Antonio Miranda set out on the road apostolically for the . . . province of Moqui. They reached the first pueblo, called Aguatubi [Awatobi], where they reduced all the natives and baptized many. Desiring to remain among them, from here they notified the Indian Don Francisco Espeleta that it was their intention to go on to the other pueblos. Upon receiving this news the said Indian Espeleta came with more than eight hundred Indians to the place where the two religious were, and the latter went out about the distance of an arquebuse shot to meet them. As soon as the Indians saw them they began to draw their bows and threaten the religious with them, but they did not fire any arrows, though some of them struck the fathers some blows with their bows.

The Indians entered the pueblo, where the religious labored more than six hours, preaching to the said Don Francisco de Espeleta and those of his chiefs who were acquainted with the Castilian language, and yet with all this they returned to their pueblos that same day indifferent and obstinate. The religious remained there some days instructing the Indians already reduced and then went back to their missions to make ready some things for their return, and to report to the prelate and to the governor, so that the latter might station some soldiers there to protect those Indians.

At this time, his people being infuriated because the Indians of the pueblo of Aguatubi had been reduced to our holy faith and the obedience of our king, he [Espeleta] came with more than one hundred of his people to the said pueblo, entered it, killed all the braves and carried off the women, leaving the pueblo to this day desolate and unpeopled.[18]

The destruction of the village of Awatobi is one of the most significant events in Hopi history. It is fortunate that in addition to Valverde's brief reference to it there are other allusions to it in Spanish records of the period. Also, several Hopi versions were handed down from one generation to another, some of which were later published. From all these sources we have pieced together the following account.

Tapolo, Chief of Awatobi, had become greatly distressed over so many of the people of his village proving untrue to the Hopi religion and the Hopi way of life. He determined upon a ruthless course of action, one utterly at variance with basic Hopi beliefs. He took this plan to the chiefs of other Hopi villages, hoping to gain their support for it. He was able to do so in the villages where hatred of the Spaniards was strong and where there was steadfast adherence to the Hopi religion. This incredible plan encompassed the complete destruction of Awatobi!

As in most crises of this kind, when ill-feeling has been engendered on major matters, there were other minor matters that served to intensify the hatred of other Hopi for the people of Awatobi. In his *Hopi Journal* Alexander M. Stephen related a Hopi legend to the effect that during one period of drought a widespread fire swept through the Hopi country, and the fields of all the villages *except Awatobi* were destroyed (there is good reason to believe that in those days there was a much more luxuriant growth of vegetation in the Hopi country east of the Little Colorado than there is today). Furthermore, the people of Awatobi had more horses than those of other villages and, it was claimed, took unfair advantage during rabbit hunts.

When the Awatobi chief visited Oraibi he took with him two small clay figures. He explained that one represented all the men of Awatobi and the other all the women. He urged the Oraibi chief to choose between them. The latter picked up the figure representing the women. By this choice it was understood that when the strife at Awatobi had ended the men of the Warrior Society of Oraibi would have the right to select whatever women they wished from among the captives. The remaining prisoners were to be disposed of as the Warrior Society men of the other villages saw fit. The chiefs of Awatobi and Oraibi then determined upon the day for the attack.

The Oraibi chief called the leaders of his Warrior Society together and announced the prepared plan for the punishment of Awatobi. When the details for the attack were thoroughly understood by the men of the Warrior Society, they went through the streets of Oraibi urging the people to busy themselves making bows and arrows and heavy shields for the assault upon Awatobi four days hence.

The Oraibi chief selected three of his nephews to carry news of the plan to the chiefs of Walpi, Mishongnovi, and Shongopovi. The messengers returned shortly with word that the Warrior Societies of all three of these villages would join in the attack and that they would form two war parties, one made up of men from Walpi and the other of men from Shongopovi and Mishongnovi. All three parties were to meet at dark on the evening of the fourth day at the foot of the Awatobi mesa.

During that night the Awatobi chief, followed by his wife carrying a great bundle of piki, joined the war party. As they ate together he suggested that when the first light of dawn came they should move to a strategic hiding place closer to the village from which they could see the housetops against the eastern sky.

Under some subterfuge or other he had arranged with all the men of Awatobi to meet together in their kivas before sunrise that day. As soon as every man had disappeared down the kiva ladders the chief's son was to stand high upon the roof of their house and so serve as a signal for the attack.

Just as the sun rose the chief's son suddenly stood in tall silhouette against its glowing disk. The raiders swept into Awatobi, surrounded the kivas and quickly pulled up the entrance ladders, trapping the able-bodied men of the village inside. When the trapped men looked up they were menaced by dozens of war arrows aimed down at them. Others of the war party quickly set fire to great bundles of firewood and threw them down among the trapped men. Others threw down armfuls of Spanish peppers, for which the Awatobi people had developed a taste. The roofs of the kivas soon caught fire and began collapsing on the dead and dying.

Chaos reigned in Awatobi as the victorious men of Walpi, Shongopovi, Mishongnovi, and Oraibi swept through the village, making captive the weeping women and children and carrying off with them such booty as struck their fancy. The village itself was not destroyed. But time, the elements, and later men from the Hopi towns in search of building materials saw to its ruin.

At Skeleton Mound (Maschomo), between Walpi and Mishongnovi, the conquering party halted with their prisoners and a dispute broke out. The men from Oraibi protested that the men from the other villages had not honored the agreement that their chiefs had made regarding the disposition of the prisoners. The warriors from the other three villages refused to surrender any of the girls and women they had captured. The leader of the Oraibi warriors in a fiery speech proposed that they should kill all of the prisoners right then and there and thus eliminate the cause of their dispute. A fierce fight ensued in which several of the captive women and children were killed before pleas for mercy stopped the carnage. Remaining women and children were then divided among the warriors of the three villages. Most (some accounts say all) of the able-bodied men of Awatobi were killed.

What appears to be confirmation of this tragic episode is contained in a paper by Christy G. Turner II, and Nancy T. Morris outlining their studies of the dentition of skulls excavated some years ago at Skeleton Mound.

The fields and grazing lands that had been Awatobi's were soon taken over by the Hopi of First Mesa. The captured women and children were absorbed into the general life of the three mesas, and the once proud village of Awatobi became an uninhabited ruin. To this day the placid sheep of both Hopi and Navajo graze in the silence of a town where Massau-u, the God of Death, reigns as village chief (Kikwongwi).

The final years of Spain's attempted domination of the Hopi cover scant pages of the few records that have come down to us. In 1701 Cubero, chafing under Espeleta's refusal to submit to Spanish sovereignty, led a detachment of soldiers against the Hopi. Several Hopi were killed and many were taken captive but later released as a matter of good policy. This action did not intimidate the Hopi. In fact, it resulted only in intensifying their determination to remain free of any Spanish influence, secular or religious.

During the years that followed Cubero's abortive expedition to the Hopi villages, Hopi from time to time traveled to New Mexico. There they often met Spaniards who wishfully thought them to be ambassadors of peace. In reality they were usually Hopi traders following their age-old tradition, bartering throughout the Southwest.

In 1716 the then governor in Santa Fe, Captain Felix Martínez, led a force of sixty-eight soldiers into the Hopi country and, according to his report, waged two fights against the Hopi in which several Indians were killed. According to the Hopi, the Spaniards succeeded only in destroying some corn fields before retreating to Santa Fe.

Ten years later the responsibility for conversion of the Hopi to Christianity was transferred from the Franciscans to the Jesuits, who seemed to be having considerable success in their missionary work among the southern tribes. However, there is no evidence that the Jesuits made any real effort to convert the Hopi, although several priestly scouts of that order occasionally looked over the area.

One rather important event took place in 1742. Two priests, Delgado and Piño, came to Tusayan and managed to persuade 514 Tigua, who had migrated to Tusayan from New Mexico following the great rebellion, to return to their old homes, the pueblos of Sandía, Alameda, and Pajarito. The priests wished to have these pueblos reestablished because the Spaniards were deeply concerned over French threats to what they considered their territory in the Southwest and also over the intensification of Navajo and Comanche raids upon their settlements. As a result, the Hopi enjoyed a long period of comparative freedom to live their own lives in their own way.

Tusayan was not entirely forgotten by the Spaniards, however. In their desire to find a satisfactory route to link Santa Fe with their settlements in California, two exploring priests later made brief visits to the Hopi.

Silvestre Vélez de Escalante was a missionary priest at Zuñi in 1775 when he received a request from the governor in Santa Fe to report on (1) the possibility of a route between Santa Fe and Monterey, the Spanish capital of California, and (2) a new plan for subjugation of the Hopi.

Escalante and a small party made a horseback trip to Walpi and on to Oraibi. At Oraibi he tried to talk to the Hopi about Christianity, but he received a very hostile reception. Returning to Walpi, he was delighted to find there a young Havasupai. Herbert E. Bolton tells of their meeting.

The friar lighted a *cigarro,* he and the Cosnina [Hopi term for Havasupai] alternately puffed on it as long as it lasted, "and then they smoked another." Meanwhile the Indian told Escalante about his homeland in the west, made him a map of the trail from Oraibe to the Cosnina settlement in Havasupai Canyon, showing the turns, the days' journeys, watering places, villages, the size of the country, the course of the Colorado River, and neighboring tribes. All this he mapped with charcoal on an equestrian breastplate, belonging apparently to one of the soldiers in the friar's escort. Escalante wrote to the governor at Santa Fe, "I do not reproduce the map here, because after I have seen all those places I hope to make one myself." The conference ended, the Cosnina said, "Padre, now my heart is at peace." With the information acquired, Escalante rode back to Zuñi and thence to Santa Fe to confer with the governor. He little dreamed what an Homeric adventure was in store for him as a sequel to that friendly smoke with the young Cosnina Indian from the Colorado River.[19]

At the very time Escalante was trying to gain a friendly reception among the Hopi, a fellow Franciscan missionary, Francisco Garcés, was exploring a route from California eastward toward Tusayan. With a horse and a Mojave Indian guide, Garcés set forth on June 5, 1776, from the Colorado River north of The Needles bound for the Havasupai and the Hopi.

After his visit to the Havasupai, Garcés journeyed on toward the Hopi. With eight Yavapai companions he reached Oraibi on July 2. As he entered he unrolled a banner bearing a vivid picture of non-baptized "heathen" suffering the torments of the damned in Hell. This was old stuff to the Hopi, and they gave him a cold reception, although they were hospitable to the Yavapai who came with him. He was not even permitted to enter a house to sleep and was not allowed any food either for himself or for his horse.

Realizing that he was gaining nothing, at midnight on July 3 Garcés wrote a letter to the missionary at Zuñi, who proved to be Escalante, giving an account of his exploration up to that point. It is possible that at the very time Garcés was writing it was early morning of that July 4 in Philadelphia when the Liberty Bell was ringing.

When morning came to Oraibi, Garcés bribed a young Hopi to see to it that his letter would be carried on to Zuñi. He then started on his long journey back to his missionary post at Yuma.

In view of the hostility of the Hopi and the Apache, Escalante was convinced that a route from Santa Fe to Monterey must be found well north of one he had taken the year before. With that in mind he and a well-organized party, headed by Escalante's superior, Francisco Atanasio Domínguez, set out from Santa Fe on July 29, 1776. One of the most important members of the expedition was a retired military captain, Don Bernardo Miera y Pacheco. He was custodian of an astrolabe with which he made astronomical observations along the way. He also was the party's cartographer and he drew a detailed map of their route. Miera also wrote a report of the journey which complements Escalante's own invaluable diary.

They managed to get as far west as Utah. There they realized that their chances of getting to Monterey before winter set in were slim. They had already experienced snow and bitter cold. They decided to turn south and return to Santa Fe by way of the Havasupai and the Hopi villages.

They crossed the Colorado at "The Crossing of the Fathers" and traveling almost due south passed through where Tuba City and Moencopi are today. There on November 14 they discovered several large herds of cattle belonging to the Hopi. Hungry as the party was, they decided against killing any of the cattle for food, as they realized this would only further antagonize the Hopi. On November 16 they struck a well-used trail that led them to Oraibi.

To their surprise, instead of the hostile reception they expected, they were received in a very friendly fashion and given food for themselves and their horses, of which they were in very great need. They visited the villages on Second Mesa where they also met with a friendly reception, but they were told frankly that although the people of Shongopovi and Mishongnovi were willing to be friends, they had no desire to become Christians.

On First Mesa they also were welcomed and spent the night in the home of the village chief of Hano. On First Mesa they met an old Indian who had come to Hano from his original home at the pueblo of Galisteo in New Mexico where he had been baptized as a Christian but later had become an apostate.

Escalante wrote:

We were told by an apostate Indian named Pedro, from the pueblo of Galisteo in New Mexico, who was now old and had great authority in this pueblo of the Tanos at Moqui, that they were now at fierce war with the Navajo Apaches who had killed and captured many of their people. For this reason, he added, they were hoping that some fathers or Spaniards would come to these pueblos in order through them to beg from the Señor Governor some aid or defence against these enemies. So they had been especially delighted when they learned that we were coming to visit them because they hoped we would aid and console them.[20]

On hearing this Escalante and his companions concluded that at long last the way might be opening for an agreement with the Hopi which would make secure the hoped-for route from Santa Fe to Monterey through the Hopi country. They also felt that the Hopi rejection of Christianity might now be weakening.

In an attempt to capitalize on this situation Escalante suggested that old Pedro persuade the Hopi to call a general meeting of their chiefs in one of the kivas at Hano. At this meeting Escalante tried to persuade the Hopi leaders to send ambassadors with him back to Santa Fe. This the Hopi leaders would not agree to, and Escalante closed his journal entry with these words: "The assembly having ended, we withdrew very sadly to our lodging, realizing that the obstinacy of these unhappy Indians was invincible. And so we decided to continue the next day to Zuñi before the passes and the roads should be closed, because it was snowing constantly, for which reason we were unable to observe the latitude of these pueblos of Moqui.[21]

Despite the friendly reception accorded them, Miera in his long report to the King of Spain recommended that,

These Moquis, for many reasons (which I shall not set forth, in order not to make this narrative too long), should be brought down by force from their cliffs. I will say only that even though they do not make war, they are obnoxious to New Mexico, for they serve as an asylum for the many apostates from the Christian pueblos of that province. On the other hand, they are Indians who are very highly civilized, much given to labor, and not addicted to idleness. For this reason, although they live in that sterile region, they lack nothing in the way of food and clothing, and their houses are built of stone and mortar and are two or three stories high. They raise cattle, sheep, goats, and horses, and weave good fabrics of wool and cotton. They live on the tops of three high and steep mesas in six separate pueblos. But they would come down from them without the shedding of blood, with only the threat of a siege of the principal cliffs of Oraibe and Gualpi [Walpi] by a company of soldiers stationed at the waterholes which they have at the foot of the cliffs, and in less than a week they would surrender and be ready to do whatever might be required of them.[22]

Following Escalante's visit to the Hopi, events occurred in both Tusayan and at Santa Fe which rendered needless Miera's harsh recommendations for forcing the Hopi to leave their mesa tops.

As a reward for his success in furthering the Spanish colonization of California, Lieutenant-Colonel Juan Bautista de Anza was appointed to the governorship of New Mexico in 1778.

The following year reports came to him that conditions in Tusayan had become desperate since the visit of the Escalante party there three years before. Hopi crops had failed, disease was rampant, raids by hostile tribes had been intensified.

Anza and his advisers, both secular and religious, decided that the situation among the Hopi was so bad that they might abandon pueblo life and join those tribes which were still harassing the Spanish settlements along the Rio Grande. They also concluded that drought and disease might well be serving to break the stalwart Hopi spirit of resistance where Spanish might and Christian persuasion had so signally failed.

In August, 1780, word came to Santa Fe that forty Hopi families were willing to abandon their high mesa homes to seek settlement along the Rio Grande provided that Anza himself would come to escort them. In September, Anza — accompanied by the priests Fernández and García — set out to visit all the Hopi towns, but before their arrival the families who had offered to migrate to the Rio Grande country had been forced by hunger to seek relief wherever they could find it. According to Bancroft, the Navajo killed all the men in the party and made slaves of the women and children.

Everywhere they went among the Hopi, Anza and his party found stark tragedy. Following his visit to the Hopi in 1775 Escalante had estimated that the villages numbered 7,494 persons. De Anza now found a scant 798. No rain had fallen in Tusayan during the past three years. The total harvest of that year for the entire Hopi country was estimated at less than 800 bushels of corn and beans, and this would have to last through the year to come. Of thirty thousand sheep that Escalante reported only about three hundred remained. The cattle were all dead and only five horses still survived.

The village chief at Oraibi was offered food to take care of the immediate wants of the few people still remaining in his ancient town, but true to Hopi tradition he refused the gift as *he had nothing to offer in return,* nor would he listen to the priests' or to Anza's pleadings. In reply he told them that apparently it was the fate of his people to face annihilation and that the few who still remained at Oraibi were resolved to die in their homes and to remain steadfast to their own religion. He did agree, however, that his people were free to do as they themselves wished.

The Spaniards finally persuaded thirty Hopi families to leave and return with them to New Mexico. Bancroft states that he was not able to find any record of what happened to these thirty families, but he concludes, "I have an idea that with them and others, a little later, the pueblo of Moquino, in the Laguna region, may have been founded."

In the closing years of Spanish domination of the Southwest we find little mention of the Hopi in Spanish historical records. A few accounts refer to a vast increase in harassing raids by the Navajo and to retaliatory military action by the Spaniards. According to Bancroft, this forced the Navajo to sign a treaty with Spanish authorities on August 21, 1819, which indirectly resulted in the Navajo settling in the country around the Hopi villages.

This move subjected the few Hopi who had survived the years of pestilence and drought to constant raids by the Navajo, who carried off not only corn and other foods the hard-working Hopi had won from the desert soil, but also large numbers of sheep. Hopi women and children were taken as slaves. Some of these were kept by the Navajo, but many were sold to other Indian tribes and to Spaniards.

Spain's influence slowly eroded and corroded away in the Hopi country. In spite of all the power of the Spanish church, of Spanish armed might, of Spanish colonial determination, and of the ravages of Spanish-introduced plagues to which the Hopi had no natural resistance, the "Little People of Peace" continued to live on in their picturesque villages on the mesa tops of the great deserts of northern Arizona.

Violence Under Mexico

WHEN IN 1810 the Mexican priest Miguel Hidalgo y Costilla sounded his inflammatory "Cry of Dolores," he ignited long-smoldering fires of rebellion against Spanish domination in the Americas — the Mexican War for Independence being the result. Revolutionary regimes followed, interspersed with short-lived empires and iron-fisted dictatorships.

Meanwhile, many high-sounding laws were enacted on behalf of the Indian by Mexican reformers with scant knowledge of the people they thought they were helping. (The Indian was not even supposed to be called "Indian" but *indigene*.) Implementing these idealistic concepts — designed to assimilate the Indians into the cultural and political lives of the far-flung provinces — proved to be more difficult than conceiving them. In the farthermost province of all (New Mexico-Arizona of today) ties of civil authority with the central government in Mexico City were particularly tenuous.

Though less remote from its command at Chihuahua, the Mexican military establishment responsible for protection of Indian and Mexican settlements in the northern provinces even so had its hands full. With a beehive of problems right on the doorstep of Santa Fe, it could have done nothing to protect the Hopi at Tusayan against the raiding Navajo even if it had wished to do so.

During the years 1823 to 1845, while a long series of Mexican governors held office at Santa Fe, most provincial settlements were under constant attack from raiding parties of various hostiles. There was fear, too, of an invasion from the Independent Republic of Texas. Dissatisfaction became so great that in August, 1837, the Mexican governor of New Mexico was temporarily deposed and a Taos Indian, José Gonzales, took his place in the Governor's Palace.

Taking full advantage of the inability of the Mexican authorities to cope with the situation, the Navajo not only intensified their raids on Hopi mesas and villages but also penetrated ever deeper into territory long considered by the Hopi to be their own.

[71]

Thousands of cattle, horses, and sheep were rustled and sold to dealers as far away as Bent's Fort on the Arkansas — dealers who knew better than to ask questions as to the source of the booty. Time after time the Hopi food supply was so decimated that virtual starvation threatened the villagers. As late as 1837 a massive Navajo raid on Oraibi, at that time by far the largest of the Hopi villages, killed or scattered virtually its entire population. It was many years before the ancient town began to recover.

In addition to Navajo harassment there were raids by Ute, Apache, and Comanche Indian parties. Many Mexican bands joined in devastating forays. Especially heartbreaking to the Hopi were the scalping and slave raids, particularly those carried on by Mexicans. Because of their intelligence and personal attractiveness, Hopi young people brought high prices in the extensive slave trade carried on at Santa Fe and elsewhere in New Mexico, Chihuahua, and other Mexican states. Frank Siemptiwa of Moencopi and Tewaquaptewa of Oraibi in 1926 related that old men they had known in their youth told how Comanche, Ute, and Apache raiders had taken Hopi scalps and laughed over the good Chihuahua silver coin paid for them.

In the January, 1944, *Plateau,* the quarterly publication of the Museum of Northern Arizona, Edmund Nequatewa told of a Mexican raid on Oraibi in which the Hopi were tragically double-crossed. In about 1846 a party of Mexicans from the Rio Grande country with horses and pack mules passed through the Hopi country on their way to some destination in the north. Some days later the party returned and to the consternation of the Hopi made camp just outside Oraibi. The village chief had the Crier ask the people of the village to be friendly to the Mexicans and to offer them food in the hope that they would leave the Hopi country without causing trouble.

During the stay of the Mexicans, three Hopi men, so desperate because of some serious personal problems that they wished to die, made a secret bargain with the Mexicans to kill them in such a way that they would not lose their reputation for bravery and good character among the people of Oraibi.

The Soyal Ceremony was in progress at Oraibi on the day the Mexican party broke camp and rode off down the horse trail on the west side of the mesa. When they reached the bottom they circled to the old foot trail up the east side; leaving their horses and mules there, they hurried back up to the top of the mesa.

The Mexicans detailed to do the killing were able to look down into the kiva where the Oraibi men engaged in the Soyal Ceremony were assembled. They tried to pick out the Hopi victims, but they could not do so in the dim light of the crowded kiva. The three Hopi saw them, however, and not wishing to pollute their kiva they climbed out. As they emerged they were shot, one by one, by the Mexicans. As the last Hopi fell another shot rang out, and one of the Mexicans was badly wounded by a bullet from a Hopi who did not know of the suicide pact.

Carrying their wounded companion, the Mexican party made a dash through the village, capturing several Hopi children and one young woman as they went. At the foot of the mesa they strapped their captives to their own bodies, mounted their horses, and rode off toward Second Mesa. On their way they came upon several Hopi herding sheep. After killing the men they drove off the sheep. This left not one flock to the people of Oraibi.

When the party reached the Rio Grande the Mexicans apportioned their captives in a way that they felt certain would make it impossible for any party of Hopi bent on rescue to locate any of them. The parents of the Oraibi captives were heartsick over the loss of their children. Wikvaya, husband of the captured young woman, persuaded some of the men of Oraibi to journey to New Mexico to see if they could gain the release of the captives. When this effort failed, Wikvaya finally journeyed alone to Santa Fe and pleaded with the Mexican governor for the return of his wife and the Oraibi children.

So earnestly did he plead that the governor ordered his soldiers to find the captives and bring them and the Mexicans who had made slaves of them to Santa Fe. There Wikvaya's wife was restored to him, and the Hopi children were given over to their care to be returned to their own parents in Oraibi. Before they left Santa Fe the governor had the Mexican raiders publicly beaten and then either shot or stoned to death.

Masavema, who told this story to Nequatewa, and his wife Quamana were among the Hopi children who were captured in this long-remembered raid.

Raiding Indian tribes penetrated deep into Mexico itself. So many children were carried off from there that governors of the northern provinces reverted to a Spanish custom of buying Indian scalps supposedly taken from the heads of such raiders. State funds were augmented by popular subscription and in the 1830s, one hundred dollars was being offered for the enemy scalp of a male fourteen years of age or older, up to fifty dollars for that of a woman, and twenty-five dollars for that of a child under fourteen.

The most notorious dealer in this tragic merchandise was a Scotch-

Irishman named Don Santiago Kirker with his "volunteer corps," which included frontier adventurers of all kinds and some Delaware and Shawnee Indians. Although Kirker's bloody band operated far south of Tusayan, there is good reason to believe that many Hopi scalps found their way indirectly, through traders and allied Indian bands, into Kirker's hands. Mexican authorities eventually became suspicious that the Kirker gang was tricking them into paying for the scalps of their own Mexican people. Officials of Durango then demanded presentation of the entire head before they would pay bounty, so as to be certain that the blood money they were expending was for the killing of enemies, particularly Apache and Navajo.

Constant raids by mounted parties of Utes during this Mexican period caused many small Hopi villages to consolidate or to join larger more impregnable villages. Kwayesha of Oraibi told Voth of one such incident.

About seven miles northeast of Oraibi there were two small villages on opposite sides of a wash which had been subjected to repeated Ute raids. When the Hopi spotted a large party of Utes camping nearby they joined forces to defend the more strategically located town and prepared themselves as best they could to repel the attack they were sure would be made upon them. When the Utes did attack, the Hopi were able to hold them off for quite a time, and several Utes were killed by Hopi arrows. However, the Ute raiders finally managed to enter the village and capture several women and children. Although the Hopi men gave pursuit on foot, the mounted Utes soon outdistanced them. Some days later the people of this village went to Oraibi and sought sanctuary which was granted them by the village chief.

The effects of the many raids upon Hopi villages during these years were tragic and far-reaching. Hopi population had been decimated, their sheep and other food sources had been depleted, and their religious ceremonials had been constantly interrupted. In their hearts there had developed a searing distrust of all things Mexican and of ways of life other than their own. More devastating than all this, however, was their growing awareness of Navajo encroachment upon their territory — their Hopi Tusqua. This was to give them ever-growing concern, and it is a problem which to this day has not been solved.

While the flag of Mexico still flew over the Governor's Palace in Santa Fe, pale-faced adventurers, traders, and trappers, sometimes alone but usually in parties of various sizes, defied Mexican law to prowl the Southwest. Few of them were lured into the Hopi country, since no tales of golden cities, streams alive with beaver, or tribes rich in peltries stirred them to brave its long and rough desert trails.

In his invaluable *Kit Carson Days,* Edwin Legrand Sabin wrote that Old Bill Williams, the colorful "Mountain Man," lived among the Hopi in 1827. If Sabin is correct, then Bill Williams may well have been the first citizen of the United States met by the Hopi. It would be difficult to imagine a more unfortunate representative of Uncle Sam's nieces and nephews than William Sherley Williams, the renegade Baptist preacher turned Mountain Man. Kit Carson once said of Williams, "In starving times no man who knew him ever walked in front of Bill Williams."

According to another Mountain Man, Joe Meek, Bill Williams was a member of a large party that had been recruited by Captain Benjamin Louis Eulalie de Bonneville to trade, trap, and explore the Rocky Mountain region. Bonneville had taken two years' leave of absence from the United States Regular Army in the hope that he would make his fortune on this expedition. Staff officers urged him to make a careful study of the various Indian tribes inhabiting the regions he would travel, as well as to ascertain the quality of soil, the possibility of mineral deposits, the climate, and the geography of the region, in the hope that his reports would make it possible for all of them to enrich themselves.

Bonneville was well financed by wealthy easterners but seems, in spite of his military background, to have been incapable of disciplined organization of his expedition. His trading stock and finances soon ebbed away. In 1833, in the hope of recouping his losses, he sent Capt. Joseph Walker, one of his guides, and a party of about forty, including several well-known and experienced mountain men, to explore the country around Great Salt Lake. Bill Williams was a member of this detachment.

Ostensibly to look for beaver in the streams of the Sierra Nevada, but doubtless to steal valuable herds of horses from the Spanish ranches, Walker's party spent little time around Great Salt Lake before striking out for California. After a winter in California, devoted mostly to attending bull fights, cock fights, fiestas, and riotous parties — but with no trapping to help reimburse Bonneville — the Walker party left California by way of the San Joaquin Valley where they helped themselves to "a likely bunch of five or six hundred head of the Spaniards' horses."

Crossing the Sierra by what is known today as Walker's Pass, they took a trail across the desert to the Colorado River. Where a tributary stream now known as Bill Williams River entered the Colorado from the east, they joined forces, according to Meek, with a detachment of Mountain Men of the Rocky Mountain Fur Company which included the famous Kit Carson.

Many of the men in the Walker party had already demonstrated their brutal contempt for any Indians encountered along their route. One of the trappers was so enraged at the loss of one of his traps that he swore to kill the next Indian he saw. Coming upon two Indians peacefully fishing, he killed one of them and would have shot the second one if the latter had not dived into the stream and made his escape. A short time later the party came upon a small band of Indians whose peaceful behavior indicated that they had never seen white men before and who certainly gave no demonstrations of warlike intent. Men of the Walker party ruthlessly slaughtered twenty-five of them in cold blood.

Such was the character of many of the men in the combined party of 200 men, along with hundreds of horses and many cattle and dogs, which took the trail eastward toward the Little Colorado and Tusayan. Considering the knowledge gained some seven years earlier when he lived with the Hopi, Bill Williams undoubtedly served as guide.

Coming upon Hopi corn and melon fields they plundered them with callous disregard of what the consequences might be to the Hopi owners. Produce not considered edible for themselves they allowed their horses and cattle to trample into the ground as they grazed. When Hopi men protested, the Mountain Men shot twenty of them before they left to continue on their way toward Taos and Bent's Fort on the Arkansas.

To the Hopi still harboring hopeful dreams of the white-skinned descendants of the Plumed Serpent God who were to return one day to befriend the Indians, these introductions to citizens of the United States must have meant further keen and bitter disappointment.

Unhappily they served only too well as prelude to much of what the Hopi could expect in the years soon to come when the Stars and Stripes would fly not only over the Governor's Palace in Santa Fe but also over United States government buildings in Tusayan itself.

Stars and Stripes
Over Tusayan

In 1846 THE UNITED STATES declared that a state of war existed with Mexico. Bancroft states flatly that the purpose of this war against Mexico was to acquire territory — particularly that which is now California, Arizona, and New Mexico. An Army of the West was organized at Fort Leavenworth with Colonel Stephen Watts Kearny, "Horse Chief of the Long Knives," as many of the Indian tribes knew him, in command. Its mission was the conquest and occupation of that wide expanse of territory extending from New Mexico to the California coast.

The advance division consisted of three hundred regular soldiers, a regiment of Missouri Volunteers, and five additional volunteer companies, including two of artillery. The total force consisted of about eighteen hundred men with a supply train of a thousand mules, augmented by four hundred wagons of the annual Santa Fe Caravan. They left Fort Leavenworth, Kansas, in June, 1846, and after stopping at Bent's Fort early in August arrived in Santa Fe at six in the evening of August 18. During the trip Kearny had been promoted to the rank of brigadier-general.

General Kearny and his forces were greeted in most friendly fashion by the acting Mexican governor, Juan Vigil, and the flag of the United States was raised over the Governor's Palace. The Army of the West encamped on the hills overlooking the town, while General Kearny spent the night in the old *palacio*. New Mexico and Arizona had fallen to the United States without bloodshed.

This bloodless victory was brought about largely through the cooperation of United States citizens residing there, and of American traders who easily convinced many of the important Mexicans and Indians that the United States government would quickly bring about effective pacification and control of the warlike tribes which had been ravaging the land for so many years. The record regarding their various diplomatic moves is far from adequate, and some wild and salty tales are current to this day as to just how the way was paved for Kearny's easy victory. Governor Armijo had fled from Santa Fe at the approach of the Kearny forces. Those who were opposed to Kearny's takeover were unprepared for his rapid advance. Although abortive attempts were made to reconquer the province, the Stars and Stripes have flown over the Governor's Palace since that day in August, 1846.

Following his peaceful night in *El Palacio,* Kearny called for an assembly of the people of Santa Fe in the plaza and read them a proclamation informing them that New Mexico was now part of the United States and that they were now its subjects. They were given assurance of the full protection of the government of the United States for their property, their lives, and their religion.

In spite of Kearny's impressive words it would be many years before the people of the Southwest, and the Hopi country especially, would enjoy even a modicum of the basic freedoms so readily promised them by General Kearny during those days of easy victory in 1846.

The raiding parties of the Navajo, the Ute, the Comanche, and the Apache continued for some years before they began to taper off as some semblance of law came to the Southwest. As these raiding parties diminished, a pageant of strange, wonderful, and ill-assorted humanity began — adventurers, trappers, sheep stealers, explorers, fugitives from the law, prospectors, surveyors, geologists, tourist parties, land-grabbers, archaeologists, anthropologists, cattlemen, sheepmen, traders, army men, missionaries, schoolteachers, writers, government agents, horse thieves, do-gooders, troublemakers, Boy Scouts, Girl Scouts, photographers, artists, nurses, doctors, bootleggers, and many more — as well as Indian friends from Zuñi, Acoma, and the pueblos along the Rio Grande. All came to visit the Hopi for reasons as varied as they themselves. In more recent years many representatives of new cultural groups in the white man's society have joined the parade.

Traditional Hopi hospitality has only too often been sadly taken advantage of. In many instances it has been grossly abused. Yet the Hopi continue to welcome visitors in accordance with their long-established way of life.

The Hopi had no opportunity to demonstrate this traditional hospitality to the first government agent whose official responsibilities included the Indians of Tusayan. It seems ironical that he never found it possible to visit the Hopi villages during his term of office.

James S. Calhoun arrived in Santa Fe in July, 1849, holding a commission as Indian agent for what in 1850 was to become the Territory of New Mexico. At that time Arizona was still included in New Mexico and remained so until it was made a separate territory in 1863. Bancroft writes of Calhoun as a zealous and intelligent official, albeit "intemperate." Certainly he manifested sincere interest in the welfare of the Indians, both his actions and his letters reflecting this attitude.

The Indians of the Rio Grande Pueblos surprised and delighted him, and he tried to curb the depredations of the warlike tribes that were still harassing them with constant raiding parties. However, he was so handicapped by lack of sufficient military forces that he could gain little protection for them.

Calhoun first mentions the Hopi in an early letter to the Commissioner of Indian Affairs in Washington:

> The Indians informed me at Jémez, there were seven Pueblos of Moquies. The best information I could obtain, in relation to these people, induces me to locate them about one hundred miles west of Zuñi, in an excellent country, through which a road must run to the Pacific. Indeed, it is said, a large number of emigrants selected that route this season. They are supposed to be decidedly pacific in their character, opposed to all wars, quite honest, and very industrious — It is said, in years gone by, these Indians abandoned a village because its soil had been stained with the blood of a human being. I deeply regret that I have not been able to visit these, and all other Pueblos in this Country — that I might be able to lay before you information, of a character, more precise and accurate.[23]

This information seems to have aroused his curiosity and he seriously contemplated a visit to the Hopi villages. However, he was strongly advised against making any attempt to do so, indeed was virtually forbidden to do so without a military escort. Yet the military, who so ordered him, would not supply him with such an escort despite many requests by him.

At a later date he wrote the then Commissioner, Orlando Brown:

> Beyond Zuñi, west, perhaps one hundred and fifty miles, the Moqui country is reached — These Indians live in Pueblos, cultivate the soil to a limited extent, and raise horses, Mules, Sheep and goats, and, I am informed, manufacture various articles —
> I am extremely anxious to visit these Indians; but it would be unsafe to do so, without a sufficient escort, as the Apaches are upon the left, and the Navajos on the right in travelling from Zuñi to the Moquies.[24]

In October of 1850 he reported further:

> The seven Moqui Pueblos sent to me a deputation who presented themselves on the 6th day of this month. Their object, as announced, was to ascertain the purposes and views of the Government of the United States towards them. They complained, bitterly, of the depredations of the Navajos — The deputation consisted of the Cacique of *all* the Pueblos, and a *chief* of the largest Pueblo, accompanied by two who were not officials. From what I could learn from the Cacique, I came to the conclusion, that each of the seven Pueblos, was an independent Republic, having confederated for mutual protection. One of the popular errors of the day, is, there are but five of these

Pueblos remaining, another is, that one of the Pueblos speak a different language from the other Six — I understood the Cacique to say, the *seven* spoke the same language, but the Pueblo in which he resided, Tanoquevi, spoke also, the language of the Pueblo of Santa Domingo — hence the error first mentioned. These Pueblos may be, all, visited in one day. They are supposed to be located about due West from Santa Fe, and from three to four days travel, North West, from Zuñi. The following was given to me as the names of their Pueblos —

1. Oriva	5. Opquive
2. Somonpavi	6. Chemovi
3. Juparavi	7. Tanoquevi
4. Mansana	

I understood, further, they regarded as a small Pueblo, Zuñi, as compared with Oriva.[25]

Although Calhoun could not manage to get to the Hopi, the Hopi made a second visit to Calhoun in Santa Fe. In August of 1851 he reported this visit in some detail in another letter to his superior:

Thirteen Indians, from these Pueblos, visited me on the 28th inst. Their object was to ascertain, whether their Great Father, and they supposed me to be him, would do anything for them. They complained that the Navajos had continued to rob them, until they had left them exceedingly poor, and wretched, indeed, did they look. They had heard of a *priest,* but never had seen one; and requested me to see one for them, and to deliver to him some *feathers,* and a powder, they called, as it was interpreted by a Santa Domingo Indian, their "Big Medicine," and to beg the priest to pray to the Great Spirit to send them rain, and to make their corn grow, that they might not perish. These Indians seem to be innocent, and very poor, and should be taken care of. The Navajos having exhausted, or nearly so, the supplies of the Moquies, are now at peace with them, and will remain so, until the Moquies increase their stores to an extent that shall awaken their cupidity. More than twelve months ago, I made an effort to visit the Moquies, but then, as now, an escort was not allowed me — You will remember, their Pueblos are situated west of Santa Fe, and at a distance from it, computed at Three hundred and fifty miles, and beyond the Navajo Country. Not very remote from the Moquies, the Gila Apaches should be made to settle; but this is a question that can not be determined before that country is thoroughly explored.[26]

Calhoun was frustrated at every turn in his efforts to meet all the Indians under his jurisdiction and to help them as he wished. Washington seems to have appreciated his ability and dedication, and, even though his health was seriously impaired at this point, he was appointed governor of the Territory of New Mexico in 1851. His inauguration took place in March of that year.

By 1852 Calhoun was so seriously ill that he had his own coffin built in Santa Fe and with it started on the long, arduous trek to his home in the East. He failed to get very far, for in June he died and was buried at Fort Leavenworth.

Despite Calhoun's interest in the Hopi as shown in his reports to Washington, it was not until 1869 that an agency was officially established for them, and even then it was located far away to the east at the army post of Fort Wingate. Unfortunately it was named the "Moqui Pueblo Agency," thus giving apparent governmental approval to the name Moqui which has always been resented by the Hopi. It was not an auspicious beginning of official relations between the government of the United States of America and the independent villages of the three Hopi mesas.

In 1871 the agency was moved to Fort Defiance and here a small school for Indian children was established. Two years later it was moved again, this time to Keams Canyon — about thirteen miles east of Walpi — where it has remained.

Thirty feet or so above the road up Keams Canyon beyond the agency buildings, cut into a smooth face of the cliff, are the following words:

1st Reg't N. M. Vol's
Aug. 13, 1863
Col. C. Carson, Comm.

This brief inscription commemorates one of the most significant incidents in the history of Tusayan.

The ravaging raids by the Navajo against the Hopi and the Pueblo Indians of New Mexico, as well as against Mexican settlements throughout the Southwest, had continued year after year, until in 1863 Brigadier-General James H. Carleton, commanding officer of the United States forces in Santa Fe, took decisive action. The famous Kit Carson was ordered to round up all Navajo and take them as prisoners to Fort Sumner on the barren expanse of the Staked Plains in the southeast corner of New Mexico.

At Fort Defiance supplies were assembled for a six months' campaign, and in June Carson arrived with his New Mexico Volunteers to take command. He called for additional volunteers, and many of the Hopi who had suffered so long from the depredations of the Navajo offered their services. One hundred Utes were engaged as scouts and Carson himself visited the Zuñi and Hopi villages to secure competent guides.

Ruth Underhill in her book *The Navajos* writes, "How willingly all these tribes gave their aid! The Ute probably regarded the white soldiers as rather green allies in a war they had been prosecuting for centuries. To the Hopis and Zuñis, the new protectors, supplied with guns and food, were like the realization of a dream. . . . The Navajos were reaping the harvest of the years they had been Lords of the Soil."

Carson with the New Mexico Volunteers and their Indian allies waged a ruthless, scorched-earth campaign in order to break the spirit of the proud Navajos and to secure their capitulation with as little bloodshed as possible.

Captain Eben Everett, an officer of the New Mexico Volunteers, kept a diary during at least a part of this campaign in Tusayan. Published in the *New Mexico Historical Review* (Vol. 21), it describes the journey north from Fort Defiance and how the troops destroyed Navajo cornfields, capturing their sheep and other livestock as they proceeded. In his entry for August 12, Captain Everett wrote:

Left one mule unable to travel to be brought up by the party tomorrow if possible, if not to be given to the Moquis who have treated us very honestly. About four miles from Camp we descended another of those precipices and entered a beautiful Canon from fifty to 200 yards in width and miles in length, abounding in cool springs and green grass, luxuries that we seldom meet with, and to our poor animals, it is indeed a Godsend for from want of water and grass they are growing very weak. Found a small corn and melon field which was soon packed off for our horses. Left one mule at Camp as it could not be found.

This is the first good pleasant Camp since we left Defiance, everything requisite being found in abundance and good quality. From the appearance of the numerous trails it must be a favorite resort of the Navajoes.

Col. Carson with the rest of the command comes up tomorrow.

August 13, Day of Rest. Laid in Camp all day. Col. Carson with the remainder of the column joined us about 9 A.M. Found a mule that I lost in our last camp in another company, slightly altered, but not enough to prevent recognition. Animals sent on the hills to graze. Soldiers washing clothing. Officers eating, sleeping, reading & gambling, and so the day passed.

August 14th, 1863. Still in Camp in Volunteer Canon. Guards in and around camp doubled and trebled last night. Co. "B" being encamped between the two Battalions of Majors Morrison & Cummings, and belonging to neither, had the full benefit of a neutral position between to [two] active powers, i.e., to furnish details for Guards and Pickets for both Columns with an extra supply for Herd Guard [sheep and cattle] and also an additional force called for directly from Hdqrs. The details were not so heavy as to cause any inconvenience but I was called on six times yesterday evening to furnish guards and every one was alerted again and again. As I am my own 1st Sergeant I didn't like it.

One of our men was yesterday at work chiseling in the face of a smooth rock on the side of the Canon the Legend, "1st Regt. N.M. Vols. Aug. 13, 1863" in letters a foot square. Ages since this may cause as much curiosity among antiquarians, as do now the old names upon the famous Inscription Rock near Zuñi, where there are hundreds of names and records of events, back to the year 1618.

Captain Everett was stretching things a bit far when he likened the inscription carved into the cliff face of "Volunteer Canyon" — the

Keams Canyon of today which has played such an important part in Hopi history — to the famous "Inscription Rock" of El Morro National Monument. However, Christopher Carson has become such a national hero that the soldier's inscription (later that August day in 1863 the words "Col. C. Carson, Comm." were added) certainly did result in one of northern Arizona's most historic markers and helped put Keams Canyon on the tourist map.

Although Carson's campaign was to defeat and imprison the Navajo, the Hopi could not help but be involved far beyond their services as guides to the Carson forces. Soldiers and their Indian allies swept through the entire Hopi country in search of Navajo squatters and fleeing refugees. Even Hopi cornfields some distance from the villages were sometimes destroyed by the soldiers in the belief that they belonged to Navajo.

On November 21, 1863, Kit Carson, with a considerable force, made camp below Oraibi mesa. In a dispatch he sent to Santa Fe some weeks later Carson wrote, "Before my arrival at Oraibi, I was credibly informed that the people of that village had formed an alliance with the Navajos, and on reaching there I caused to be bound their Governor and another of their principal men and took them with me as prisoners."[27]

According to certain leaders of Old Oraibi, Kit Carson within a few days became convinced that he had been misinformed regarding the attitude of the Oraibi people toward the Navajo, and his two Hopi captives were released.

Noting in fact that the Hopi and Navajo were at odds over "some injustice perpetrated by the latter," Carson told of recruiting representatives from all the villages except Oraibi "to accompany me on the warpath," and added, "My object in insisting on parties of these people accompanying me was simply to involve them so far that they could not retract; to bind them to us, and place them in antagonism to the Navajos. They were of some service and manifested a great desire to aid us in every respect."[28]

As he traversed the Hopi country, Carson was deeply disturbed by the condition of the Hopi people. In the same dispatch he wrote:

... I would respectfully represent that these people, numbering some four thousand souls, are in a most deplorable condition, for the fact that the country for several miles around their villages is quite barren, and is entirely destitute of vegetation. They have no water for purpose of irrigation, and their only dependence for subsistence is on the little corn they raise when the weather is propitious, which is not always the case in this latitude. They are a peaceable people, have never robbed or murdered the people of New Mexico, and act in every way worthy of the fostering care of the government. Of the bounty so unsparingly bestowed by it on the other Pueblo Indians — aye even on the marauding bands — they have never tasted. And I earnestly recommend that the attention of the Indian Bureau be called to this matter. I understand that a couple of years annuities for the Navajos not distributed are in the possession of the Superintendent of Indian Affairs at Santa Fe, and I consider that if such arrangement would be legal, these goods should be bestowed on these people.[29]

Unfortunately Kit Carson's recommendation for Hopi relief was only partially carried out and then not until late in 1864 when the starvation period of 1863–64 was over. Hopi crops had been poor that year and the destruction of many of their fields by the troops, in the mistaken idea that they were the property of the Navajo, added to their misery. There was much hunger and sickness in the villages until well into spring.

The winter saw the defeat of the Navajo, and, hungry and cold, band after band surrendered to Carson at Fort Defiance and by March began the "Long Walk" to their concentration camp at the Bosque Redondo, a grove of cottonwoods near Fort Sumner.

With the great mass of Navajo now captive at Fort Defiance, or on their way to Fort Sumner, many Utes and other Indians who had a part in their defeat waged heartless raids against small scattered remnant bands of the once arrogant tribe which called itself "Diné" — *The People*. These raiding parties often joined forces with Mexican slavers. Since the women and older children were easy to control and brought good prices, Navajo men found with their family groups were shot and old women and babies were either killed or cruelly left to starve or freeze to death. These raiding parties also often captured Hopi women and children when they came upon them herding sheep or searching for food on the desert beyond their villages. It was a bad winter indeed for both the Navajo and the Hopi.

Over the years the Kit Carson inscription on the cliff in Keams Canyon has served as a constant reminder to Hopi visiting their agency there that, at least for a time, Navajo intruders into their country had once been effectively curbed.

Mormons and Other Visitors

THE SPANIARDS were not the only Caucasians who, upon coming to the New World, felt that it was their duty to civilize the Indian by converting him to their variety of Christianity. Attempts to Christianize the Indians were made all during the British colonial period in eastern North America.

In President Washington's annual address to Congress in 1791 he offered a six-point program as basic to future dealings between the newly created United States and the Indians. One of his points was the undertaking of "national experiments for imparting to the Indians the blessings of civilization." These "blessings of civilization" were to include conversion to Christianity. As early as 1776 the Continental Congress gave this concept formal approval in a resolution that provided for the propagation of the gospel and directed the commissioners for Indian affairs to investigate places in Indian country for the residences of ministers and teachers.

As the frontier of the United States extended farther and farther west, Christ's admonition to his disciples, "Go ye into all the world and preach the gospel to every creature," served to motivate many and varied Christian sects to undertake missionary work among the innumerable tribes being brought under the Stars and Stripes.

Mormon Expeditions

The first American missionary to contact the Hopi was Jacob Hamblin, a dedicated member of the Church of Jesus Christ of Latter-Day Saints (the Mormons). He served not only as a missionary and an astute political agent for his church and its vigorous leader, Brigham Young, but also as a courageous and indefatigable explorer of the Southwest.

The interest of the Mormons in converting the Indians to their faith dates back to the publication in 1830 of their basic scripture, *The Book of Mormon*. According to this, ancestors of the American Indians came from Palestine some six hundred years before the time of

Christ and built a truly remarkable civilization on the North American continent. Later, because of their neglect of their religious laws and the resulting degredation, many of them were cursed with dark skins and became known as "Lamanites." These Lamanites waged a long series of wars against their "civilized" brothers, who had remained true to the faith, and eventually wiped them out. Since these Indians, or Lamanites, were "of the blood of Israel," a promise was held out to them by the Mormons that some day their descendants might be converted and become "a white and delightsome people."

When young Jacob Hamblin became a Mormon by baptism into the Church of Jesus Christ of Latter-Day Saints on a cold day in March, 1842, in the then wilds of Wisconsin, the Mormons gained one of their most heroic figures. Early in 1858 in Salt Lake City Brigham Young appointed Hamblin as Territorial Sub-Indian Agent. In September of that year, while at his farm at Santa Clara in southern Utah, he received instructions from Brigham Young to take a group of his fellow Mormons to visit the Hopi. Brigham Young had come to the conclusion that it would be advantageous to the Mormons in southern Utah to persuade some peaceful and friendly Indians to settle north of the Colorado and thus form a buffer state against more hostile tribes. Hamblin was instructed to ascertain if the Hopi might be willing to make such a move.

The party of twelve which Hamblin selected included a Spanish interpreter, for he was sure that some of the Indians where they were going would understand that language. A local Indian named Naraguts acted as guide. The Colorado was forded at Ute Ford — "the Crossing of the Fathers," as it is more generally known. Within a few days they came to some terraced gardens watered by a good spring (probably the Hotevila Spring). A few miles farther on they came to an "Oraibi village."

Hamblin's own account of his first visit to the Hopi is worth quoting at length:

After our arrival in the village, the leading men counseled together a few minutes, when we were separated and invited to dine with different families. A man beckoned to me to follow him. After traversing several streets, and climbing a ladder to the roof of the first story of a house, I was ushered into a room furnished with sheepskins, blankets, earthen cooking utensils, water urns, and other useful articles. It seemed to me strangely furnished, yet it had an air of comfort; perhaps the more so, for the reason that the previous few days had been spent in very laborious traveling, on rather low diet.

The hostess made a comfortable seat with blankets, and motioned me to occupy it.

A liberal repast was provided. It consisted of stewed meat, beans, peaches and a basket of corn bread which they called *peke*. It was about the thickness of brown paper, dry and crumbling, yet quite palatable.

Jacob Hamblin, Mormon missionary to the Hopi.

Arizona Historical Society

The hostess, apparently surmising that I would not know how to partake of the bean soup without a spoon, dexterously thrust her fingers, closed tightly together, into the dish containing it, and, with a very rapid motion carried the soup to her mouth. Then she motioned me to eat. Hunger was pressing, and a hint was sufficient. . . .

The people generally used asses for packing all their supplies, except water, up the cliffs to their dwellings. The water was usually brought up by the women, in jugs, flattened on one side to fit the neck and shoulders of the carrier, and this was fastened with a strap which passed around in front of the body.

Most of the families owned a flock of sheep. These might be seen in all directions going out in the morning to feed, and returning in the evening. They were driven into or near the towns at night, and corralled and guarded to keep them from being stolen by the thieving Navajoes.

We found a few persons in all the villages who could speak the Ute language. They told us some of their traditions, which indicate, that their families knew the Mexicans, and something about the Montezumas.

A very aged man said that when he was a young man, his father told him that he would live to see white men come among them, who would bring them great blessings, such as their fathers had enjoyed, and that these men would come from the West. He believed that he had lived to see the prediction fulfilled in us.[30]

When Hamblin decided to return to make his report to Brigham Young, he left four of his party, including one of his brothers, to live with the Hopi, "to study their language, get acquainted with them, and, as they are of the blood of Israel, offer them the gospel."

These four had lived at Oraibi only a short time before a serious dispute broke out among the Hopi upon being advised of Brigham Young's suggestion that they abandon their ancient village and establish their homes on the other side of the Colorado River. Hopi ceremonial leaders expressed grave doubts as to whether these Mormons were the hoped-for white men prophesied by their ancient leaders. During the winter the controversy became so bitter that the village chief and his councillors advised the four Mormons to return to their own people. Before they left one of the Oraibi leaders prophesied that the time would soon come when the Mormons would be settling along the Little Colorado, south of the Hopi villages.

Early in 1859 Brigham Young again summoned Hamblin from his home in Santa Clara to Salt Lake City and informed him that their Mormon brother Marion J. Shelton had been "called" to live with the Hopi to learn their language and to teach and labor among them. One particular task upon which Brigham Young insisted was that Shelton make a genuine effort to teach the Hopi the Deseret Alphabet, which the regents of the University of Deseret had invented and which the Mormons hoped would become a universal means of communication between the people of diverse languages, both European and Indian, who were becoming converts to the Mormon faith. Hamblin also was ordered to select a companion to remain with Shelton in the Hopi country.

This small party of Hamblin and six men left Santa Clara on October 4, 1859. On their long and arduous trip one amusing incident occurred, amusing to all but the man personally concerned. On Sunday October 23, before they had reached the Colorado, one of the party, Thales Haskell, recounts:

Traveled on till sundown and camped. Brs. Shelton and Pierce not having arrived we began to feel uneasy about them and were afraid they were both lost. We were just preparing to fire a gun when they came in sight. We now got supper and after satisfying our appetites stretched ourselves on the ground before a big pine fire. While spinning yarns, br. Shelton's pants caught fire, causing him to jump and dance in such a manner as to set the rest of us into roars of laughter. He however burnt his hands so bad putting it out that we had to let up. Br. Hamblin while on guard killed a badger and roasted it, and we managed to eat it, one after another, as we came on guard. Plenty of feed and good timber at this place but no water. Called it 20 miles from Mountain Springs to this place.[31]

They arrived at Oraibi early in November. Hamblin decided upon Thales Haskell as the one to remain with Shelton at Oraibi, then he with the rest of the party went to visit other Hopi villages. Upon their return to Oraibi, Hamblin and his three companions bade goodbye to Shelton and Haskell on November 17 and started on their return to Santa Clara.

The two young Mormons obtained permission from a man of Oraibi, whose name Haskell spelled Thuringwah, to sleep in his kiva which he designated as his "workshop." Later Thuringwah's wife agreed to their use of a small room, twelve by eight feet by four feet high, with an entrance through the roof, for living quarters, and they made such preparations as they could for the winter.

The Mormons found the Hopi friendly, but aloof when it came to matters of religion. True to Mormon concepts of missionary work, they helped the Hopi in every way they could — sharpening saws, building ladders by splitting cottonwood poles, carding wool, making powder horns, bullet molds, and so forth. In return, the Hopi often invited them to eat with them and to witness their spectacular religious ceremonials. The latter thoroughly mystified the young Mormons.

The winter proved to be hard and lonely for them, as these extracts from Haskell's journal bear witness:

Sunday 25th — Went down to the wolf trap but had caught no wolf. Came home. Found br. Shelton preparing Christmas dinner. Got it ready and invited three of the head men of the village to eat with us. Had boiled mutton, stewed peaches, suet dumplings, pancakes, and peek. After dinner we smoked then sung a hymn and had some conversation with our Indian friends. They appeared to enjoy themselves very much. In the afternoon we saw another Indian performance which took place in second story of old Thurs house. 15 or 20 young bucks naked to the breechclout went up there while the old woman and her two girls stood by and dashed cold water over them. They went into the back part of the house and got melons and other nicknacks which they threw down to the crowd below, yelling at the same time scandilous.

Monday 26th — Made a pair of bullet moles out of sand rock and run some balls for my yauger. Appearance of snow.

Tuesday 27th — Got some leather off my saddle and half soled my shoes. Visited the Indians. Slight snow fell during the day.

Wednesday 28th — Snow fell 3 or 4 inches during the night. Spent most of the day in the hut, it being very cold.

Thursday 29th — I sit on top of the hut sewing while br Shelton works below at his fiddle. Pleasant day.

Friday 30th — Finished my garments [L.D.S. garments] and felt lonesome.

Saturday 31st — Spent the day in the shop with the Indians, it being the day before New Years got to thinking about home and got the blues scandilous.[32]

Since the Hopi men no longer had to spend long hours in their fields the Mormons showed them how to make deadfalls to trap "wolves" and joined them on hunting trips for antelope and rabbits.

As the winter slowly wore on Navajos were frequent visitors to Oraibi, and Shelton and Haskell had many of their scant and valuable possessions stolen by them. Eventually they decided that they would make better progress in learning the Hopi language and teaching the Hopi the Deseret Alphabet if they separated and went to live with different families.

In spite of frequent illness Shelton finished his fiddle. Then he and Haskell spent many an evening wandering through the streets of the old village singing Mormon hymns and songs to its accompaniment. This amazed and delighted the Hopi.

One of the villagers of old Oraibi most friendly to the Mormons was "Tuby" [Tuba], who was later to play such a prominent part in the Mormon settlement near Moencopi.

On February 19 Haskell wrote in his journal, "Learned today that the Oraibes six years ago used to have a White Chief of their own tribe. They speak of him as being a very good man." It would be interesting indeed to know if this "White Chief" was an albino Hopi, as Haskell's phrase "of their own tribe" would seem to indicate.

During early spring Haskell became seriously ill and in the concluding pages of his journal we read:

March 1st — Unwell all day. Windy weather.

Tuesday 2nd — Navihoes in town. My friend Tuby traded a robe and Buckskin for a pony with one of them and made me a present of it. I prevailed on him to except my gun, rather against his will however. He said when he made his friend a present he did not wish anything in return.

Wednesday 3rd — Got ready to go to the Movincapy [Moencopi].

Thursday 4th — Started. Went 15 miles. Camped.

Friday 5th — Traveled 18 miles and arrived at the Movincapy. This is a small stream where the Oribes raise cotton and they recommended it to us as a good place to build a mill and for the Mormons to make a small settlement.

Saturday 6th — Went exploring. Did not find a very good prospect.

Sunday 7th — Started back to the village.

Monday 8th — Arrived and made preparations to start home.

Tuesday 9th — Made a start about noon. Oribes cautioned us to beware of Navihoes and be shure to hold on to our lariets when we camped till we got out of the country. Traveled till after dark. Camped, talked over our condition and as we had no fire arms except an ancient shooter concluded to trust providence and take the chances. Hobbled our ponys. Made a big fire and went to bed and slept sound and I will say that we never saw a human being till we got to the Rio Virgin.[33]

In the autumn of 1860 Hamblin was directed to make still another effort to establish a mission in the Hopi country and to take along as a member of his party George A. Smith, Jr., the son of one of the important Mormon leaders, Apostle (later President) George A. Smith.

Hamblin left Santa Clara in October with a party of nine men, including, besides Hamblin and Smith, Thales Haskell, Ira Hatch, and

Hamblin's younger brother Francis. With them also was an experienced Paiute guide named Enos Tutsegavits. Feeling that they would help in establishing friendly relations with such Indians as they would meet along the way, Jacob Hamblin and Hatch took along their Indian wives Eliza and Sarah.

The mules were heavily laden. Three beeves had been well fattened and slaughtered and the meat dried. A knocked-down boat was lashed to the sides of one mule. The trip to the Colorado was uneventful and the crossing made without incident. It seemed good to have the women along if only because their ability to cook was far superior to that of the men, Hamblin reported.

They had not proceeded far into the Navajo country when serious trouble began. They ran out of water and were warned by some of the Navajos that if they went on to the next watering place they would all be killed. Hamblin realized that if they did not press on to water they would die of thirst. Hamblin and Enos remained behind while Haskell and the rest of the party went on to a waterhole which they knew of just a short distance ahead. More and more Navajos joined in the parley with Hamblin. They demanded that he turn over the two Indian women to them, promising that they would then allow the Mormons to return home without further harassment. This Hamblin refused to do, whereupon the Indians then demanded that Hamblin trade all the goods his party had brought with them, including their ammunition. If they did this, they would be allowed to cross the Colorado and return home in peace.

Realizing that their situation was desperate, Hamblin agreed to this demand, and the next morning the trading began. While this was going on Hamblin ordered some of his men, including young Smith, to take their animals to water. On the return Smith's horse turned off on a side trail and he went after it. When all the Navajos suddenly left and Hamblin realized that Smith was not yet back, he sent two men after him. A mile or so from their camp they found him with three bullet wounds in the lower part of his body and four arrows between his shoulders. Realizing that young Smith was in a desperate condition, Hamblin had him carried into camp on a blanket.

Advised that a band of about forty Navajos had gathered at a strategic place to block their journey to the Hopi, Hamblin knew that there was nothing for them to do but return to Santa Clara. Smith begged them to leave him behind, but they placed him in a saddle on one of the mules with one of the men behind him to hold him.

Fearing attack from the Navajos at any moment, they started sadly back toward the Colorado. By the end of the day Smith was dead. Wrapping his body in a blanket, they laid him in a depression by the side of the trail and hurried on in fear of their own lives.

Later that winter Hamblin led a party to bring in the remains for proper burial.

Following the tragic death of Apostle Smith's son, Mormon interest in missionary expeditions across the Colorado River cooled for a time. Jacob Hamblin became so involved in the soul-wrenching, heart-breaking tasks the Mormon pioneers were facing in Utah's "Dixie" that even he could not consider any further trips into Tusayan. Intense heat, bitter-cold winter winds, drought, and cloudbursts plagued the settlements of St. George, Washington, and Santa Clara.

It was not until the autumn of 1862 that Brigham Young's curiosity about the Hopi and his determination that they should be converted to membership in the Church of Jesus Christ of Latter-Day Saints persuaded Hamblin to lead another mission party to the Hopi.

Brigham Young ordered Hamblin to seek another crossing of the Colorado south of St. George and again to make every effort to find a suitable route for wagons from the Colorado to the Hopi villages. A new crossing was found south of Grand Canyon.

This was a relatively large party of twenty Mormon men, the Indian wives of Ira Hatch and Jacob Hamblin, and three converted Indians — Enos Tutsegavits, his wife, and Hamblin's adopted Indian son Albert. They also had with them an Indian guide, but he turned back as soon as they came in sight of the San Francisco Peaks, presumably fearful of the desert stretches ahead.

When they arrived at Oraibi on December 18 they found the Hopi in desperate circumstances. At Oraibi alone twenty-four men and twenty-two women had died from starvation due to a long period of drought. In spite of this, the friendly Hopi managed to welcome them with a few crumbs of *piki* and some precious drinking water.

Ceremonies were in progress to unite the villagers in prayers to end the drought and to bring good crops in the next growing season. In these the Mormons participated, adding their prayers to those of the Hopi. Hamblin at once made heavy inroads on his own precious food supplies to help the desperate Indians.

Almost immediately upon their arrival at Oraibi, Tutsegavits and his wife left on a mission to the country of the hostile Apache to bear the Mormon faith to them. Jahiel McConnell, Ira Hatch, and the indefatigable Thales Haskell remained at Oraibi. Hamblin cut deeply into the supplies he badly needed for his trip back home in order to supply the three missionaries so that they would not need to depend upon the meager provisions the Hopi had to sustain them until the next harvest.

Hamblin tried to persuade several Hopi to return with him to Utah to visit Salt Lake City and meet with Brigham Young, but he found none willing to go with him. As he prepared to leave, Hopi ceremonial leaders pleaded with him to remain at Oraibi at least for a few more days as they were certain their prayers for rain would soon be answered with a heavy storm. Ignoring this storm warning, Hamblin and his party left Oraibi in late December.

The first night out the storm which had been forecast struck and they spent a cold, wet, miserable night under such shelter as an overhanging rock provided. In the morning they found the ground well covered with snow, making grazing difficult for their animals. To their great surprise, three Hopi joined them there, saying that after a long council their leaders had decided to send them to visit the great Mormon leader and to see the places in Utah Hamblin had told them about.

The entire trip back to Santa Clara was a tough one. There were ice floes in the Colorado and the crossing was particularly hazardous. Because they were running out of food, Hamblin sent two men ahead on the party's best horses to bring relief. They were literally eating crow before the relief supplies arrived. The Mormons were deeply impressed when the Hopi, virtually starving as they were, refused to eat until they had made proper prayers by offering portions of food to Sun.

When advised that three Hopi had accompanied Hamblin back to Utah, Brigham Young was delighted. He placed Hamblin in charge of their visits throughout the Mormon settlements and ordered that the Hopi should be treated as honored guests wherever they went. When the three Hopi were introduced to Brigham Young he treated them with the utmost courtesy and handed each of them a shiny red apple, which the Hopi accepted and ate with amazement and pleasure. Brigham Young informed the Hopi that he hoped to send at least a hundred missionaries to their country and he invited the entire nation to take up residence on the Mormon side of the Colorado River.

The Hopi were treated royally during all their days in Salt Lake City. The leaders of the Church took turns inviting them to dinner. Welsh converts questioned them several times in the hope they could find some similarity between the Welsh language and that of the Hopi. The Hopi told some of the Mormon leaders that long, long ago, ancestors of the Hopi had made "books." This led some Mormons to speculate that this statement might be some vague and distant reference to their ancestral life as one of the Lost Tribes of Israel, and others to wonder if it might not possibly indicate some equally vague and distant tradition based on the codices of Montezuma's day.

In the years that followed Jacob Hamblin frequently interrupted his farming and family responsibilities in southern Utah to continue his exploration and missionary efforts in the Hopi and the Navajo country. Not long after the Navajo were released from their captivity at Bosque

Redondo in New Mexico — during the summer of 1869, numbers of them began settling in Tusayan — the Hopi were harassed constantly by hostile bands of them. Although Jacob Hamblin had established friendly relations with several Navajo leaders, the missionary and colonization projects he wished to continue and develop in the Hopi country were often in serious jeopardy. Some Hopi from Oraibi had been encouraged by Hamblin and other Mormon leaders to reestablish a Hopi community at Moencopi and in the 1870s hostile Navajo proved a constant threat to it. The Navajo do not call themselves "Diné," The People, for nothing, although in fairness it must be said that not all of them accent the "the."

In 1872 Hamblin persuaded Tuba and his wife Pulaskanimiki to return with him to Santa Clara for a visit. While there Hamblin saw to it that they were duly impressed by the various industries that had been established at St. George and other Mormon settlements in Utah's "Dixie." Tuba and his wife were indeed awed by them. The flour mill made Pulaskanimiki recall the long hours she had to spend over her corn-grinding stones, while Tuba himself marveled at the cotton mill with its hundred spindles turning out more cotton thread in a moment than he could spin with his hand spindle in a long lifetime. It is small wonder that later on Tuba would favor the Mormons' establishing a settlement alongside Moencopi, once he was assured that their plans included a spinning mill.

To this day the women's gardens below the Hopi springs and the fields of the men contain food plants that serve well to remind the Hopi of the pioneer Mormon missionaries and their leader. Turban squash, safflower, sorghum, and many other foods that added variety and nutriment to the Hopi diet were all introduced by the Mormons of those early days. In turn, many peach trees grown from seeds taken home by him from Hopi villages grew and flourished on Hamblin's various farms even as they had flourished in the Hopi country when the Spaniards originally brought the seeds from their ancestral trees in distant Spain.

Jacob Hamblin was by far the most influential of all the many missionaries who went to the Hopi country. He died in 1886 at Alpine, Arizona, where he was in hiding from agents of the United States government then sweeping the Mormon country in its efforts to stamp out polygamy. Surely an ignominious death for a truly heroic figure whose name is now so proudly borne by many places throughout the widespread landscapes of the Southwest.

Major J. W. Powell

Sixteen years before his death Hamblin escorted to Tusayan a man who is honored as a hero by Hopi and *Bahana* alike for his pioneering exploration of the mighty canyons of the Colorado River. Tiyo, founder of the Snake Clan, whose legendary exploits on the Colorado form the background material of the famous Snake Ceremony, is matched by Major John Wesley Powell, the first white man to explore the Colorado from one end of its many canyons to the other.

Powell's exploration work along the Colorado undoubtedly became known to the Hopi while his first party was still in the canyons, so when word reached them late in the summer of 1870 that the one-armed major was on his way to visit them there was very considerable curiosity among the villages as to what manner of man he would prove to be. Even more important to Hopi religious leaders was what he might have to tell them about their sacred places in the canyon country. Had he journeyed up the Little Colorado above its junction with the main river to that most sacred of all Hopi shrines at Sipapu, the entrance to the Underworld?

The Hopi proved to be a distinct surprise to Major Powell. Never had he seen such Indians, and at first he seems to have been rather disappointed in them. Strange to say, he did not like the way the Hopi men wore their hair cut in even, low bangs across their foreheads. Possibly this style of haircut made it difficult for the ethnologist in him to judge, at a glance, their cranial development! However, he immediately applauded the picturesque whorled hair styles of the young Hopi maidens and the neat dresses of all the women.

In fact, Powell became so interested in the Hopi that he remained with them for nearly a month. This necessitated changes in some of his major plans for further exploration work in the high plateau country of the Southwest.

He traded with the Hopi for all kinds of artifacts to carry back for display in Washington. He took in every possible Hopi ceremony. He gathered an extensive vocabulary of Hopi words and was the first to recognize the place of the Hopi language in the great Uto-Aztecan (Shoshonean) family of languages.

Powell and his party, guided by Hamblin, came first to Moencopi which they found deserted. After an overnight camp near a pool of water in a canyon above the deserted settlement, they traveled on to Oraibi. Powell's account of his days with the Hopi contains several interesting notes.

In a street of Oraibi our little party is gathered. Soon a council is called by the "cacique," or chief, and we are assigned to a suite of six or eight rooms for our quarters. We purchase corn of some of the people, and after feeding our animals they are intrusted to two Indian boys, who under the direction of the "cacique," take them to a distant mesa to herd. This is my first view of an inhabited pueblo, though I have seen many ruins from time to time. . . .

After we have looked about the town and been gazed upon by the wondering eyes of the men, women, and children, we are at last called to supper. In a large central room we gather and the food is placed before us. A stew of goat's flesh is served in earthen bowls, and each one of us is furnished with a little earthen ladle. The bread is a great novelty to me. It is made of corn meal in sheets as thin and large as foolscap paper. In the corner of the house is a little oven, the top of which is a great flat stone, and the good housewife bakes her bread in this manner: The corn meal is mixed to the consistency of a rather thick gruel, and the woman dips her hand into the mixture and plasters the hot stone with a thin coating of the meal paste. In a minute or two it forms into a thin paperlike cake, and she takes it up by the edge, folds it once, and places it on a basket tray; then another and another sheet of paperbread is made in like manner and piled on the tray. I notice that the paste stands in a number of different bowls and that she takes from one bowl and then another in order, and I soon see the effect of this. The corn before being ground is assorted by colors, white, yellow, red, blue, and black, and the sheets of bread, when made, are of the same variety of colors, white, yellow, red, blue, and black. This bread, held on very beautiful trays, is itself a work of art. They call it "piki." After we have partaken of goat stew and bread a course of dumplings, melons, and peaches is served, and this finishes the feast. What seem to be dumplings are composed of a kind of hash of bread and meat, tied up in little balls with cornhusks and served boiling hot. They are eaten with much gusto by the party and highly praised. . . .

In the evening the people celebrate our advent by a dance, such it seemed to us, but probably it was one of their regular ceremonies. After dark a pretty little fire is built in the chimney corner and I spend the evening in rehearsing to a group of the leading men the story of my travels in the canyon country. Of our journey down the canyon in boats they have already heard, and they listen with great interest to what I say. . . .

One afternoon they take me from Oraibi to Shupaulovi to witness a great religious ceremony. It is the invocation to the gods for rain. We arrive about sundown, and are taken into a large subterranean chamber, into which we descend by a ladder. Soon about a dozen Shamans are gathered with us, and the ceremony continues from sunset to sunrise. It is a series of formal invocations, incantations, and sacrifices, especially of holy meal and holy water. The leader of the Shamans is a great burly bald-headed Indian, which is a remarkable sight, for I have never seen one before. Whatever he says or does is repeated by three others in turn. The paraphernalia of their worship is very interesting. At one end of the chamber is a series of tablets of wood covered with quaint pictures of animals and of corn, and overhead are conventional black clouds from which yellow lightnings are projected, while drops of rain fall on the corn below. Wooden birds, set on pedestals and decorated with plumes, are arranged in various ways. Ears of corn, vases of holy water, and trays of meal make up a part of the paraphernalia of worship. I try to record some of the prayers, but am not very successful, as it is difficult to hold my interpreter to the work. But one of these prayers is something like this:

"Muingwa pash lolomai, Master of the Clouds, we eat no stolen bread; our young men ride not the stolen ass; our food is not stolen from the gardens of our neighbors. Muingwa pash lolomai, we beseech of thee to dip your great sprinkler, made of the feathers of the birds of the heavens, into the lakes of the skies and sprinkle us with sweet rains, that the ground may be prepared in the winter for the corn that grows in the summer." . . .

In the evening we return to Oraibi. And now for two days we employ our time in making a collection of the arts of the people of this town. First, we display to them our stock of goods, composed of knives, needles, awls, scissors, paints, dyestuffs, leather, and various fabrics in gay colors. Then we go around among the people and select the articles of pottery, stone implements, instruments and utensils made of bone, horn, shell, articles of clothing and ornament, baskets, trays, and many other things, and tell the people to bring them the next day to our rooms. A little after sunrise they come in, and we have a busy day of barter. When articles are brought in such as I want, I lay them aside. Then if possible I discover the fancy of the one who brings them, and I put by the articles the goods which I am willing to give in exchange for them. Having thus made an offer, I never deviate from it, but leave it to the option of the other party to take either his own articles or mine lying beside them. The barter is carried on with a hearty good will; the people jest and laugh with us and with one another; all are pleased, and there is nothing to mar this day of pleasure. In the afternoon and evening I make an inventory of our purchases, and the next day is spent in packing them for shipment. Some of the things are heavy, and I engage some Indians to help transport the cargo to Fort Wingate, where we can get army transportation.

October 24. — Today we leave Oraibi. We are ready to start in the early morning. The whole town comes to bid us good-by. Before we start they perform some strange ceremony which I cannot understand, but, with invocations to some deity, they sprinkle us, our animals, and our goods with water and with meal. Then there is a time of handshaking and hugging. "Good-by; good-by; good-by!" At last we start. Our way is to Walpi, by a heavy trail over a sand plain, among the dunes. We arrive a little after noon. Walpi, Sichumovi, and Hano are three little towns on one butte, with but little space between them; the stretch from town to town is hardly large enough for a game of ball. The top of the butte is of naked rock, and it rises from 300 to 400 feet above the sand plains below by a precipitous cliff on every side. To reach it from below, it must be climbed by niches and stairways in the rock. It is a good site for defense. At the foot of the cliff and on some terraces the people have built corrals of stone for their asses. All the water used in these three towns is derived from a well nearly a mile away — a deep pit sunk in the sand, over the site of a dune-buried brook.

When we arrive the men of Walpi carry our goods, camp equipage, and saddles up the stairway and deposit them in a little court. Then they assign us eight or ten rooms for our quarters. Our animals are once more consigned to the care of Indian herders, and after they are fed they are sent away to a distance of some miles. There is no tree or shrub growing near the Walpi mesa. It is miles away to where the stunted cedars are found, and the people bring curious little loads of wood on the backs of their donkeys, it being a day's work to bring such a cargo. The people have anticipated our coming, and the wood for our use is piled in the chimney corners. After supper the hours till midnight are passed in rather formal talk. . . .

Two days are spent in trading with the people, and we pride ourselves on having made a good ethnologic collection.[34]

Major Powell's visit to the Hopi was one of great significance. The Hopi found in him a man whom they instinctively trusted. Powell not only delighted in the richness of Hopi culture but, unlike many Americans who came to Tusayan, he treated the inhabitants there like fellow human beings. Wallace Stegner, in his *Beyond the Hundredth Meridian,* says of Powell's unusual ability in dealing with the Hopi, as well as other Indians: "Powell respected them, and earned their respect, because he accepted without question their right to be what they were, to hold to the beliefs and institutions natural to them. To approach a strange culture and a strange people without prejudice, suspicion, condescension, or fear is common enough among students now; it was not too common in 1870."[35]

Beyond this characteristic, however, Major Powell came to the Hopi a mature, experienced, well-educated gentleman. Born in 1834 at Mt. Morris, now engulfed by New York City, he avidly gained what education he found available in the life sciences of his day. He began the geological survey of the Colorado River in 1869, and in later years became director of the United States Geological Survey. In 1879 his interest in the American Indian led to his being appointed the first director of the Bureau of American Ethnology.

During his stay with the Hopi, Powell and Tuleta Tca'akmongwi (Crier Chief) at Oraibi, became friends. When the major learned that Hamblin was planning to take Tuba and his wife back to Salt Lake City to visit Brigham Young, he invited Tuleta to accompany him back to Washington. Tuleta accepted Powell's invitation with alacrity.

Powell described Tuleta:

... who is well mounted on a beautiful bay, is a famous rider. About his brow a kerchief is tied, and his long hair rests on his back. He has keen black eyes and a beaked nose; about his neck he wears several dozen strings of beads, made of nacre shining shells, and little tablets of turkis are perforated and strung on sinew cord; in his ears he has silver rings, and his wrists are covered with silver bracelets. His leggings are black velvet, the material for which he has bought from some trader; his moccasins are tan-colored and decorated with silver ornaments, and the trappings of his horse are decorated in like manner. He carries his rifle with as much ease as if it were a cane, and rides with wonderful dexterity. We get on with jargon, and sign language pretty well. At night, after a long ride, I descend to the foot of the mesa, and near a little lake I find the camp. The donkey train has not arrived, but soon one after another the Indians come in with their packs, and with white men, Oraibi Indians, Walpi Indians, and Navajos, a good party is assembled.[36]

Powell left on October 28, his original party greatly increased by a cavalcade of burros bearing the collection of several hundred Hopi artifacts which he had collected at the various villages and which still form part of the permanent collection of the Smithsonian Institution. A number of Hopi men and boys acted as freighters. Unfortunately for Tuleta somewhere between Fort Defiance and Santa Fe his horse was stolen by some Navajo. The party was in a hurry and could wait only one day while he tried to recapture it. When that day had passed and Tuleta did not return, Powell reluctantly gave word to resume the journey to Santa Fe.

Tuleta was so anxious to make the trip to Washington with Powell that he secured another horse somewhere, somehow, and galloped after him as fast as he could; but the stagecoach bearing the major had been gone a good hour when he reached Santa Fe. Tuleta had no paper to show that Powell wished him to go to Washington, so sadly and reluctantly he began the long ride back to Tusayan.

Powell's weeks with the Hopi won for them an invaluable and influential friend in Washington. Frequently it was only Powell's influence that served to curb the Indian Bureau of that day from putting into effect some of the unfortunate plans it was considering for the Hopi, plans which Powell realized would have been decidedly detrimental to their welfare.

Hopi Tusqua

BUREAUCRATIC INERTIA AND APATHY, often called typical of the Bureau of Indian Affairs, are all too well exemplified by the fact that it was nearly forty years after its without-your-leave takeover of the Hopi before the bureau took any action to safeguard Hopi lands from growing encroachment by both Navajos and whites.

Many of the former, returning from the Bosque Redondo, were reunited with fellow tribesmen who had eluded capture. Concurrent with the rapid increase in their numbers, the Navajo began to build their hogans in Hopi country.

In 1875 the Mormons had established a community near Moencopi. About the same time other Mormon settlements began along the Little Colorado River. The Atlantic and Pacific Railroad, now the Santa Fe, would soon cross into Arizona some sixty miles south of the Hopi villages. Thus the isolation which had granted them at least precarious seclusion from the white man was gradually being eroded.

The need to block these invasions of the Hopi country prompted Agent W. B. Truax, in his 1876 report to the Commissioner of Indian Affairs, to urge that a reservation for Hopi be established. This suggestion was acted upon almost at once — largely due, no doubt, to the then anti-Mormon attitude of both the Indian administration and the military.

On December 16, 1882, President Chester A. Arthur, in an Executive Order consisting of just one long sentence, set up a Hopi Reservation. This order read as follows:

Executive Mansion, December 16, 1882
It is hereby ordered that the tract of country in the Territory of Arizona, lying and being within the following-described boundaries, viz., beginning on the one hundred and tenth degree of longitude west from Greenwich, at a point 36 degrees 30" north, thence due west to the one hundred and eleventh degree of longitude west, thence due south to a point of longitude 35 degrees 30" north, thence due east to the one hundred and tenth degree of longitude,

and thence due north to the place of beginning be, and the same is hereby, withdrawn from settlement and sale, and set apart for the use and occupancy of the Moqui and such other Indians as the Secretary of the Interior may see fit to settle thereon.

CHESTER A. ARTHUR

In his report for 1882 the Commissioner of Indian Affairs published a map of the newly established reservation. This map showed the southwest corner of the reservation reaching to the Little Colorado, and it also included Hopi butte country in the reservation, thus bringing it fifteen or twenty miles closer to the railroad line. Unfortunately, this map was not approved, and the commissioner's 1883 report shows a map of the reservation exactly as it was outlined in President Arthur's Executive Order.

The concluding phrase of that order, "for the use and occupancy of the *Moqui and such other Indians as the Secretary of the Interior may see fit to settle thereon*" (italics added) was only too often slipped into various kinds of regulations establishing Indian reservations. In all, or nearly all cases, it has resulted in controversy and trouble.

There is absolutely no record to show that the Hopi themselves were consulted in any way regarding the reservation that was set aside for them in this peremptory fashion. Furthermore, Arthur's Executive Order allowed the Hopi only the *use* of the lands designated. It in no way recognized their right to ownership. The Hopi had no knowledge whatever that lines were being drawn on maps in Washington limiting them to the use of a certain area of the extensive country which they for centuries had believed to be their own.

It is unlikely that even the few whites living in that part of northern Arizona knew where the boundaries of the newly created reservation were. There was no way the representatives of the government in Arizona could protect the Hopi from encroachment on the reservation. Even the Hopi agency, established thirteen years earlier, was given up in the autumn of 1882 and was not reestablished until 1887. To further complicate matters for the Hopi, from 1882 until 1899 it was administered as part of a joint Moqui and Navajo Agency.

The Hopi themselves have always considered as theirs the lands occupied by their ancestors where they have shrines, such as the one near the summit of Mt. Thomas in the White Mountains of Arizona; and lands with natural features of a sacred nature, like the salt deposit in the Grand Canyon of the Colorado and various eagle-nesting sites. This area can be bounded, roughly, by the junction of the San Juan River with the Colorado in the north, the Arizona-New Mexico state line on the east, the Mogollon and Zuñi rim on the south, and the San Francisco Peaks on the west.

When one considers that these conceptions of the Hopi as to what constitutes their country were totally ignored when "their" reservation was established and that the order for its establishment also provided for its use and occupancy by other tribes, it is small wonder that down through the years the constant encroachment of the Navajo into the area has proved not only a serious threat to the very existence of the Hopi in their own land, but also multiple thorns in the flesh of conscientious agents at Keams Canyon.

When the first Spanish came to the Southwest they spoke of the Hopi country as being part of the province of Tusayan, but to the Hopi it has always been the Hopi Tusqua, the land.

The Hopi have long been aware of how intimately their lives are bound up with the ecology of their land. The fact that their ancestors settled there so many centuries before the first white man saw what was to him the New World has made Hopi roots grow deep and hold fast to the lands they consider theirs.

In 1951 many important members of the various clans and religious societies of Shongopovi drew up a statement which was presented to the Commissioner of Indian Affairs, outlining the boundaries of the area they have traditionally considered to be theirs. This document also set forth in their own words their depth of feeling regarding that land.

> Always vital to us is the subject of our land. In times far back before your history we were taught truthful and peaceful living, which remains with us in the traditional life way of the Hopi people. We could not remain here in selfish tenant. In our traditional life we are strong against selfishness and tyranny, and are to be governed in our traditional way so we might have prosperity, happiness, honor and peace, not only for ourselves but for all people including our white brothers.
>
> Many times we have talked with officials of the United States Government on the matter of our land. In April of 1939 we presented a map of our land to the Commissioner of Indian Affairs but have not received acknowledgment of our claim. . . . In this effort we have failed to find where you gave us any legal way or rights or title to the land which was ours from times long before you came among us.
>
> Thus, realizing that inasmuch as you have not given us legal entrance to the problem we must humbly and with deepest thought and sincerity present our claim to the Hopi land (Tusqua) as it is fixed by our traditional life and which we must use in our traditional way in carrying out our traditional practices and regulations. . . .

THE LAND AND ITS PURPOSE

The Hopi Tusqua (land) is our Love and will always be, and it is the land upon which our leader fixes and tells the dates for our religious life. Our land, our religion, and our life are one, and our leader, with humbleness, understanding and determination, performs his duty to us by keeping them as one and thus insuring prosperity and security for the people.

1. It is from the land that each true Hopi gathers the rocks, the plants, the different woods, roots, and his life, and each in the authority of his rightful obligation brings to our ceremonies proof of our ties to this land. Our footprints mark well the trails to these sacred places where each year we go in performance of our duties.

2. It is upon this land that we have hunted and were assured of rights to game such as deer, elk, antelope, buffalo, rabbit, turkey. It is here that we captured the eagle, the hawk, and such birds whose feathers belong to our ceremonies.

3. It is upon this land that we made trails to our salt supply.

4. It is over this land that many people have come seeking places for settlement, and finding Shungopovi established, asked our leader for permission to settle in this area. All the clan groups named their contributions to our welfare and upon acceptance by our leader were given designated lands for their livelihood and for their eagle hunting, according to the directions from which they came.

5. It is from this land that we obtained the timbers and stone for our homes and kivas.

6. It is here on this land that we are bringing up our younger generation and through preserving the ceremonies are teaching them proper human behavior and strength of character to make them true citizens among all people.

7. It is upon this land that we wish to live in peace and harmony with our friends and with our neighbors.

We realize that within the area of the Hopi land claim there are towns and villages of other people. It is not our intention to bring disturbance to the people of these places, for our way requires us to conduct our lives in friendship and peace, without anger, without greed, without wickedness of any kind among ourselves or in our association with any people; and in turn to have guaranteed that there will be no disturbance to us in the carrying out of our traditional life.

Although we are small in numbers, scarce in money and without wide knowledge of your ways and your laws, with humble hearts but strong determination we state the traditional claims of the Hopi people, who are joined as one on this question of land through their commitments to our leader and his assignment of land for their use in fulfilling their obligations and maintaining their life. Our authority to present the claim is in the traditional organization of the Hopi people. By custom long established and observed it is known to all true Hopi that authority and responsibility for the security of the land belongs to their leader, and all individuals, groups, clans, villages, in return for the land assigned to them for use are obligated to support this authority. And none, whether through self-will, ignorance, or through any other means, are free to take authority over the land into their hands. We are aware that through ignorance of our ways certain Hopi individuals, groups and villages have been encouraged in directions in opposition to the traditional government of the Hopi people, and that they may take it upon themselves to act in respect to this land claim of the Hopi people. It is our responsibility to point out this situation, not in anger, not in ill-will, but only to have it clear that we alone are authorized by the traditions of the Hopi people to represent the people on this matter of the Hopi Tusqua (land). . . .

At the present time and for some years we have been forced from these boundaries inward and it has been only with difficult effort and strong faith in our way of life that we have managed to survive. Our petition to you is for full restoration of the land to us and the freedom to govern its use. We cannot, by our tradition, accept coins or money for this land, but must persist in our prayers and words for repossession of the land itself, to preserve the Hopi life.

Our claim — based upon our occupation and use in the conduct of our traditional life under the traditional order of the Hopi people joined as one through long established custom, and through agreements whereby all clans are pledged to their traditional leader and in turn are supported by their leader — is for our rights to the full use of our resources, our ceremonial shrines and hunting areas.

Through many dark hours we have come to this time and have lived through the times of anger, confusion, ignorance, fear, and misunderstanding, supported by the strength of our traditional life, and it is our confidence that you in the spirit of justice and honor will recognize this traditional claim of the Hopi people, that we may live together in peace with one another.

BOUNDARY MARKS OF HOPI TUSQUA (LAND)

1. Sak wai vai yu (Chevelon Cliffs)
2. Honapa (west of Sedona)
3. Tusak Choma (Bill Williams Mountain)
4. & 5. Po ta ve taka (Point Sublime, Grand Canyon, to junction of Colorado River and Escalante River) Polungoihoya
6. Tukuk navi (Navajo Mountain)
7. & 8. Ky westima (east of Keet Seel and Betatakin)
9. Nei yavu walsh (Lolomai Point)
10. Nah mee toka (Lupton — mouth of Canyon)
11. Tsi mun tu qui (Woodruff Butte)

*   *   *

[SIGNED:]

Clark Talahaftewa (Fingerprint)	Kikmongwi (Bear Clan)	Sakwalenmongwi (Blue Flute Society)
Dick McLean Quanavama (Signed)	Katcinmongwi (Katcina-Parrot Clan)	Dowmongwi (Singers Society)
Franklin Coochyestewa (Fingerprint)	Sun Clan	Kwanmongwi (One Horn Society)
Viets Lomaheftewa (Signed)	Water Clan	Al mongwi (Two Horn Society)

Ralph Selina (Signed)	Corn Clan	Wuwucim mongwi (Wucucim Society)
Otis Polelonema (Signed)	Snow Clan	Mas len mongwi (Grey Flute Society)
Louis Tewanima (Fingerprint)	Rope Clan	Tchuf mongwi (Antelope Society)
Wadsworth Nuvangoitewa (Fingerprint)	Sunforehead Clan	Chumongwi (Snake Society)
Andrew Hermequaftewa (Fingerprint)	Bluebird Clan	Advisor

*   *   *

Leaders of other Hopi villages may differ in some degree as to the boundaries defined by these men of Shongopovi. Such differences are not serious enough to preclude the acceptance of this statement in order to gain some concept of the wide expanse of territory the Hopi have for so long felt to be theirs and why they feel the reservation that was designated for them seems so inadequate.

Washington Comes
to the Hopi

ON MAY 26, 1887, several heavily loaded wagons left the railroad
station at Holbrook, Arizona, for the long haul over the rough road
across the Painted Desert to Keams Canyon. Whatever Hopi there may
have been at Thomas Keam's trading post at the canyon must have
watched with keen curiosity as James Gallaher, the first representative
of the government of the United States to establish his official residence
in Tusayan, arrived with such supplies as were deemed necessary for
his purpose.

Superintendent Gallaher soon found that he had his hands full
trying to put the buildings which had been rented from Keam into suitable
shape to house his office, a school, and living quarters for himself and
his staff.

Back in Washington, Indian Commissioner J. D. C. Atkins had
received a petition signed by twenty Hopi leaders asking that a school
be opened in their country and pledging that if this was done they would
"gladly send our children." Among those signing the petition were
Supela of Walpi and Honani of Shongopovi. Gallaher had been ordered
to comply with this request.

In his report for this first year he gave the Hopi population as 2,206
and estimated their livestock to consist of 20,000 sheep, 1,500 goats, 300
cattle, 750 horses and 15,000 burros — an average of about seven
burros for every man, woman, and child!

Time after time, all during the year, the Navajo raided the Hopi
fields and stole their livestock. Gallaher was constantly forced to make
long trips to the various villages and widely scattered Navajo hogans in
what soon proved to be futile attempts to protect the Hopi from Navajo
depredations.

Building supplies necessary for the reconditioning of the rented
buildings had to be hauled by wagon from the railhead at Holbrook

over roads that often were rendered virtually impassable by cloudbursts. Such shipments of supplies as did arrive were often found short of many items deemed absolutely essential. However, by hook or crook, Gallaher and his staff managed to open school on October 1, 1887, with fifty-two pupils.

Uncle Sam was in Tusayan to stay.

Because of almost dictatorial powers exerted by the various men who over the years represented the United States government to the Hopi, either as school superintendents or as superintendents of the Hopi Agency at Keams Canyon, the names of many, if not most, of them are still well remembered in Tusayan.

During his term of office Leo Crane made a digest of the reports of his predecessors, which were then on file at Keams Canyon. From Crane's report and several other sources we have attempted to list the names of these various officials and the dates when they took office.

Successors to Gallaher, acting as school superintendents at Keams Canyon but answerable to the agent at Fort Defiance, were:

S. C. Baker	1889
Ralph P. Collins	1890
C. W. Goodman	1893
Samuel L. Hertzog	1895
Ralph P. Collins	1896

The volume of reports for 1897–98 "is missing from the records of the Keams Canyon Agency," according to Crane. "This has probably been stolen, as it no doubt contains the recital of the smallpox among the Hopis." (So far as we have been able to determine, it is missing from the files of the Washington office as well.)

Later the following men acted as school superintendents and U.S. agents, answerable directly to the Bureau of Indian Affairs in Washington:

Charles E. Burton	1899
Theodore G. Lemmon	1904
Horton H. Miller	1906
Abraham L. Lawshe	1910
Leo Crane	1911
Robert E. L. Daniel	1919

In 1923 the name of the Keams Canyon office was changed officially to the Hopi Agency and the men holding the top posts dropped the title of "School Superintendent, acting as Indian Agent," and were known from then on merely as superintendents.

The list from then to the time of this writing is as follows:

Edgar J. Miller	1924
Ernest H. Hammond (acting)	1934
Alexander G. Hutton (acting)	1935
Alexander G. Hutton	1936
Seth Wilson	1939
Burton A. Ladd	1942
James D. Crawford	1948
Dow Carnal	1951
Clyde W. Pensoneau	1954
Herman E. O'Hara	1956
Clyde W. Pensoneau	1965
Joseph Nucero (acting)	1967
Homer W. Gilliland	1968
Francis J. Boger (acting)	1972
Guy McIntosh	1974

Only too frequently, especially in the early years, the men appointed to such jobs were little better than political hacks who in turn surrounded themselves with lesser breeds of political parasites. Nepotism and graft were widely accepted by these men as their way of life.

It is little wonder that General Nelson A. Miles, the famous Indian fighter and commander-in-chief of the Army, once wrote to his wife: "There has been no branch of the government so corrupt and disgraceful to the Republic as that which has had the management of our Indian affairs."

In reading over the annual reports of the men who have served at Keams Canyon it is all too evident that the majority came to Tusayan with deep-seated prejudices against the Indian, with intolerance for his religious beliefs, and with a determined dedication to do everything within their power to make the Hopi over into an imitation and second-class white man, rather than the best type of Hopi citizen.

Down through the years these agents found the Hopi determined to hold fast to his religious beliefs and to his concepts of how a true Hopi should live. He would not conveniently die off and thus become a "good Indian," according to the white man's frontier concept. The greater the pressure applied to get him to abandon his ceremonies and adopt the white man's way of life, the more tenaciously he remained friendly but absolutely adamant in his refusal to abandon what he considered the proper Hopi way of life. To have done so would have rendered him *Kahopi* — not a Hopi at all.

From reading their reports, it becomes equally clear that many of the men sent to carry out the plans and policies of the Bureau of Indian

Affairs — "Washington" to the Hopi — were sincere, and likely even honest, in their attempts. The fact that the early officials were frequently harassed by directives proclaiming policies and programs that were entirely unsuited to the Hopi and the Hopi country cannot be blamed on the Keams Canyon agents themselves. Moreover, much of their time was devoted to problems which had little bearing upon the Indians for whose well-being they were responsible.

Personnel problems among ill-paid employees — who came to the Hopi country with no conception of the circumstances under which they would live and work or the culture of the Indians whom they were to work with and for — demanded hour after hour of the superintendent's time. Only too often the Civil Service Commission and the Indian Office in Washington were absolutely unable to fill the vacancies which occurred frequently in the reservation staff.

Building construction that was slipshod and ill-suited to the climate and terrain required endless repairs and construction. A frustrating amount of time had to be devoted to such planning and supervision as this work required.

More and more visitors were coming to Tusayan. In the early days the majority took lodgings with trader Thomas Keam, who conducted them about the reservation. Many of these visitors were there just to see the sights. A great number of them, however, were scientists, ethnologists, anthropologists, archaeologists, surveyors, geologists, biologists, and men and women of many other scientific disciplines. There were also writers, artists, and photographers among them, as well as assorted odd-ball characters so colorful that they added many a vivid tint to the Painted Desert landscape.

None of these early white visitors to Tusayan forced their way into Hopi history as did the aggressive anthropologist Matilda Coxe Stevenson, whose papers regarding Zuñi are to be found in the early volumes of the Bureau of American Ethnology *Annual Reports*. Mrs. Stevenson was determined that she was going to visit one of the Hopi kivas. The Hopi were determined that she was not. As a result, the decidedly formidable Mrs. Stevenson won for herself a place in the *Illustrated Police News* for 1886 — a distinction not shared with any other anthropologist.

Most of the men in charge at Keams Canyon were suspicious and often resentful of visitors. Too many of them, they felt, became friendly with the dissident Hopi. Some even openly sympathized with the Indians in their stand to preserve their own way of life. A few visitors even wrote letters to their congressmen!

A great cause of misunderstanding and friction was the language barrier between the men sent out from Washington and the Hopi. Interpreters who were fluent in both languages were scarce. Nevertheless, the

Smithsonian Institution, National Anthropologist Archives

Matilda Coxe Stevenson, anthropologist, supported by her husband, stages a violent demonstration when the Hopi protest their prying into ceremonial secrets. (From an engraving published in *The Illustrated Police News,* March 6, 1886)

fact that the administration for control and management of the Hopi and their lands was set up without agreement of any kind with the Hopi themselves, or with the leaders of their independent villages, was the single greatest source of trouble.

Radically different viewpoints regarding the land itself, even to this day, have been the cause of endless friction between the men of Washington and the Hopi. The latter's deeply religious concept of the land made many things done with it and to it by white officialdom seem sacrilegious to the Hopi. The white man's ideas as to individual and corporate ownership were foreign to the Hopi. The actions of superintendents and agents in giving or granting the use of land to missionaries and traders was naturally considered high-handed and dishonest by the Hopi.

It is only too evident that the men who came out as representatives of the BIA did not even consider the age-old indigenous system of government the Hopi had worked out for their villages. Certainly, no attempt was made by these government officials to work through the traditional leaders of the villages.

Although many of these village leaders had petitioned for a school, almost immediately after the one at Keams Canyon was opened friction developed between school officials and Hopi parents. Hopi mothers and fathers could not understand why, since their children did not have to go to school on Sundays and other days deemed sacred by the white man's religion, school officials made such strenuous objection when the children were kept out of school for important Hopi religious occasions.

Various jobs — freighting, road building, police work, construction work, and the like, for which government officials could hire Hopi — were much sought after for the substantial boost the meager wages could effect in the standard of living of those fortunate enough to be hired. This situation soon came to be used for the leverage it offered in persuading such Hopi employees to Washington's way of thinking. Every effort was made to persuade these employees to send their children to school and to become converts to Christianity in opposition to their clan and religious leaders. Thus the old policy of divide and conquer was put to work in Tusayan.

What follows is a short account of happenings on the Hopi Reservation based on reports of the school superintendents at Keams Canyon and of the Indian agents at Fort Defiance from 1890 to 1899. This has been taken from "History of the Moqui Indian Reservation" (compiled by Leo Crane from annual reports) in the manuscript collection of the Museum of Northern Arizona in Flagstaff.

In 1890 Agent C. E. Vandever at Fort Defiance reported that a number of Hopi had been taken to Washington and to the Carlisle Indian School in Pennsylvania and that some of the Hopi were impressed with Carlisle and were credited as being in favor of having a school like it established in their own country.

The persistent objections of the people of Oraibi to their children's attending school, largely because of its interference with their proper participation in Hopi religious observance, prompted School Superintendent Ralph P. Collins to request troops from Fort Defiance. On December 28 the soldiers entered the old village and captured 104 youngsters. While the troops were in Tusayan the superintendent put them to good use in driving out several Navajo families he considered trespassers on Hopi territory.

As the representatives of Washington came to realize that preservation of the Hopi way of life and especially their religion lay to a great extent in the social structure of their village communities, they decided on a plan to break up the villages. This plan began to take form in 1891 when a contract was awarded for a survey designed to make it possible to allot land below the mesas to individual Hopi. To encourage the Hopi

Thomas V. Keam. (From a
painting by Julian Scott,
November 1890)

David M. Brugge

to move to these allotted lands, the government promised to furnish
lumber and other supplies for families willing to do so. During the year
fifty houses were started.

Earlier, on July 13, 1889, Thomas V. Keam had "quit-claimed
unto the Secretary of the Interior, for the use of the government of the
United States and its assigns, all that particular tract of land known and
described as Keams Canyon, within the Moqui Reservation, in Arizona,
the consideration being $10,000." Although an appropriation to cover
this transaction was made in 1889, it was not until 1892 that the deal
with Keam was consummated, a deal in which the Hopi were given no
consideration whatever.

All during 1892 Superintendent Collins continued to fight with
bitterness the increasing Hopi objection to their children's attending the
white man's school. In spite of his use of the troops to enforce attendance, Oraibi children did not return to school when the summer vacation
was over. Collins reported tersely that the situation was "still requiring
a demonstration of force to compel them."

In a further attempt to break down Oraibi opposition, eight children
— despite the objections and pleas of their parents — were sent away
from the village to school in Lawrence, Kansas.

That same year twenty-six houses were furnished with roofs, floors,
windows, and doors at a cost to Uncle Sam of $145 each! Thus began
the ill-conceived plan to break the solidarity of the Hopi villages by
attempting to get them to desert their mesa-top homes in favor of living
in frame houses down on the desert.

Keam's Ranch about 1890. The man in the foreground may be Keam.

The report of Agent Shipley at Fort Defiance gives us the additional information that a model farm — to teach the Hopi how to grow corn — had been established and that he had issued a "decree prohibiting the Navajo from approaching within a fiftten-mile radius of the village of Machongnovi." He also reported one hundred houses well under construction and a number of allotment farms surveyed and staked out.

When C. W. Goodman replaced Ralph Collins at Keams Canyon on December 3, 1893, he found little to reassure him regarding the government's program for the Hopi. In his report for 1893 he stated that two adobe buildings had been completed at Oraibi for a day school and that this had been opened in March by a doctor and a field matron. In May a regular teacher took over. He further reported that there was great opposition to the school and only thirty children were in attendance. The attendance at the Keams Canyon School averaged ninety-three.

One hundred twenty thousand acres of land had been surveyed and allotted to such Hopi as would accept allotment, and twenty houses had been equipped with stoves, beds, and so forth, but these were being occupied only spasmodically. He estimated the Hopi population at 2,029.

Just one year after the allotment program had been completed, Commissioner D. N. Browning was forced to report (1894): "The work of allotting lands in severalty to the Indians of this reservation (Moqui) has been discontinued. All but a few of the Indians had made their selections ... but a small number continued their opposition to the allotment work. This opposition together with formal objections to the approval of any of the allotments presented to this office by friends of the Indians, led to a discontinuance of the work in February last."

In his 1893 report Superintendent Goodman also referred to the water development program, paying particular notice to a good well that had been developed for the Polacca Day School, which opened on January 15, 1894, in a building bought from Tom Polacca.

Acting Agent 1st Lieutenant S. H. Plummer, with rare intelligence, reported:

No improvement in condition of Hopis during the past year ... the plan of building houses in the valleys for these Indians, with the view of persuading them to abandon their overcrowded pueblo dwellings on the high mesas, does not seem to be as successful as desired. Many of the houses built in the valleys are unoccupied the greater portion of the year. Their habits, customs and general mode of living are so intimately connected with the conditions of life on the mesas that it is doubtful whether anything else than compulsion will cause them to abandon their pueblo dwellings. It has been the custom for years for these people to cultivate their lands in common. Owing to the shifting nature of their planting grounds, it would be almost impossible to maintain any allotment to individuals. It is believed that the best interests of the tribe would be promoted by granting the petition.

The petition referred to was one asking discontinuation of the allotment plan.

Lieutenant Plummer also recommended that a separate agent be appointed for the Hopi, a recommendation which was acted upon six years later.

The divide and conquer policy first created a serious crisis at Old Oraibi. There, for the first time, those Hopi who followed the desires of the government officials and the missionaries were spoken of in official reports as the "friendlies" and those who stood fast to their Hopi way of life, were the "hostiles." School Superintendent Samuel L. Hertzog reported that the so-called "hostiles" at Oraibi and Moencopi were taking the fields away from the "friendlies" and that once more troops had been called in from Fort Defiance to restore order.

Chief Lomahongyoma and the others at Alcatraz.

1. Komaletstewa	7. Karshongnewa	14. Wongnehma
2. Yoda	8. Kochventewa	15. Unidentified
3. Naquatewa	9. Beephongva (?)	16. Polingyouma
4. Kochyouma	10. Poolegoiva	17. Hahvema
5. Soukhongva	11. Lomahongyoma	18. Masatewa
6. Sekaheptewa	12. Lomanankwosa	19. Quoyahoinema
	13. Kochadah	

Captain Constant Williams, Acting Agent at Fort Defiance, gave further details in his report to the Commissioner of Indian Affairs: ". . . the troubles at Oraibi resulted from the disposition on the part of the hostiles to drive the friendlies from their fields. In the fall they drove the friendlies from the fields at Moencopie and in the spring, threatened to do the same thing at Oraibi. Nineteen ringleaders were arrested by U.S. troops and sent to Alcatraz Island, in San Francisco Harbor. This action settled the question, at least for the present."

The Hopi prisoners were received at Alcatraz on January 3, 1895, and were released for good behavior on August 7 of the same year.

In 1894, Superintendent Goodman had built a brick kiln at Keams Canyon in which fifty thousand bricks were made during that year and this work was continued over the next year. In 1896 the old buildings which had been bought from Keam were abandoned as unsanitary; the school, the offices, and the living quarters were moved into the new buildings built with these bricks.

Collins returned to Keams Canyon and resumed the office of school superintendent. In his report for 1896 he wrote that the Hopis who had been imprisoned at Alcatraz now claimed that they were told there that they were not to be forced to send their children to school. In opposition to this, Acting Agent Captain Williams in his report for the same year stated that the prisoners were released from Alcatraz upon their promising to obey all orders given them. It may very well be that the language problem was responsible for this misunderstanding, as had been true in the past, and often still is in relations between the Hopi and the white man.

Superintendent Collins estimated that the 1896 Hopi population was 2,050 and that they possessed 500 cattle, 5,000 sheep, 3,000 goats and 3,000 horses, mules, and burros.

Smallpox which had ravaged the Hopi in 1780, 1840, and 1853 continued to be a scourge. The Hopi, like other Indians, had developed no natural immunity to many of the diseases introduced into the New World by the white man. In 1897–98, an epidemic began which raged through Tusayan for several years. Hopi and Navajo deaths reached into the hundreds.

The government's program of enforced vaccination, which was carried through with little attempt to educate the Indians as to its purpose, led to still deeper rifts between "Washington" and the Hopi, as well as between the "hostile" and "friendly" Indians.

Masau-u and Spider Woman
Confront the U.S. Army

THE INADEQUACY OF REPORTS to Washington by Keams Canyon officials during this period is underlined by a crisis which occurred in 1891 — a crisis that would profoundly affect all the Hopi villages.

Brief reference was made in foregoing excerpts from official reports to a proposed survey of the Hopi country preparatory to initiating an allotment program. Nowhere in the reports of that year is there a hint that this was to result in a confrontation with the Army of the United States.

The mysterious and incomprehensible — to the Hopi — actions of the 1891 survey party aroused grave suspicions and profound apprehensions among the Indians. The latter feared desecration of the earth they held as sacred. Would their many and sacrosanct shrines be violated?

Destruction of the offending survey stakes was the only action they could envision, and they began to tear them down as rapidly as they were set in place.

By June of 1891 the situation had reached such a point that again a small detachment of cavalrymen, this time under Lieutenant L. M. Brett, was sent to Oraibi from Keams Canyon. Brett reported to the assistant adjutant general in Los Angeles:

"Came to Oraibi to arrest several Oraibis, who have destroyed surveyor's marks and threatened to destroy the school. When we entered the village we were confronted with about fifty hostiles armed and stationed behind a barricade. They openly declared hostility to the government, and a fight was barely averted. A strong force should be sent here with Hotchkiss guns, as I anticipate serious trouble if the hostiles are not summarily dealt with."

Lieutenant Brett's plea for reinforcements gives no concept of the colorful and dramatic confrontation at Oraibi reported by Fewkes and other informants. As Brett and his men approached the village, they were met below the mesa by Lololomai who urged them not to enter the village. Brett paid no attention to the warning and, upon meeting men he understood were of the hostile faction, he put them under arrest. Placing one of these prisoners beside each of his men, he ascended the mesa to be greeted by wildly shouting Hopi warriors.

Suddenly the shouting stopped and an ancient Hopi woman hobbled slowly forward to confront the startled soldiers. This was really a man personifying Spider Woman, mother of the twin War Gods of the Hopi. Although her words were unintelligible to the lieutenant and his men, her gestures and the force of her declamation left them in no doubt as to her meaning. She warned of serious trouble if they did not leave Oraibi at once.

A few moments later Spider Woman was joined by a Hopi representing Masau-u, the God of Death. He made a dramatic entrance wearing a fearsome black mask and carrying, among other objects of a ceremonial nature, a bowl filled with liquid "medicine." Solemnly he passed along the line of soldiers and with a large feather sprinkled some of this "medicine" on each of them, being careful that none of it touched any of the Hopi prisoners. He then warned the soldiers, even more forcefully than had Spider Woman, that they must leave Oraibi immediately before the most fearful of the Hopi War Gods led his warriors against them.

As Masau-u finished, the warriors back of their barricade flourished their old guns and bows and arrows and yelled defiance of the white man. From time to time their leader could be seen — a massive man, his face streaked with paint — who wore a strange woven helmet crested with a tuft of feathers painted red, and carried an ancient war shield.

Lieutenant Brett, utterly confused by these proceedings and well aware that he was greatly outnumbered, withdrew from Oraibi and returned to Keams Canyon.

A still more terrible creature was being held in reserve by the Hopi if a final desperate attempt had been needed to persuade Brett to retreat. This was a representation of Kua-tu-ku-e, a spirit of such ferocity that to this day many Hopi are fearful of trying to describe it. It took the form of a monstrous eagle-like creature and is sometimes referred to as Knife Wing or Killer Bird. Its name is sometimes written as Kwakata and Kwotoko; the spelling followed here (Kua-tu-ku-e) is that favored by Titiev. There is a pictograph symbolic of it on First Mesa, and it is known to the people of Acoma and Zuñi as well.

The next military move on the part of the whites was the arrival at Keams Canyon on June 30 of Colonel H. C. Corbin with four troops of cavalry and two Hotchkiss guns, the semiautomatic machine guns

Kua-tu-ku-e. The figure is cut ⅛ to ¼ inch deep, in a detached block of sand-stone. The lines are from ¼ to ⅜ inch wide; the wing is 2 feet long. Ovals mark the number of victims. The rock and the design were complete in 1865.

From Stephen's Hopi Journal

of that day. Thomas Keam was requested to accompany the detachment to Oraibi, which he agreed to do but apparently with some reluctance.

His eyewitness account of what happened is contained in Keam's letter of July 16, 1891. This is given in Thomas Donaldson's invaluable *Extra Census Bulletin — Moqui Indians of Arizona* Government Printing Office, 1893.

After consultation we decided to get an early start on July 1 and go to the west side of the village of Mishongnavi, where the large spring is, and camp midway between it and a large spring at the foot of the village of Shimopavi. We got an early start and reached camp in good season under a broiling hot sun, and fortunately found sufficient water in the first spring for our whole command. Here we met a courier from Oraibi, who informed us that the bad Oraibis had threatened to kill La-lo-la-my on sight of the troops and were prepared to fight. In the evening we decided to leave all baggage, food, etc., except a lunch, in camp, and start for Oraibi at 3 a.m., July 2, so as to be near the village shortly after daylight. After a cup of coffee, promptly at 3 a.m., on the 2d of July, with Eone and I leading, we moved up the sides of the Shimopavi mesa, over it and into the Oraibi valley, and on and to within 3 miles of the village. Here a halt was made, and after consultation with those in command I volunteered to go to the mesa, send for the hostiles, and, if possible, get them to come back with me to where the troops had halted. I rode up close to the village and sent "Honani" of Shimopavi to inform the leaders I desired to see them. He returned saying they would not come. I again sent him back to tell them that serious trouble would result if they did not meet me at once. This brought 6 of the leaders down. . . . After saying a few words to them, I escorted them to the troops, where they were made prisoners and heard some good advice from Colonel Corbin. They were quite sullen and refused to answer questions. The order was now given to mount, and we rode up into the village, taking the whole command, with the 2 Hotchkiss guns. Here we took the war chief and his son prisoners. Both were finer and better looking men than any of the others. The son, on being asked what he had to say, replied: "I was prepared to fight the few soldiers that were here some days ago, because I thought we could kill them and drive them away; now, however, it would be useless. I never saw so many Americans before, You have my friends prisoners and I am not able to fight all these soldiers; take me, as I am in your power." The troops were then arranged in front of the village, and after Colonel Corbin had explained to the people what was to be done with the prisoners, and impressed them with obedience to their chief, La-lo-la-my, he said would show them what would have been done with the Hotchkiss guns if they had offered resistance. I had started toward the guns to witness the firing, when I heard loud shouting, yelling, and screaming from the Indians, and as I turned saw an Indian pursued by a soldier jump off the mesa. It was one of the prisoners escaped, and the excitement was great for a while. He succeeded in getting away, and has not yet been caught. A strict guard was kept on the others, who were brought safely to camp and well guarded that night. Next day we reached the cañon. The troops proceeded to their different stations, the 11 prisoners being taken to Wingate. A small detachment with an officer remains here until everything is quiet.[37]

Dr. J. Walter Fewkes, who had camped at Toreva Spring below Second Mesa, with Major Corbin, his officers, and their black troops along with several Navajo serving as interpreters and trackers, was an eyewitness to what later happened. According to his account in the *American Anthropologist* for July–September, 1922, they left Toreva Spring at two o'clock the next morning. A detachment of men was sent ahead with a small cannon to take a position commanding Oraibi. The rest of the party arrived at the main spring of Oraibi just before sunrise. Lest the spring had been poisoned, orders were given that no one should drink from it. The soldiers were drawn up about the spring and a messenger was sent to the mesa top demanding that six of the foremost leaders of the village come down and submit to arrest.

After a wait of about a half hour six Hopi leaders, obviously concerned, presented themselves before Major Corbin. The leader of the Hopi showed Major Corbin a stone bearing a number of pictographs.

This was passed around among the officers, and the Hopi who had handed it to them was asked for an explanation. He told them it defined the boundaries of the lands granted the Bear and its related clans by Masau-u on their arrival at Third Mesa. The stone was then returned to the Hopi and the six of them were put in charge of soldiers and marched back up the narrow trail by which they had come.

The remainder of the troops took a longer trail to reach the main entrance to the village. As this group approached Oraibi, the way was blocked by a middle-aged man imposingly costumed as a chief of the Warrior Society. By his side was a youth similarly garbed. The older man was queried as to who he was and if he wanted to fight the entire detachment of soldiers. The older man replied that he was the Chief of the Warrior Society of Oraibi and that the younger man was his son who would succeed him as War Chief. The War Chief then went on to explain that the men of the Warrior Society were willing to fight but that the people of the village, true to Hopi tradition, were not. He then requested that they take him and his son as hostages and do whatever they wanted with them but not destroy their people. (Fewkes always remembered the admiration he felt for the courageous old War Chief of Oraibi and his son.) With this the two Hopi were put under arrest and marched into the village followed by the troops.

Oraibi seemed deserted. Doors and windows were plastered over with adobe and even the usual horde of dogs was absent. There was not a sign of a living thing. Word came to Major Corbin that the villagers were all assembled out on a point of the mesa. Thereupon the soldiers marched through the village and out toward the end of the mesa. There huddled together was the entire population of Oraibi. The women and children were crying and the men, drawn up to face the troops, were silent and determined. Many of the Hopi carried baskets and bundles.

Major Corbin ordered the soldiers to form a line across the mesa between the village and the place where its inhabitants were crowded together. Those in charge of the cannon were ordered to prepare to fire.

The chiefs among the Hopi were then invited to come forward for a smoke and a talk. After this invitation had been repeated several times a few Hopi men came forward and sat with the six who had been brought up under guard from the spring. These Hopi were told that the cannon was to be fired to show them how futile it would be for them to resist, and at a signal the cannon began firing into a distant Hopi peach orchard. As a result of the explosions one of the six arrested at the spring suddenly jumped away from the guards and dashed to the edge of the mesa and threw himself over the cliff. Although pursued by several of the soldiers and some of the Navajos who shot at him, he managed to escape unharmed.

In spite of Colonel Corbin's suggestion that the people of Oraibi should accept Lololomai as their leader, the band of prisoners taken to Fort Wingate evidently included him as well as Patupha, the leader of those opposing Lololomai. Apparently the prisoners were well treated at Fort Wingate. They were put to work in the gardens of the officers and given plenty of clothing and food. Evidently Lololomai and some of the others were soon allowed to return to Oraibi, for by October, 1892, there were only five remaining at Fort Wingate.

It is also evident that the official treatment meted out to the Hopi was being seriously questioned by many important government officials. Thomas Donaldson was not the only one to question the legality of making prisoners of any Hopi who objected to sending their children to school or of imprisoning them without court commitment. He concludes his statement regarding the Oraibi campaign with these words:

Are the lessons of history worthless? . . . The shadows of murdered and poisoned priests and Spaniards hover around and about the Moqui country. They were killed because they attempted to civilize the Moquis in Spanish fashion. Why should we be more fortunate than the Spaniards, or shall we be compelled to keep a garrison of 250 to 300 men at the Moqui pueblos in order to educate 100 to 200 children at a distance from their homes? We began with soldiers and Hotchkiss guns. Are we to end in the same way? Such civilizing has not heretofore been a pronounced success.[38]

Crusade Against
Superintendent Burton

THE POWERS granted a man commissioned as an Indian agent are fantastic in their variety and their scope. As Agent Leo Crane later put it, "His rule is quite feudal and absolute." Only too often the actions of the men appointed tended to prove the truth of Lord Acton's famous saying, "Power tends to corrupt; absolute power corrupts absolutely."

Certainly the multiplicity of judgments that an agent to the Hopi must make every day of his term in office is often far beyond the sphere of competence of most men. It is not surprising, therefore, that so few men have filled that position with success and honor.

When in 1900 School Superintendent Charles E. Burton also became the first "Agent to the Moqui Reservation" he was only twenty-seven years old. He soon found that he had taken over a Pandora's box of trials and tribulations to which were added more of his own making. These came to a dramatic climax in 1903 when Belle Axtell Kolp, a teacher at Oraibi school, resigned after having been in the Hopi country only seven weeks. Mrs. Kolp was a niece of Samuel B. Axtell, one-time governor and later chief justice of New Mexico.

Agent Burton had issued an order to the effect that all Hopi men and boys who refused to cut their hair would be subjected to having it cut by force. The way this order was being enforced, the brutal treatment exercised by Burton and his assistants in their administration of the Hopi Reservation, and the general conditions she observed during her brief residence there all made a deep impression upon Mrs. Kolp. Burning with indignation, she journeyed to Los Angeles and sought out Charles F. Lummis, the well-known writer who knew and championed the rights of the many Indian tribes of the Southwest.

Associated with Lummis in his Sequoia League, the purpose of which was "To Make Better Indians," were some of the most respected men and women of that time — people like David Starr Jordan, C. Hart Merriman, George Bird Grinnell, Phoebe Hearst, F. W. Putnam of the

Peabody Museum, George A. Dorsey of the Field Columbian Museum, Frederick Webb Hodge, Hamlin Garland, Washington Matthews. Many of these were authorities on the American Indian.

Then, too, Lummis and Theodore Roosevelt had become friends while students at Harvard. Lummis, more than anyone else, was responsible for gaining Roosevelt's interest in trying to get a decent deal for the Indian. Thanks to Lummis and his Sequoia League, Roosevelt personally intervened to secure suitable lands for the dispossessed Indians of the Warner's Ranch area in southern California. This had been a signal victory.

Lummis had not listened long to Mrs. Kolp before he seized upon the situation on the Hopi Reservation as an ideal basis for another crusade to bring justice and humane treatment to the Indian.

He led off in the April, 1903, issue of *Out West* with an eight-page prelude to the campaign he was to wage throughout the year to secure an investigation of Mrs. Kolp's charges. In the June issue Lummis wrote a long and well-illustrated article, "Bullying the Quaker Indians," giving some of the historical background of the Hopi and castigating Agent Burton as "the pinhead official . . . this oppressor . . . Czar over the lives of 1800 Hopi . . . that bully."

In the July issue of *Out West,* Lummis printed the affidavit of Mrs. Kolp. This contained important evidence which led to an investigation of Burton's administration. Since this is one of the most important documents pertaining to the conduct of representatives of the United States government among the Hopi, it is worth quoting in full:

As a teacher from the Government day school at Oraibi, Ariz.; as one who has "seen with her own eyesight" the cruelties inflicted upon the Hopi people there; as a sympathizer with these oppressed people; as an American — I offer, unsolicited by anyone but these poor, persecuted wards of the United States Government, my services in this fight for right, justice, and humane treatment for the Hopi Indians. In doing this I am but keeping a promise which I made to them. Among the last words they said to me were these: "Tell our friends how hard it is for us — tell them to help us."

I began my work as teacher in the day school at Oraibi, Dec. 31, 1902; I resigned from the service Feb. 5, 1903. I resigned that I might be free to speak and act according to the dictates of my own conscience with regard to the persecutions which the Hopi people were compelled to endure from those in charge of the school at Oraibi, John L. Ballinger and wife, and from the Reservation Agent, Chas. E. Burton. I left Oraibi Feb. 17, 1903. Although there a trifle less than seven weeks, I witnessed more of "Man's inhumanity to man" than I ever saw before or ever hope to see again. And all done in the name of the "Big Chief at Washington." Whenever a punishment was threatened or carried out, it was represented to the Indians that it was by "Washington's" orders. I have heard both the principal of the school, John L. Ballinger, and his wife, so talk to the children; and Mrs. Ballinger told me that

"Mr. Burton was going to get United States soldiers to come on to the Reservation to put a stop to the Indians' dances." By permission of Mr. Burton I attended one of these dances. I saw nothing immoral or improper. Most of these dances are religious ceremonies which have been carried on for hundreds of years. They are as sacred and as solemn to these people as religious ceremonies in our churches are to us.

When I began work at Oraibi, the daily attendance at the school was about 125 children. When I left, there were 174 children in the school, and still two teachers — one of them having in her charge 96 children, whose ages ranged from less than four years to others who were 18 or 20. One of the latter — a girl — was said to have been married. The school age is from 5 to 18. There were, when I left at least a dozen little ones in school who were not more than four years of age. They were not strong enough to walk the mile which lay between the village where the Indians live and the schoolhouse. These children, with others, were taken forcibly from their homes by an armed body of Government employees and Navajo Indians under leadership of C. E. Burton — not for the purpose of "making better Indians," but for the benefit of those in charge. Mr. Ballinger wanted to establish a boarding school at Oraibi to take the place of the day school. This would permit drawing more rations and a better salary; also allow him a clerk — which position his wife was to take; so that instead of being school-cook at a salary of $30 per month, or teacher at $52 per month, she would draw from the Government $100 per month. I know these things, for it was all discussed in my presence.

After consultations with Mr. Burton, a raid — or, as Mr. Ballinger called it, a "round-up" — was planned and decided upon. About 10 o'clock on the night of Feb. 2, 1903, the raiding party — consisting of Agent Burton, Physician Murtaugh, Carpenter Stauffer, Blacksmith Copeland, and a squad of Navajo Indian "policemen" — arrived at the school grounds from Government headquarters at Keam's Cañon. The Navajos, armed with rifles, were sent to surround the Hopi village in the night. The next morning — Tuesday — the white men previously named, and Mr. Ballinger, joined the Indian guards up on the mesa, about 5:30 o'clock. I do not know whether all of the white men were armed, but I saw revolvers on Burton, Ballinger and Stauffer. The snow thickly covered the ground, and was still falling. Those children who could be found who were not already enrolled in the school, were sent down to the school under guard. The attendance at school on the fourth was about 150. That was not enough. "I know there are more children up there," said Mr. Ballinger. "We must go after them again." The Indian police were reinforced by more Navajos — seven, I think, came up from Little Burro Spring — and this time the raiders made a "clean sweep." This took place in the early morning of February 5th. Men, women and children were dragged almost naked from their beds and houses. Under the eyes and the guns of the invaders they were allowed to put on a few articles of clothing, and then — many of them barefooted and without any breakfast, the parents and grandparents were forced to take upon their backs such children as were unable to walk the distance (some of the little ones entirely nude) and go down to the school building, through the ice and snow in front of the guns of the dreaded Navajos. They were kept there all day, until after six in the evening, while clothing could be made or found for the children. Before being allowed to go back to their homes these orders were given them by Mr. Burton through his Indian interpreter — "You must have these children in school every day. If the weather is very stormy, or if they are not able to walk to school, you must carry them here and come down and get them when school is out. They must be in the school. If they are not, we will take them away from you." That same evening a meeting of the school employees was called, and I gave in my resignation. I could not be with those Hopi people and withhold my sympathy from them, as I was ordered to do by Mr. Burton. (You will find enclosed letter to me from Mr. Burton to that effect.) I never found that being sympathic and friendly made these people "sullen and hard to manage."

On that Monday following the raid (Feb. 9th), some of the little ones were not in school. The next morning they were not present at roll call. As I had been up to the village on Monday afternoon to visit some of the children who were ill, I knew the dangerous condition of the trail, and when I told Mr. and Mrs. Ballinger that those little ones could not walk down or up it — that I had carried three of those who had been brought down to school in the morning, and who had been turned out of school earlier than usual, up the steps, and that I had fallen several times (I found these children standing in the trail, crying and half frozen). That they did not have sufficient clothing, and would he please not insist upon their being in school until the weather moderated. "That does not make any difference," said he, "they are better off here — after they get here — and they must come to school. Their parents or some of the larger children can carry them." So he took the horses and wagons and with the school "policeman" (father of Nellie Kiwani), rode up to the village, found the children, and made the parents go down to the school with the children on their backs, while he rode down in the wagon.

Rations and clothing for about 125 children were allowed that school when I was there. When I left, bread for 174 children was made once a week from 150 pounds of flour. (Less than one pound of flour per week for each child.) And sometimes the bread was so poorly made that nothing save a hungry dog or a starving burro could or would eat it. The only thing many of their children had for their breakfast was a handful of parched corn. All that was allowed them for their dinners on school days was a slice of bread, a few stewed prunes, dried peaches or molasses, and a part of a teacup of boiled beans, cornmeal mush, or a tiny piece of boiled beef, goat or salt pork. *Absolutely* nothing else, except a cup of water.

If it were a rule to cut the hair of the Indian boys, that rule was never enforced while I was there (with the larger boys), except in case of punishment. One morning Mr. Ballinger came to me and said, "I do not want you to sympathize with Bryan. I cut his hair just now, and I had to use him pretty roughly. He nearly got the best of me." Bryan had indeed been used "pretty roughly," judging from his bruised face. Though he was a new recruit, he was one of the best boys in my school. The children were all truthful with me.

A physician is provided by the Government for these people, but he is stationed at Keam's Cañon, 40 miles away from Oraibi. I know of the death of two of the school children who died without having any attention from Dr. Murtaugh, although his attention was called to both cases. One of the school boys — Henry — about eight years of age, had his leg broken

Bryan Kayahviniwa, a victim
of the haircutting incident.

Southwest Museum

on the afternoon of Friday, Jan. 30th, while on his way home from school,
about two hours before the departure of Mr. and Mrs. Ballinger for Keam's
Cañon, where they went to plan with Mr. Burton for the "round-up." Mr.
Ballinger saw the boy as his father was carrying him home from the place
where the accident occurred; but neither Mr. Ballinger nor his wife paid any
attention to the child further than to stop on their way and tell the missionary,
Mr. Epp, of the accident. Dr. Murtaugh was notified on Saturday, but he
did not come to Oraibi until Monday night with the raiding party; and then
the boy was dead and buried. Another of the school children — Lena, aged
about fourteen — was ill for five weeks or more, and died without having
been seen by the doctor. A few spoonsful of cough syrup were sent to her
from the school medicines. The doctor was at the village while she was
sick; but I know that he did not see her, for I asked him what he thought
of her case and he said he had not seen her. Lena died and was buried on
Feb. 15th. Though rations were drawn for these children, they never received
them. All that Lena had from the school stores during her illness was a loaf
of bread and one change of clothing, besides the cough syrup.

An employee . . . told me that she had seen Mr. Ballinger break sticks
on the boy's backs when whipping them in the school dining-room.

Mrs. Ballinger told me she whipped the children in her school-room
when they needed punishing.

In my room, which was my living-room (as I did my own house-
keeping at Oraibi), I had many pictures — paintings and photographs —
which the school children took great delight in looking at and asking questions
about. It was all new to them, and I enjoyed explaining things. One day, after
they had been coming to my room for three or four weeks, Mr. Ballinger
said to me, "Don't you know that you are breaking school rules by allowing
the school children to visit you in your room?" I replied that "I knew that

rule applied to boarding schools." "It applies to this school, if I want to enforce it," said he. Then I asked him if he objected to their visits to me, and if so, why, since they were learning of things outside their little world. His reply was, "We do not want them to know too much, and they must stay away." And he gave those orders to the children, with threats of whipping if they disobeyed. I was told of these threats by several of the children, both boys and girls. It must have been so, for they did not come any more, except to look in the doorway, smile and shake their heads.

A Hopi man — La-pu — who has a wife and two children — who lives, dresses and speaks "American," and who sometimes is interpreter at chapel services for the missionaries, was fined by Agent Burton for leaving the reservation to earn money to support his family. He was made to work out that fine by doing work in the Government school kitchen, and in the living-rooms of the Principal's family — scrubbing, washing, etc.

A few days after beginning my work at Oraibi, Mr. Burton came to me and said, "The Indians here will find out that you are from Pasadena, and will ask you questions about Mrs. Gates. I do not wish you to talk with them about her." On my asking him who Mrs. Gates was, and why I was not to talk of her, he explained that "she was a lady from Pasadena who had been out there, and that she had done things which made it necessary for him to request her to go." Subsequently, I learned that Mrs. Gates had done nothing but what was helpful in every way to the Hopi people, and the Hopi people all loved her. I have recently become acquainted with the lady, and know her to be a very superior woman — one who would do nothing but what was good. I was told by Mrs. Ballinger that if Mr. Burton heard me tell the Hopi that Mrs. Gates was "paslolomai" (the Indian term for all that is good) he would discharge me.

While at Cañon Diablo, on my way back from Oraibi to my home in California, I met a missionary among the Navajo Indians. He told me of former troubles at Oraibi, and that he had bought from a Hopi Indian there a blanket which had been cut into shreads; and had also seen remains of pottery which had been broken by H. Kampmeier — a former principal at Oraibi under the Burton regime. These things were destroyed because of parents not sending children to school.

On Feb. 18th, I was told by a trader on the Navajo Reservation . . . about what occurred up at the Indian village of Oraibi at the time of the school raid of Feb. 5th. The Navajo assistants who went from Little Burro Spring told him "what fun they had." They also told him that Mr. Burton would not dare to do such things with *them* (the Navajos). Mrs. Ballinger also told me of some of the situations up on the mesa — (she had her information from the whitemen). While the raid was going on, she said to me, "I'd like to have been up there this morning to have seen the fun when the Hopi woke up and saw the Navajos with their guns. I wonder what they thought?" What occurred at the school I saw for myself, I am grieved to say; and I only wish that those who have it in their power to change and make better the conditions for the Hopi people, could have seen it as I did. When I asked Mrs. Ballinger why the raid was made in such a storm, she laughed and said, "Why, so the Indians can't get the children away and hide them in the rocks. They can be tracked if they try to run through the snow."

These people need neither guns, clubs, force, nor brutality to make them "better Indians." Justice and mercy — kindness and friendship — will lead them any place. It will cost less; and these abused, embittered people will love, instead of hate, the name of "Washington."

BELLE AXTELL KOLP

Subscribed and sworn to before me this 2nd day of June, 1903.

ROGER S. PAGE
Notary Public
In and for Los Angeles County, State of California.

The report of the investigation that was made following Lummis's crusade contained a reprimand for Agent Burton for neglect of duty in having failed to notify the department of Kampmeier's conduct, or Ballinger's unfitness. It further reprimanded him for his "ill-advised and improper method of carrying out the hair-cutting order." Furthermore, he was warned that in the future, no threats or force of any kind were to be employed regarding haircutting and that he must trust entirely to persuasion and example. The report recommended that Kampmeier, who already had been transferred, be dismissed from the Indian Service, as he was in 1904, and that Ballinger be removed to a less responsible place.

Lummis and Mrs. Kolp at first were deeply disappointed by the report. They were out for Burton's scalp and felt the Sequoia League had been very poorly represented. In *Out West,* however, Lummis cried "Victory!" "To the People of Peace," he wrote,

the Hopi Indians of Moqui, the League's congratulations. They don't Have to Cut their Hair until, with self-respect, a respect for their short-haired instructors shall lead them to desire to resemble the latter. No one will dare shear them again against their will. It will be a long time before another government teacher shall smash their furniture and crockery, cut up their blankets, kick their children, bully their women, or indulge in any of the other little pleasantries of the gentlemen whom the government has dismissed from the Service or removed to humbler spheres as a result of the League's efforts. The Hopi will no more be insulted nor maltreated by any one. And that is what the League was after.

The fact remains that Burton continued on the job. Basic policies were not changed and harsh and brutal methods of enforcing ill-advised policies went on and on until relatively recent years.

The national publicity given the whole affair certainly served to bring the Hopi to the attention of many people who likely had never heard of them before. The determined tenacity of the Hopi leaders in fighting for their traditional way of life brought them moral support from their friends in many of the pueblos of New Mexico, as well as from a number of white scientists, artists, and writers who were becoming more and more frequent visitors to Tusayan.

Civil War at Oraibi

THE SEEDS which finally germinated and developed into open warfare at Oraibi were planted at least as far back as the time in 1834 when a party of trappers raided the Hopi cornfields and shot twenty of the men who attempted to protect their property.

A certain amount of antagonism may have existed before that time between the various clans that eventually divided into the two factions known to government officials as the Hostiles and the Friendlies, depending upon their attitude toward traveling the white man's way.

Talaiyauoma was village chief at the time the incident with the trappers occurred and he was infuriated by it and passed on his hatred of Americans to his successor, nicknamed "White Man" because he was an albino Hopi. He never married, and the young man whom he had selected and trained to follow him as village chief died before him. When he did die, two young brothers of the Bear Clan were chosen to take his place. However, as they were considered too young to act, their father Kuyingwu of the Water Coyote Clan served as regent and temporary head of the Soyal Ceremony until 1880.

These brothers, Sakhongyoma and Lololomai, grew up to share the general feeling of antagonism toward Americans. In 1880, Lololomai, the younger of the two, was recognized as village chief, but Sakhongyoma shared in the important leadership of the village as head of the Soyal Ceremony.

During his early years as chief, Lololomai continued the decidedly anti-American policies of his predecessors. A complete about-face occurred in Lololomai's attitude as the result of a trip to Washington arranged by Thomas Keam, the trader, who apparently at that time was acting as some sort of government adviser regarding the Hopi. At Keam's own suggestion and endorsed by Agent C. E. Vandever at Fort Defiance, he was authorized in the 1880s to conduct a group of Hopi leaders to Washington to discuss with officials there the serious problem of Navajo encroachments upon Hopi country. The Hopi selected by Keam for the trip were, besides Lololomai, Honani of Shongopovi, to represent the villages on Second Mesa, Sima and Ahnawita to represent the First Mesa villages, and Tom Polacca of Hano to act as interpreter.

During their visit in Washington it was suggested to the Hopi leaders that one way to meet the Navajo problem would be for them to persuade their people to desert their mesa-top villages and relocate around various desert springs. Apparently each of them made a choice of some areas for that purpose. However, little if any effort was made by them to try to convince their people to consider such a move, for they knew it would be opposed as contrary to Hopi tradition.

Although this effort by government officialdom to break up the Hopi communities failed, the trip to Washington by such respected leaders as Lololomai, Honani, Sima, and Ahnawita did have far-reaching effects upon all Hopi people for years to come.

Upon the party's return to Tusayan, Lololomai not only abandoned his anti-American attitude but, along with his companions on the trip, initiated a program of cooperation with school authorities and even, in some cases, with the Christian missionaries.

Lololomai admitted to Special Agent Julian Scott that on his trip to Washington in the 1880s he had seen so many wonderful things which came about as a result of the education white children received he had changed his mind about Oraibi children going to school.

Lololomai's change of heart hit the people of Oraibi like an earthquake. Within a few days after his return the people of Oraibi who shared, or came to share, Lololomai's views began to line up behind him as village chief and head of the Bear Clan, while those in opposition turned to Lomahongyoma as their leader.

Lomahongyoma was head of the Spider Clan and thus, because of its close relationship to the Bear Clan, according to Hopi custom was considered a "brother" to Lololomai. Furthermore, Lomahongyoma was married to a woman of the Water Coyote Clan to which Lololomai's father had belonged. Lomahongyoma was also a ceremonial leader of the Blue Flute Ceremony and a member of the Warrior Society. All these affiliations made Lomahongyoma a formidable antagonist despite Lololomai's important clan connections, ceremonial prominence, and position of leadership.

In support of his position Lololomai cited details of Bear Clan traditions regarding the emergence of the Hopi people from the Underworld and of the clan migrations that followed. However, Lomahongyoma and his supporters contended that Lololomai was sadly mistaken in his belief that the Americans were the true *bahana* who, according to tradition, were to come one day as brothers to the Hopi. Real *bahana,* he claimed, would be familiar with the Hopi language and would possess a certain inscribed stone which would complement those brought by Matcito from the Underworld, then in possession of Lololomai as head of the Bear Clan. Since the Americans had not presented this important evidence, Lololomai therefore was misled in thinking that they were the *bahana* of ancient Hopi prophecy.

Among the clans allied with Lomahongyoma and the Spider Clan was the Kokop Clan, considered the most aggressive of all Hopi clans. Its most important leader was Patupha of the Warrior Society. He was considered even by those Hopi who opposed him to be a man of almost fearful "power."

The controversy between the two factions grew in intensity. Christian missionaries found themselves involved along with such government officials as teachers and field matrons.

In November, 1890, Thomas Keam and certain government officials visited Lololomai at Oraibi to discuss with him the problem of school attendance. After some discussion Keam asked the chief to point out to him the leaders of the hostiles. Lololomai directed them to a kiva where they arrested Patupha and his younger brother, Youkeoma. This action so inflamed the hostiles that they threatened Lololomai's life and imprisoned him in a kiva where he remained until released the following month by soldiers sent from Keams Canyon for that purpose.

Upon the death of Lololomai at the turn of the century, Tewaquaptewa, who had been chosen by Lololomai and trained by him to be his successor, became village chief of Oraibi. Lololomai apparently chose Tewaquaptewa over the latter's older brothers because he believed that he would prove to be a more dynamic leader than either of them.

When Tewaquaptewa took office, Lomahongyoma, head of the Spider Clan, allowed Youkeoma to become the aggressive leader of the anti-American faction. The latter's opposition, not only to school attendance for Hopi children, but also to everything suggested by "Washington" for the benefit of the Hopi, became more and more bitter as the years went by.

Like Lololomai, Tewaquaptewa was a firm believer that in all matters of cultural and religious importance the Hopi must remain true to their own way of life. He also, like his predecessor, felt that a compromise could be made with the representatives of Washington by which the Hopi could benefit without endangering their integrity as good Hopi — the children could attend school; American visitors could be met in friendly fashion; Hopi could avail themselves of wagons, metal, tools, and other helpful articles in exchange for labor.

Even before Youkeoma and Tewaquaptewa became the accepted

Lololomai, Village Chief of Old Oraibi.

Honani of Shongopovi, a ceremonial leader in the late 1800s and early 1900s.

FOUR HOPI LEADERS WHO TRAVELED WITH THOMAS KEAM
TO WASHINGTON IN THE 1880s. *Photos – Courtesy Viets Lomaheftewa*

Sima, Village Chief of Walpi.

Ahnawita,
an important war chief at Walpi.

Tewaquaptewa, Village Chief at Old
Oraibi and head of the Friendlies. This
picture was taken in the 1930s.

Youkeoma, leader of the Hostiles at
Old Oraibi. He founded Hotevila in
1906.

Harry C. James   *Courtesy Viets Lomaheftewa*

leaders of their factions, the breach between them had become so great
that as far back as 1899 Youkeoma's group had built a new kiva, the
Kiacsuc Kiva, where they planned to duplicate the important ceremonials
— the initiation rites and the great Soyal — which Lololomai and his followers celebrated at the Hawiova Kiva. All the people of Oraibi, even
those foremost in the leadership of the opposing parties, developed a
deep sense of impending catastrophe as a result of the duplication — a
violation of long-established religious custom.

Tewaquaptewa frequently expressed an almost oriental sense of
destiny as the reason for proceeding as he felt obligated to do, well aware
that his actions might lead to the eventual disintegration of Oraibi. In
1904 the schism in the old village began to reach its crisis.

To swell the ranks of his followers Youkeoma persuaded about
thirty members of a dissident group from Shongopovi, led by Tewahong-
miwa, to join him at Oraibi. Naturally Tewaquaptewa objected to this
sizable reinforcement of Youkeoma's adherents, especially since it had
been a bad year for Hopi crops and there was every prospect of a severe
water shortage. However, Lomahongyoma of the Spider Clan reasserted
his authority at this point and had the newcomers given farm plots in the
fields which belonged to Tewaquaptewa's Bear Clan. Also, despite Tewaquaptewa's violent protests, they were assigned places in Oraibi on which

to build houses. The presence in Oraibi of this Shongopovi group greatly intensified the hostile feelings in the village.

In 1906 Tewaquaptewa went to Keams Canyon to confer with Superintendent Lemmon. Lemmon agreed that the Shongopovi people had no right to be at Oraibi. He informed Tewaquaptewa that he was within his rights to expel them and that Washington would support him in such an undertaking. However, Tewaquaptewa, who still hoped for a more peaceful way of settling the problem, a way more in keeping with fundamental Hopi philosophy, hesitated to take such ruthless action.

In the summer of 1906 both factions celebrated the Niman, the great summer ceremony depicting the annual departure of the kachinas from the Hopi villages. Tewaquaptewa's more aggressive supporters persuaded him, against his will, to protest the use by the opposing faction of the shrine where, at the end of the ceremony, the kachinas remove their costumes and make their prayers for the safe return of the spirit kachinas to their homes. In this way (from the Hopi viewpoint) Tewaquaptewa was led to take the first belligerent action in the long-drawn-out controversy.

From this point on there were almost constant meetings in the kivas and elsewhere of the leaders of the two parties. Time after time the followers of Tewaquaptewa urged him to follow the advice of Superintendent Lemmon and expel the Shongopovi people, but still the chief hesitated.

Late that summer, because of the continuing jibes of Youkeoma's supporters and the constant urging of his own advisers, Tewaquaptewa agreed to take action. The Snake Ceremony was to be performed in a very short time. Not wanting the crowd of white visitors who usually attended that event to be witness to the disturbance which he was certain would result, he and his leaders planned for the expulsion of the Shongopovi dissidents to take place a few days ahead of the ceremony.

To counterbalance Youkeoma's reinforcements from Shongopovi, Tewaquaptewa sent a request to the leaders of Moencopi, considered a colony of Oraibi, to send what men they could to his support. Moencopi responded by sending a very considerable force.

The days before the Snake Ceremony were filled with acrimonious debate and several scuffles occurred between individuals belonging to the opposing associations. So bitter were the disputes becoming that bloodshed seemed inevitable in spite of the Hopi's long-held opposition to warlike action. Leaders of each side urged their followers against the use of violence, at the same time cautioning them to have their weapons ready in case of attack by their opponents. What guns they had were cleaned and oiled; knives, clubs, and, according to Tewaquaptewa, even bows and arrows were made ready, just in case.

On September 6 there were meetings far into the night, each side sending men to spy on the other. Thus Tewaquaptewa overheard the leaders of the opposing party agree that there was to be no bloodshed, and he persuaded his own followers to a similar agreement.

During the night Francis E. Leupp, then Commissioner of Indian Affairs, who was in Tusayan looking into Navajo land problems, talked with both Tewaquaptewa and Youkeoma and threatened to summon troops if they did not settle their differences without bloodshed. As Superintendent Lemmon's superior, he let Lemmon know that he did not approve of the backing he had given Tewaquaptewa.

By morning Tewaquaptewa's party had decided on their course of action. They would drive the Shongopovi people from Oraibi, and if Youkeoma and his people offered interference they would be driven out too. It was assumed by many of the leaders on both sides that if Youkeoma had to leave Oraibi he and his people would go north to Kawestima.

Very early in the morning Tewaquaptewa and a group of supporters marched to the house of one of Youkeoma's leaders where many of the Youkeoma men and Youkeoma himself were eating. In accordance with Hopi custom, Tewaquaptewa as village chief was not permitted to take an active part in what followed. A spokesman for him three times ordered the Shongopovi men to leave Oraibi. They refused and a bitter argument ensued. Finally Tewaquaptewa's men seized several Shongopovi men and threw them out of the house. Youkeoma's men tried to help their allies.

With this Tewaquaptewa's men shouted, "They are helping the Shongopovi people! Now we can drive them to Kawestima!" Thereupon they seized Youkeoma and threw him out the door.

In the hours that followed Oraibi was the scene of a feud which grew in intensity. Several missionaries and lesser government officials stood helplessly by, at a safe distance, certain that at any moment shooting would begin.

Late in the afternoon of September 8 the two brawling groups faced each other on the level ground a short distance northwest of the village. Youkeoma gave a shout, and the men of both sides paused to hear what he had to say. With his big toe, he drew a line east and west on the sandy earth and grouped his men north of the line behind him. Tewaquaptewa grouped his forces on the other side of the line with their backs to Oraibi. Youkeoma stepped back across the line toward Oraibi and challenged his opponents to push him over the line, declaring that if they could do so, he and his followers would leave Oraibi forever.

Humihongniwa of Tewaquaptewa's party took a position face to face with Youkeoma. These two placed their hands on each other's shoulders and their men grouped themselves, more or less in the shape of a fan, back of them. It took a few moments for all the contestants to get in position, then at a signal the great push was on. At times the

Tewaquaptewa, Village Chief of Old Oraibi, reminiscing in the 1950s as he views the record on the rocks at the site of the September 8, 1906, confrontation with Youkeoma. Lower photo shows detail of inscription in rock.

pressure was so great that Youkeoma was forced up high into the air between the contestants. According to many witnesses he took quite a beating. One spectator watching from a nearby housetop got so excited that he fell off the house. Finally Youkeoma acknowledged that he had been fairly pushed back over the line and the "civil war" at Oraibi was over.

The defeated faction was given permission by Tewaquaptewa to take with them what food and other possessions they could carry. As the sun was setting, Youkeoma led his people to a site with good springs where they started the Hotevila of today.

The next day Superintendent Lemmon met with Tewaquaptewa and drew up an agreement with him stipulating that Youkeoma's people, but not more than three at a time, were to be permitted to return to Oraibi to gather up what personal property they may have left behind. Tewaquaptewa also agreed that the people of Oraibi would not harass them.

While this conference was going on Poli Payestewa of Moencopi and some friends went out on the flat rock near where Tewaquaptewa had won the bloodless battle and carved a short straight line in the hard stone. Beside it they chiseled this inscription, "Well it have to be this way now, that when you pass me over this LINE it will be DONE. Sept. 8, 1906." They also cut a bear's claw, the symbol of Tewaquaptewa and the Bear Clan, and a death's head to symbolize Youkeoma and his Masau-u Clan affiliation. In this way is commemorated the unfortunate crisis that speeded the disintegration of Old Oraibi, which for so long had been the largest of all the Hopi villages. In her book *Me and Mine* (UA Press, 1969), Helen Sekaquaptewa states that this inscription was made by Robert Selena, on vacation from the school at Keams Canyon.

A month or so later two troops of cavalry arrived to take charge of affairs at Oraibi only to find that the Hopi had already settled their differences in their own way. The soldiers then went on to Hotevila and, rounding up the Shongopovi people there, returned them by force to their own village. Youkeoma and several of his leaders were arrested and imprisoned at Fort Wingate.

The victory of Tewaquaptewa and his followers over Youkeoma and his forces had a bitter aftermath for the people of Oraibi. In the autumn of 1906 Commissioner of Indian Affairs Leupp ordered that Tewaquaptewa was to be deprived of his chieftainship temporarily and that he and his wife and children and Frank Siemptiwa of Moencopi and his wife and children were to be taken to Sherman Institute in Riverside, California, to be taught the English language and American customs.

The Commissioner also decreed that Oraibi was to be governed by a commission consisting of the teacher in charge of the day school, the War Chief of Oraibi (who had been acting as Hopi judge), and a second judge hostile to Tewaquaptewa. Before leaving Oraibi Tewaquaptewa appointed his brother Sakwaitiwa, also known as Burt Fredericks, to take his place as village chief during his absence in Riverside.

Of course, this ill-advised setup did not work. Sakwaitiwa soon had violent differences of opinion over the government of Oraibi with the commission appointed by Commissioner Leupp.

Nor were things any better at Hotevila. It was already autumn and the growing season was past. The little food which the Youkeoma group had been able to take with them from Oraibi was not sufficient to sustain them during the winter ahead, even though friends and clan relatives in the villages on First and Second Mesa shared what they could spare from their own scant supplies. Much work was necessary to build up the new village. By winter Hotevila was desperate.

Upon his return to Hotevila from the imprisonment at Fort Wingate Youkeoma began to quarrel with Lomahongyoma, who now felt that they ought to try to effect a reconciliation with the people back at Oraibi. As a result, late in 1906 Lomahongyoma led a group of moderates back to their old village where they reoccupied their former homes. Sakwaitiwa objected to their return but perpetrated no acts of physical violence against them. However, they were constantly subjected to mockery from Tewaquaptewa's followers.

For Youkeoma the years following the establishment of Hotevila were bitter indeed. In spite of his protestations that he and his people wanted only to be let alone, "Washington" and missionaries followed them to Hotevila. A school was built there and time after time virtual raids were made through the village to collect the children and enforce their attendance. Over and over again Youkeoma was arrested and confined for months at a time in the Keams Canyon jail. When he died in 1929 considerable controversy developed as to who should be his successor. Apparently the old man had not designated anyone to succeed him. Eventually Poliwuhioma of the Spider Clan became recognized by most of the villagers as their *kikmongwi*.

When word of the return of Lomahongyoma's group reached Tewaquaptewa at Riverside he was deeply concerned and began preparing messages to Sakwaitiwa urging him to force them to leave. Learning of this, government authorities at Sherman Institute conferred with Washington and then took action to nullify any move that Tewaquaptewa might make to gain the expulsion of Lomahongyoma and his faction from Oraibi.

Chief Youkeoma and the others arrested at Shongopovi, 1906, en route to Fort Wingate.

1. Glen Chorswytewa
2. Tawahongnewa
3. Edward Tawanimptewa
4. Archie Komaletstewa
5. Naquavema
6. Louis Tewanehma
7. Kochventewa

8. Lomawonu
9. Mack Yoywytewa
10. Wallace Kochhoyouma
11. Rutherford Tuvawyma
12. Albert Tewaventewa
13. Washington Talayamtewa
14. Navajo

Southwest Museum

15. Gashhongva	22. Youkeoma
16. Unidentified	23. Talawesewma
17. Kochadah	24. Talaswongnewa
18. Sekayouma	25. Lolmaewma
19. Talangynewa	26. Pongyaquaptewa
20. Joshua	27. Andrew Homequaptewa
21. Unidentified	28. Naqualetstewa
29. Masahongewma	

Tewaquaptewa always claimed that Harwood Hall, superintendent of Sherman Institute, and a military man by the name of Perry who somehow was involved, took advantage of his lack of fluency in the English language to wheedle him into signing a statement whose meaning he did not comprehend. This statement was a virtual repudiation of the action of his brother Sakwaitiwa and a plea to the people of Oraibi to do everything that the government officials wanted them to do.

Sakwaitiwa, certain that this statement had been made under duress (a suspicion soon verified by word-of-mouth messages from Tewaquaptewa), continued his program of opposition to the Hotevila refugees. Finally in October, 1907, Lomahongyoma and his people left Oraibi and formed a settlement of their own at Bacobi Spring, about a mile southeast of Hotevila. His lieutenant, Kuwannimptiwa, now took over the leadership of the new community and succeeded in gaining assistance from the agency at Keams Canyon for building the new village of which he became village chief.

In 1910 Tewaquaptewa and the other Hopi who had been sent to Sherman Institute were returned to Oraibi and their homes. If government authorities had labored under the supposition that the experiences of Tewaquaptewa and Frank Siemptiwa would make them supporters of government policies and wholeheartedly willing that their people should become Christian converts, they were in for a rude surprise. Both men returned to their villages deeply antagonized by their experiences at Sherman. To the time of his death in 1960 Tewaquaptewa spoke with bitterness of how he had been tricked into signing the statement referred to earlier.

During his absence in Riverside many of his own faction at Oraibi had been converted by Mennonite missionaries and either were building houses on the mesa in the style of the white man or else were moving down from the mesa to the growing community around the school and the trading post. Even his brother Tuwahoyiwma, Charles Fredericks, who had been away for many years at the Indian School in Phoenix, Arizona, had become a Christian. This further disquieted the village chief and he became as confirmed in his opposition to Christian missionaries as to officials of the government. This growing hostility even led to his being thrown into the Keams Canyon jail for a short period. When later on the Mennonite chapel on the mesa top next to the rapidly crumbling ruins of the deserted portions of Old Oraibi was struck by lightning, the now aging chief took it for a certain sign that he was right and supernaturally justified in his position.

As the years passed Tewaquaptewa's bitterness toward the people of Hotevila gradually wore away. After Youkeoma's death he often attended ceremonies at Hotevila and was hospitably treated there. In 1932 he boasted to Mischa Titiev, on his return from one such occasion, that he had been invited to eat and drink coffee there eight different times.

Deep, far-reaching, and permanent as were the results of the dissension which culminated in the 1906 Tewaquaptewa-Youkeoma confrontation, they served only as a prelude to what was to follow.

In time Tewaquaptewa moderated his inimical feeling toward the people of Hotevila, but, at the same time, he developed an ever-growing hostility toward many of the people of his own village. At first he went to some trouble to conceal this hostility as being improper for a Village Chief. It became increasingly difficult for him to do this as more and more Hopi moved down to New Oraibi to take advantage of such conveniences available there, as a better water supply and proximity to schools and stores. Indeed, as time went on, many Hopi left Old Oraibi chiefly to escape from what they considered the old man's domination of their lives.

Tewaquaptewa became increasingly convinced that it was his destiny to serve as *kikmongwi* of Old Oraibi until it ceased to exist as a viable community. This conviction was reinforced by suggestions that his ancient village should be rebuilt and established as a national monument — a cultural center for all Hopi. To such suggestions he would reply sadly, "Wait until I am dead."

Despite his conviction that Old Oraibi would die with him, he continued to give consideration as to who should succeed him as *kikmongwi*. During the summer of 1929, in discussing the matter of a successor, he informed this author that he already was training Myron Polequaptewa to take his place. Seemingly this choice was confirmed when in 1933 he appointed Myron to substitute for him in the important winter solstice ceremony, the Soyal. At Oraibi the Village Chief, by tradition, impersonates the Soyal kachina. Certainly, by having Myron assume this prestigious position as part of his training, Tewaquaptewa gave public recognition that Myron was to follow him, both as Village Chief and as a leader in the Soyal ceremony.

However it was generally known among the Old Oraibi people that Tewaquaptewa had been preparing his adopted son, Stanley, then still a boy, to assume some position of leadership in the village.

In the late 1940s, because of some trouble with his eyes, apparently due to trachoma, the old chief announced that Myron would take over as *kikmongwi*. There was some opposition to Myron's doing this, because of his domestic problems. Friends of Stanley felt that he should return from Los Angeles, where he had gone to live, and take over as Village

Chief. Stanley and his family, however, were well established in California and remained there. Again Old Oraibi was "a house divided against itself."

Some years before his death Tewaquaptewa showed many of the signs of serious deterioration due to age, and he was indeed a pathetic figure — virtually blind, his mind wandering, as he attempted to fashion kachina dolls to sell to visitors to the village. In spite of his condition, around 1956 he announced that he was resuming his position of *kikmongwi* of Old Oraibi.

When Tewaquaptewa died in 1960, his adopted son, Stanley Bahnimptewa, was still in Los Angeles, and Myron Polequaptewa was not living at Old Oraibi. Now Mina Lansa began to assume the prerogatives of *kikmongwi,* and she refused to relinquish them to Myron when he returned to Old Oraibi to claim what he considered to be his rightful position.

In a letter from Los Angeles to the author dated January 10, 1973, Stanley Bahnimptewa sets down his reasons for claiming the chieftanship.

He explains his adoption by Tewaquaptewa and his wife which was agreed upon with his mother, Mary Mase, before he was born. He states that at that time Tewaquaptewa promised that the child would one day rule over Oraibi.

Years later, still according to Stanley, Tewaquaptewa became very ill and sent for him to come to Oraibi, which he did promptly. In his letter he states, "Mina and I were both present when Tewaquaptewa handed me his rights." To this he adds poignantly, "We should have had someone else there."

His letter explains that, following the death of Tewaquaptewa, for a period of nearly four years Thomas Jenkins, or Banyacya, David Monongye, and John Lansa kept going to see him in Los Angeles to try to persuade him to relinquish his rights at Old Oraibi to his sister Mina Lansa.

Growing tired of this constant harassment, Stanley writes that he finally agreed to allow Mina to act for him, but on a purely temporary basis and with the clear understanding that she was to consult with him regarding whatever problems confronted her. At first, Stanley claims, Mina did this, but as time passed she stopped consulting with him and claimed that she herself was *kikmongwi.*

He concludes, "Now the people are all disappointed in her and she does not know where to turn — she has not called me so it's up to her to 'clean her own house,' as they say."

The most tragic aspect of this latest schism in Old Oraibi is the further breakdown in the clan system. As at Hotevila following the death of Youkeoma, it has become impossible for Oraibi to follow the traditional procedure in such circumstances of holding a meeting of certain clan leaders, a "Chief's talk," in the hope of finding a solution to the problem.

The masses of ruins creep cancer-like across the mesa top of Old Oraibi. A few of the people who once lived there occasionally return for one reason or another, but they stay only briefly. Many of them find satisfaction in being able to participate in a Butterfly Dance or in one of the important ceremonies taking place in other Hopi villages.

There is still a vague hope that even yet Old Oraibi may be rebuilt — a sort of "Hopi Williamsburg," testimony to the days of greatness of the oldest continuously inhabited community within the United States.

Two Outstanding
Missionaries

FOLLOWING JACOB HAMBLIN and his associates there was a lull in missionary activity among the Hopi, but toward the end of the nineteenth and the beginning of the twentieth centuries representatives of church after church and sect after sect came to Tusayan to preach their versions of the gospel. Hopi living in accordance with their own religious beliefs likely were closer to the precepts of the Sermon on the Mount than any other Indian tribe, yet for years missionaries reaped a scant harvest of Hopi souls.

Many truly dedicated men and women devoted themselves to Indian missionary work and led lives of hardship and self-sacrifice. The work of their educators, doctors, and nurses throughout the entire western United States in most cases demonstrated the spirit of Christianity. They lived and practiced the Golden Rule, "As ye would that men should do to you, do ye also to them likewise."

Unfortunately, the hostility to each other evinced by some of the Christian sects proved decidedly confusing to the Hopi. Also, the opposition — often, alas!, violent opposition — of many of the more fanatical missionaries toward the Hopi's own religious beliefs and ceremonial practices was often a cause of serious misunderstanding and even of tragedy.

Furthermore, through the help of Indian Bureau officials, missionaries to the Hopi were granted land on which to build their churches and their homes. This action in taking over land which the Hopi rightfully felt belonged to them was another cause of bitterness between the Hopi and the missionaries which exists to this day among many Hopi.

Many missionary endeavors during this period were short-lived and have already faded from Hopi memory. Two missionaries, however, played prominent roles which had far-reaching influences on Hopi life. They are Mennonite H. R. Voth and Presbyterian Dr. Clarence G. Salsbury.

Without question Voth was one of the most dedicated of all Christian missionaries to the Little People of Peace. Many Hopi leaders objected to his work among their people; nevertheless, to accuse him, as has been done, of being responsible for the quarrel at Oraibi that led to the disastrous division of that village in 1906 is a mistake. That this schism existed long before his arrival in Tusayan is clearly brought out in traditional Hopi history as well as in Voth's own account of his first years at Oraibi. The "civil war" which climaxed the controversy did not occur until four years after Voth left Oraibi. At first we were led to believe that he had started it all by statements made to us by a few Hopi who, we later discovered, were using his name to cover the activities of two or three missionaries who came to the Hopi after Voth had left. The fact that these allegations so quickly gained acceptance proves both that the people are sadly inclined to believe what they want to believe and that the "moccasin telegraph" is a highly successful, but questionably accurate, method of communication in the Indian country.

Heinrich R. Voth

By one of history's curious quirks the action of Catherine the Great of Russia in offering sanctuary to the persecuted sect known as the Mennonites eventually came to have repercussions in far distant Tusayan. In 1786 seven Mennonite groups emigrated to Russia from Germany and were permitted by the "Empress and Tsarina" to establish colonies there and to practice their religion undisturbed.

One of these Mennonite colonies was established at the village of Alexanderwohl on the Molotchna River in South Russia. There on April 15, 1855, was born Heinrich R. Voth, who came to play such a vital double role in Hopi life — that of dedicated Mennonite missionary and conscientious anthropologist.

He attended the village school at Alexanderwohl but eagerly augmented what education he secured there by voraciously reading everything that came his way. While still in Russia, having great facility in language, he added both English and Russian to his native German.

In 1874 Voth and the entire Mennonite congregation left Russia for the United States and became a member of the German Mennonite colony — again named Alexanderwohl — north of Newton, Kansas. There he found his knowledge of English of great value, since he was the only member of the colony who could communicate freely with neighboring settlers. For two years he taught at a school in Alexanderwohl, but in 1877 he gave this up to attend Wadsworth Academy in Ohio. To prepare himself still further for his work as a missionary, he studied for two semesters at the St. Louis Medical School.

H. R. Voth and convert
Fred Qoyawayma.

Mennonite Library and Archives.
Courtesy of Mrs. Martha Dyck.

It was not until 1893 that Voth's work as a Mennonite missionary brought him to the Hopi country, specifically to Oraibi. His own account of his ten years there is set down here thanks to the permission of his daughter, Mrs. Martha Dyck, and to the cooperation of the General Conference Mennonite Church, Newton, Kansas.

HISTORICAL NOTES OF THE FIRST DECADE OF THE MENNONITE MISSION WORK AMONG THE HOPI OF ARIZONA, 1893–1902

By H. R. VOTH

The actual beginning of our Mission work among the Hopi Indians in Arizona dates back to the fall of 1892 but the beginning of its preparation commenced several years before that. Sometime before 1892 Bro. P. Stauffer who had been one of our mission workers among the Arapahoes in the then Indian territory, had accepted a position in the government service among the Hopi of Arizona. Bro. Stauffer measured the needs of the Red Man — as all did — not only from the standpoint of civilization, but also from that of Christianization. He realized that those benighted people needed more than the white man's clothing, houses and education, that they needed the Gospel of Jesus Christ. So he tried for some time to interest the Foreign Mission Board of the General Mennonite Conference in the Hopi Indians and to get them to establish a mission work among them. The first was soon accomplished but to do the latter was more difficult on account of lack of funds and workers. But it soon became apparent that He, who had said: "Go ye into all the world" was behind this movement and had begun to pave the way towards its realization.

In 1891 the Mission Board had given to the writer of this sketch a six-months leave of absence after he had labored ten years as missionary among the Arapahoe in the Indian Territory. This leave carried with it the permission to visit his old home in Russia, the Holy Land, etc. During his absence the Lord wrote further chapters in the introduction of the Mission work among the Hopi. Owing to the opening of the Cheyenne and Arapahoe reservation to settlement, certain changes in the mission work in various ways seemed advisable and later became necessary. That made it possible to spare some of the older workers in Oklahoma. This caused the Mission Board to consider the call from Arizona more seriously, and finally decided to take up the work if the churches would furnish the necessary funds and as to the first workers the Board sent an inquiry to the writer, who was still in Europe, whether I would be willing to take up the new work upon my return. It is needless to say that I replied in the affirmative. On my return trip after having visited my old home (in Russia), Palestine and other countries and had had the privilege to preach the gospel in many Mennonite churches in Southern Russia also going into Switzerland, I stopped off at Dalton, Ohio. Here it was my privilege to receive from the Lord's hands in the person of Miss Martha Moser, a former mission worker in Darlington, a second help-mate for the one He had seen fit to take from my side in Darlington. Miss Moser knew from several years practical experience in mission work what it meant to be a missionary. On August 18th we were married, and a few days later we proceeded to Alexanderwohl, Kansas, where I had left my daughter Frieda with relatives while I was abroad.

The Mission Board had in the meantime decided that its president, Bro. C. Krehbiel and myself, should go to Arizona and investigate the new field and to size up and report on the whole situation. This we did. Upon our return Bro. Krehbiel laid the matter before the Board and through our papers before the churches the latter were asked to prayerfully consider the matter and to pledge the necessary funds if they wished the Board to take up this new work. The response was very encouraging. While these preliminary arrangements were made during the winter and the following spring we stayed with my parents in Alexanderwohl and it was my privilege, during this time, to preach the Gospel and to lay the mission cause on the hearts of the people at many places, also to lecture on my travels abroad.

In the spring of 1893 the funds for the new undertaking had so far been pledged that at a meeting of the Mission Board in the home of Bro. H. Richert in Alexanderwohl definite plans for the work could be made and we were instructed to move to Arizona, erect a mission house, large enough for the family and for meetings for the present and to take up the work. On July 10th we left, stopped off at Albuquerque, where we purchased some tools, a stove, utensils and other equipments and then proceeded to Gallup where we met Lt. Plummer, the agent for the Navaho and Hopi, with whom we arranged certain matters regarding our work. On July 14 we arrived at Holbrook, then the railroad station for the Hopi reservation, where we had to remain several days to attend to various matters in connection with our proposed work. A Mormon then took us and our freight with a double freight train to Keam's Canyon where the Government School and Sub-Agency for the Hopi was located. We had been traveling a whole day and the whole night, the trains having been changed in the evening. In the morning the road was quite sandy so that we had to walk part of the time.

At about 10 A.M. we arrived at Keam's Canyon, and the very cordial reception we received from our old Darlington friends, Mr. and Mrs. Collins, the Superintendent, made up for the hardships of the trip. At their invitation we stayed here about two weeks, during which I spent much of the time among the Hopi villages, at the three mesas. We finally decided definitely to locate at Oraibi, about 35 miles west of Keam's Canyon, where we moved on the 3rd and 4th of August. There we were kindly received by the government day school teacher and his family and many of the Hopi. The next few days we established ourself in a Hopi house that we had rented. I got out my carpenter tools and my knowledge of carpenter work (for which I shall always be deeply indebted to my saintly father), and some shelves, a crude table, bench, etc., were the result. My splendid practical wife soon had the stove in commission and in a few days the machinery of our simple, very simple home life and household was in motion. The diary of my wife — who finally was to find her last resting place in that desolate country — frequently says: "We had many visitors" or "our house swarmed with Indians" or "there were many Indians here." But that was what we were there for. From our trip of investigation the previous fall I had brought with me a small note filled with words and sentences in the Hopi language that Brother Stauffer had given me and which I had memorized in Kansas. And how very handy that little knowledge of Hopi came to us now! And between my tools and wood chips lay another note book with a pencil and while I was using saw and hatchet I also used tongue and pencil and it seemed to give our new friends no little delight thus to act as our teachers. We soon felt at home although we were 35 miles from the P.O. and nearest store, (Keam's Canyon), 125 miles from our railroad station, 75 miles from the nearest telegraph office, drug store, hardware store, etc. This was at Winslow to which place we opened up communication several years later.

We soon found that the people in Oraibi, among whom we went to labor were divided into two factions, the liberals or friendly under Chief Lololomai and the conservative or hostile, under Chief Lomahunga. The first took kindly to the efforts of the government to civilize them, to the schools, mission worker. Lololomai had been in Washington and was ever ready to support any reasonable efforts of the white man. The other party was opposed to all of this and serious trouble had barely been averted several times and arrests had been made of some of the leading men when the government had tried to force them to send their children to school. This deep-rooted divergence between these two factions had led to much bitterness and to many quarrels among themselves in their daily life, their close relationship, their religious societies and religious ceremonies, and made the position of the missionary a difficult one in many ways. We also found, that in a general way this tribe differed very much from the Cheyenne and Arapahoe. The Hopi lived in houses and villages, the latter in tents and camps. The Hopi supported themselves, the C. & A. were partly supported by the government. Moreover the religious conditions were very different. The religious systems among the Cheyennes and Arapahoes, though yet strong, were more or less disintegrated, much of their religious paraphernalia had been destroyed and lost in their migrations and wars. Among the Hopi the various religious organizations and systems were more intact yet. The same ceremonies, they held hundreds of years ago were essentially the same yet, the same altars, idols, symbols, etc., that they put up then, they unwrapped and erected now yet; the same songs they had chanted then, they sang now, though some partly, others entirely, in an obsolete language. These are a few indications of the situation that met us, of course, some of these details we discovered by and by, and to some extent these conditions still exist among the Hopi although material changes have taken place. The greatest difference that we found, however, was that Christianity had gained a much deeper foothold among our Oklahoma Indians than here. There we had many school children under Christian influence, about twenty had been baptized in our mission. . . .

As soon as we had somewhat arranged our simple household we commenced to plan the new Mission home. First of all we had to have a location. And right there we were confronted by a peculiar difficulty. A government allotting agent and a surveyor were on the reservation, surveying the land to allot it to the Hopi in severalty. But the only land that anything could be raised on was in the valleys and along the "washes." And as there was only a limited quantity of this tillable land the allotments had to be in 10 and 20 acre lots. And to make matters worse, all this land had long ago been carefully divided and allotted to the many different clans according to ancient Hopi customs and clan relationships. All this would be demoralized and broken up by these new plans of "Washington" to which the people of all clans, villages and of both factions, mentioned above, were desperately opposed. And now came a white man, a stranger to all of them and also asked for a piece of land for a home. And not only that, but if we wanted to have our own well we had to have our allotment near the wash where it probably would interfere with some clan's land. And the white agent, whom they disliked so much, would have to survey it and allot it to us. And it took much counseling with the chiefs, and heads of clans; also the assistance of the chiefs, Bro. Stauffer, the Supt., the Agent and some correspondence with the Indian Dept. in Washington before we finally secured a 20 acre tract, west and one east of the Wash. The first, on which the Mission station now is located, was less sandy and less exposed to the sweeping sandstorms of the wash. The other was more sandy, but gave the hope that we could raise something on it as the Indians did on land just like it. And above all, the splendid government well being close to this east tract we had good reasons to believe, that we could get good drinking water there. Wells were, and are to this day, very scarce around Oraibi and in order to find out the locations where we probably could get a good well, Bro. Stauffer and I planned to make tests at various places before we decided on a location. With this we commenced about 10 days after we had moved to Oraibi. An old well borer, which drilled a hole about two feet in diameter, was placed at my disposal and the first place we tried was near if not on the very spot where we about six months later selected our 20 acres west of the wash. But the borer, a large heavy clumsy concern, broke down several times and proved entirely unfit for hard ground like that. So finally, after much counseling with Mr. Stauffer and others we decided to build on the east 20, a piece in the wash. First of all we tried to get a well. We dug down about 20 feet, found good water, put in a new pump but did not get any water. Upon investigation we found that we had struck water in a clay adobe that closed up the holes in the pump point airtight and would not let the water through. We lowered a bottomless perforated barrel and packed stones around the pump point, this helped it some but we were compelled later on to dig two other wells near the house which furnished us with the necessary water after we had driven in three points. In two wells I very nearly lost my life through the carelessness of my Indian helpers in lowering rocks into the one, lumber into the other. In the second case Bro. Stauffer too might have lost his life. In the meantime we had also been hauling rock, some Indians made some adobes. The lumber and hardware had to be freighted from Flagstaff, 100 miles away, partly through a desert country at the freight rate of $1.25 per 100 pounds. As I had been allowed only $650.00 for the mission house and barn it may easily be figured out that I had not much money to spend for labor. Except some occasional help by some government employees at the wells and the house and some Indian labor I had to do all the mason, carpenter and other work myself assisted by a young Hopi named Tabo and my faithful wife. Fortunately the Indians worked for cheap wages. We worked in good weather and in sand storms (when even the Indians stayed at home). Dr. Warnek speaks in one of his works about the "Building distress of the missionaries." We found out what that means. Our lumber freighters too. I found in my wife's diary of those days under April 26, 1894: "Mr. Stowell and Mr. Gardner at last came with the lumber. As the road had been covered with sand they had several times lost the way. Were nine days on the road from Flagstaff and had to leave two loads behind although they had hitched up 20 horses and only brought two loads."

At last on July 10, just one year after we had left Kansas we could move into our own home. To be sure, this was not finished yet by a long way and my dear wife and I with some Indian help, have practically worked about a year yet, finishing the house, building a small barn, etc., for which the Board afterwards appropriated a small sum yet, I think $50.00. Of course, we did not neglect during this time our main mission work — the language, meetings, visiting the sick, etc.

On September 26, 1896 during the night the "wash" broke through its banks in the end near the station. There had been a heavy rain. In a comparatively short time the wash had formed a wide new bed, and for a while it looked as if our station would be destroyed. That was a dark, dreary night; but the dear Lord answered our prayers, the water fell, but the barn that had been built of palisades we thought best to tear down and rebuild at another location. In this work, my brother Peter, who was visiting us rendered us valuable assistance. But our first well, which already had proven to be very valuable for us and the Indians was destroyed by the flood, also the splendid government well.

We have, in the course of years, made many efforts to raise something, my wife vegetables, myself feed for our cow and two small mules, but almost entirely without success. We did not have the time to go to so much trouble about these matters as the Indians did; to build windbreaks and to scratch away the accumulated sand (from every plant); to replant to try to save the plants. We had too much work of more importance to attend to. We purchased some of our feed from the Indians, some from the Mormons, some from the traders. The baled alfalfa cost us $39–$42 a ton, grain from 2–3 cents a pound. . . .

Although I had just made that trip to Europe, and arrived in splendid health on the reservation, I was more or less a sick man during the fall and winter of 1893 probably owing to the high altitude and the change in the climate in general. Later I found out more from my wife's diary, how sick

I really had been, how high the fever, how great sometimes her apprehension about my recovery had been. Fortunately the Lord gave me my health back when spring came with the many vexations and such hard work already mentioned.

Also during the entire "building period" we carried on our studies and our work as much as we could. In the second year already I was frequently requested by representatives of the government, at their councils with the Indians, to·assist their interpreters to get the right meaning of what they were to interpret and from the third year, for a number of years, I had to do most of the intepreter's work. How imperfect it must have been, I found out the longer the more as I got better acquainted with the spirit and the intricacies of the language.

I have already stated that we began the study of the Hopi language in Kansas, from a small vocabulary that I had made, with Bro. Stauffer's help, on Bro. Krehbeil's and my trip, and also, that I took up this task even when we were unpacking our goods, the sentence, "Pam hin matschiwa," (how is that named?) became my first key to unlock the secrets of the language that we knew we had to learn before we could fulfill our mission. If good interpreters had been at my disposal the task would have been easier. But the children, who could have assisted us were almost all in school 35 miles away, and nearly all had but an imperfect knowledge of English. Of course, I made use of them when opportunities offered themselves. No writing existed in Hopi except a few phrases and words in some ethnological writings that I found somewhat later. So I was mostly thrown on my own resources. One I have already mentioned: the picking up, jotting down and memorizing of words and sentences obtained direct from the people. One other· was, to make desperate efforts to use what we know, to talk with the people correctly, or incorrectly.

But while we could make ourselves fairly well understood in everyday life I knew that much that we could need in our religious work was hidden in the songs, prayers, speeches and symbolism of their secret religious performances. And in order to get it genuine I would have to get it where it was — in the religious ceremonies in their underground chambers (kivas). What little I could pump out of the priests, was as I soon found, misleading, distorted, unreliable. The priests were not very anxious to furnish me anything that I wanted to use to undermine their religion. But religious paraphernalia, what I could get of their songs, prayers, etc. To be sure in the beginning I could only get into some of their performances but as the people got better acquainted with us, found out, that we were willing to take care of their sick, could extract aching teeth better and quicker than their doctors, that their children their poor could get pieces of cloth as gifts and many favors, and especially that *I did not mock and sneer at their religion and kick their sacred objects with my feet as one of the early missionaries (of another denomination, is said to have done)*, they more and more opened their kivas (when ceremonies took place) and their knowledge and their hearts to us. Then we learned of their myths and traditions concerning their origin, the creation, of their conceptions of the hereafter, of their many, very many deities and their purposes and of the manifold relations to these deities their duties towards them, their fears of them. In short, here we learned to understand the people among whom we were placed and their soul-life. *What a pantheon, what a religious system, what a rich language, what traditions, what organization!* And yet, how utterly little to satisfy the longings of the soul, to give peace to the heart for this life and a hope for eternity. Stacks of straw and chaff with here and there a grain of truth as is the case in all religious systems. . . . Here I had splendid opportunities to have heart to heart talks with the priests and if space and time permitted I could tell of the gradual development of a new knowledge, of the doubts in that empty religion and how the light from Jesus Christ had slowly illuminated the benighted souls of some of the priests that passed into eternity with doubts in the old and outstretched hands to the new religion seeking souls. Others finally accepted Jesus Christ as their Savior. I tried as much as I could to imitate the method of Paul in Athens: "For as I passed by and beheld your devotions, I found an altar with this inscription, To the unknown God. Whom therefore you ignorantly worship, him declare I unto you."

As I passed through and around their villages, their kivas I found altars and shrines, myths and traditions, indicating an unknown God. And Him and His Son, our Saviour Jesus Christ, I tried to preach unto them in our home, on the streets, in their kivas and houses and in our chapel when, after years of waiting we finally got one. . . .

I had soon discovered that many of the decorations on the pottery, altars, slabs, kilts, masks, dolls, etc., were symbols of religious ideas, deities, forces of nature and the like. So I began to study them and found them a valuable source of information in various ways. To be sure, text-books, a good dictionary of reliable teachers would have been more convenient and valuable. But I did not have them. So I began to collect these things as my limited means permitted. This collection became in a certain sense my library. As others would study their books I would discuss with the Hopi, often with the priests these symbols and hieroglyphics. The gain was many-fold: The practice in the use of the language, the obtaining of new words, phrases and ideas as one symbol would lead us into the botanical kingdom, another into the mineral, one into various phases of everyday life, another into the conceptions of the existence after death or into the very many phases of the Hopi religion and last but not least these studies, which by no means always took place "under four eyes" but often in the presence of smaller or larger audiences afforded me many opportunities to compare their vague ideas with the positive clear revelations in the Word of God, to supply from the plan of salvation the answers to their question marks, to show them the remedy against their ills and greatest of all evils — sin, to tell them of the God of love which their pantheon with its hundreds of deities does not have, and of His Son Jesus Christ who died for their sins to save them and give them eternal life.

It is well known that practically all that we know, for instance, about ancient Egypt has been obtained in a similar manner from the hieroglyphics, symbols, pictures and found on the papyri, pottery, temples and other objects of that strange-country.

These were some of the resources and methods that we had to employ to prepare us for the human side of accomplishing the mission, assigned to us; the spiritual preparation and equipment, that we certainly needed day after day we had to get in the schools of our Master through which He sent us, in our prayer closets when we could commune with Him at the Throne of Grace where He gave us daily what we needed: grace, strength, humility, faith and love.

Lest someone should, from this compact description, receive the idea that I spent most of my time in ceremonies or in ethnological studies and linguistic and religious researches in my library: I wish to say that such was not the case at all. In Oraibi there were only seven or eight religious organizations. Most of these had their secret ceremonies only every other year, some once, some twice that year. So the interval was practically two years. And then often I could not be present even then on account of other duties. Furthermore I did not get the permission to attend all of them right at the beginning, it took several years before I had gained the confidence of the conservatives sufficiently to be permitted to their ceremonies. Of course, during the nine days that these religious performances were in progress I often had to spend many a night hour in the kivas as most of the important and to them sacred ceremonies took place at night. As to the very complicated katchina cult, with its varied symbolism and significance this also only takes place mostly — say from December and during spring with many intervals. And as my "library" referred to, it often took days, even weeks that I got any new specimens and many a one was simply put away for comparison or corroboration studies as the occasions required.

Had I not these resources it would have been simply impossible with the means and interpreters at my disposal at that time to master the language sufficiently in these years to do any mission work without an interpreter as a rule and to act as interpreter on many occasions myself. With a grammar and dictionary and teachers that is not an unusual thing at all, but those I did not have.

Our work was essentially a pioneer work, and my dear wife and myself were practically alone to do it. Many times villages on other mesas were visited, very many visits to families were made. Many sick people were looked after and treated. One time I treated 80 cases of measles. A very good general knowledge of the Hopi religion, manners and customs was obtained, and later published at great cost by the Field Museum of Chicago in eleven smaller or larger volumes, some profusely illustrated of which I was glad to furnish free of charge to those missionaries who wished to have them as long as my extra copies lasted. Of the language I had discovered and could give my successors many fundamental laws and rules that govern it and often regretted, that I could have put more of my language studies in writing or even in print than I had done. But in the first place during the last years we had reasons to hope that we would receive help and it was my plan to do the compiling, sifting, systematizing in company with the new, so much hoped for, workers, as I had the privilege to do in company with Bro. J. B. Epp for one year. And so I thought best to devote my time as much as possible to follow up the many clues that I had found in my various studies described in the preceding pages. I thought it best to check up, verify and sift my studies before I spent much time in writing down and perhaps preparing for print what afterwards might have proved to be full of errors. Secondly, it was the untimely death of my beloved wife that upset and changed many of my programs and plans.

On May 3, 1901 a little daughter was born to us and on May 6 the Lord, who always knows best, took my devoted wife, who had so bravely stood by me in all our trials, labors, adversities, to Himself. She was getting along so well and was happy and cheerful until she was suddenly seized by an attack of puerperal eclampsia which continued with interruptions for about 12 hours, leaving her in an unconscious state with the exception of one time for about half a minute. The doctor was 35 miles away and before a message could reach him and he could get there in a buggy she was beyond help. We buried her the following day near the station. A few government employees, my sister and some Indians were present. When the men filled the grave little Esther, about 2½ years old, tore herself from my hand, rushed to the nearly filled grave and began to scratch the sand back, crying, "Those men must not put so much sand on Mama." Three weeks later I took sister Mary with the baby to the railroad 65 miles away through a desert country, leaving Frieda with the two little children, Albert and Esther in the care of a trusted Indian; the government teacher and his wife promised to look after them. They were one mile away, no one lived nearby, that promise was badly kept; when I returned on the fifth day the three children came running through the sand and met me about ¾ of a mile from the station. My sister Susie came with me and stayed with us for about five years, the first year in Oraibi, during which I assisted my successor, Bro. J. B. Epp to somewhat get acquainted with the people, the language and the work. I then resigned my work to which the Lord had called me, that had become very dear to me and which I had hoped to spend my life. It seemed to be my first duty to care for and to educate my four motherless children. But to sever all those ties that had been formed in those ten years between us and our Hopi friends, that was the hardest task of all. How many hundreds of times had I talked to them about the one thing needful, and pleaded with them to accept Christ. I knew that the seed sown by my sainted wife and myself, in our simple way had taken root and was sprouting in some hearts, because we had the proofs. Would it continue to grow and bear fruit? Or would they slide back? Some have accepted Christ as their personal Savior soon after, others have not done so to this day. And they were not far from the Kingdom of God. One of the priests, for years the head man of one of the secret orders, had already renounced his "office" and it was a source of joy to me when a few months later the Mission Board wrote me, that this man desired to be baptized by me and in case I should make a trip to Oraibi soon to perform this service. But when I came there my old friend told me: "Ikwatchi (my friend), you know our ways and rules. You know, that So and So is our first chief, So and So the first priest, So and So is our war chief and then come I, now, ikwatchi, you know that I cannot go around or past these three and be baptized first; but when they are ready I shall be ready too. But, if you will baptize me here in the mission upstairs I am ready." Of course, I could not do that. I knew at once that the other chiefs had discouraged, perhaps accused him. But he was baptized not very long afterwards and is now a living witness for the power of the Gospel and the regenerating influence of the blood of Christ. And how well I remember observing for years the gradual breaking through of the light of a new knowledge in the hearts and the lives of several others who are now devoted Christians. "But where are the nine?" Why so few?

It was source of great satisfaction to me that the mission got a chapel yet before I left and that I could take an active part in putting it up. If we only had this chapel six or seven years sooner!

These ten years were probably the hardest of my life. May the dear Lord bless what was done in weakness, forgive what was done amiss. With regard to man's work here on earth the great divine principle will probably also stand: "Man looketh on the outward appearance, but the Lord looketh on the heart." 1 Sam. 16:7. When He will once separate the "gold, silver, precious stones" from the "wood, hay, stubbles" (Cor. 3:12), it will be done according to His great fundamental law: "Moreover it is required by stewards, that a man be found faithful." (II Cor. 4:2)

H. R. VOTH

Goltry, Oklahoma, January 29, 1923.

The building of the chapel to which Voth refers has been the subject of much controversy. According to Mrs. Dyck, entries in her father's journal indicate that he planned to begin its construction on September 11, 1901. Just as work was about to start certain Hopi religious leaders protested that one corner of the building would lie directly over the path traditionally taken by the kachinas in their ceremonies. Voth and his fellow workers willingly changed the plan for the chapel so that the pathway of the kachinas remained unobstructed. Funds for the building had been collected by the Mennonite constituency in Kansas, and Voth supervised its construction with the help of a carpenter who had come out from Kansas. Entries in Voth's journal indicate that he had more Hopi help with the project than he could use to advantage. Yet, long years after the chapel was finished and even after it was almost completely destroyed by lightning in 1912 (or thereabouts) many Hopi continued to regard it as bewitched and would not venture close to its crumbling walls.

Voth's dedication to making converts was in the honest belief that he was doing so in the best interests of the Indians he converted. Nowhere in his writings is there the slightest evidence of contempt for the Hopi. On the other hand, there is every evidence of his sincere respect for the Hopi's own religious beliefs. To thoroughly understand those beliefs, he mastered the complex and difficult Hopi language. He won many friends among the Hopi by his unfailing willingness to use the medical knowledge he had acquired to help the sick and injured who came to him for treatment. Opposition to military service is one of the fundamental beliefs of the Mennonite Church, so one can appreciate the empathy Voth must have felt with the Hopi, the People of Peace.

Voth was a man rich in the humanities. Also, he was by nature a scholar who found the intricacies of Hopi ceremonial life an intellectual challenge. This prompted his ready acceptance in 1899 of an offer by George A. Dorsey, then Curator of the Department of Anthropology of the Field Columbian Museum, that he act as a collector with the Museum's Stanley McCormick Hopi Expedition. The artifacts he secured for the Field Museum form one of the most valuable Hopi collections possessed by any museum. The ten papers he wrote describing Hopi ceremonial life were published by the Field Museum at the turn of the century. They are invaluable additions to scientific literature on the Hopi and a lasting monument to this dedicated man.

John F. Schmidt of the Mennonite Library and Archives wrote in his paper *Heinrich R. Voth, 1855–1931* that "Voth's research activities encountered suspicion and growing resentment among the Hopi and loss of confidence on the part of the mission board." As a result, Voth had to leave Tusayan in 1902 and became a home mission worker in Oklahoma until his retirement in 1927. He died four years later.

It seems sadly ironical that when, because of the schism at Old Oraibi, Pamimptewa assumed the direction of the Powamu ceremony there, for verification of important details in this highly important religious rite he turned to a 1901 publication of the Field Columbian Museum — "The Oraibi Powamu Ceremony" by that maligned missionary Heinrich R. Voth.

Dr. Clarence G. Salsbury

Although the mission established at Ganado, Arizona, by the Board of Missions of the United Presbyterian Church of the United States is about fifty miles east of Keams Canyon and the Hopi villages, it has played a prominent part in the life of the Hopi.

In 1901, at the urging of the Presbyterian Church in Flagstaff, four men — George Logie, its pastor, Frank C. Reed, an elder, Thomas C. Moffett, a former pastor, and William R. Johnston, an early missionary to the Navajo — went on a scouting expedition to locate a site for the mission they were so eager to establish in Tusayan. After investigating many locations proposed to them, they decided upon Ganado.

The first missionary appointed to Ganado was Charles Bierkemper. Lorenzo Hubbell, the trader there, welcomed him and supplied him with living quarters, a team of horses, and a buckboard. In time, Mrs. Bierkemper gathered together a few students and established the first school at Ganado in the home Hubbell had donated for their temporary use. Later a small adobe house was built, and the Bierkempers shared this with a medical missionary and his wife who came to Ganado in 1905 to start the medical work which soon became such an important phase of the work there.

From the beginning the objectives of the Ganado Mission were Indian education and health services, and conversion of the Indians to Christianity. Among the various men who participated in the religious missionary work was Shine Smith, who, after a break with the Presbyterian Church, became well known in Arizona for his individual missionary efforts.

In 1920 the Reverend Fred G. Mitchell was operating a Bible training school at Tolchaco Crossing north of Leupp, Arizona. When his school was completely destroyed by fire, he was appointed to head the Ganado Mission. Taking his staff with him, he became the first superintendent there in 1921. Various doctors took charge of the medical work at Ganado, but by far the best known of all of them was Dr. Clarence G. Salsbury. He really put the Ganado Mission on the map.

Salsbury was born in Moira, Ontario, and was educated at the Union Missionary Training Institute in Brooklyn, New York, where he met petite Cora Burrows, whom he eventually married. They must have presented an odd couple — the tiny Miss Burrows alongside the towering "Mr. Canada," as Salsbury was known at the Brooklyn school. From the training school for missionaries Salsbury went on to the College of Physicians and Surgeons in Boston, and Cora Burrows, to the Philadelphia School of Nursing. They were married in 1909 and Salsbury continued to work his way through medical school. In 1914, the Presbyterian Board of Missions assigned the two of them to Hainan, an island off the southern coast of China. They remained in China until 1926, when they returned to the United States on furlough, with every intention of returning to China.

When his year's vacation was over Salsbury stayed close by the church headquarters so as not to waste any time when the orders came through for them to return to China, but troublous times there caused considerable delay. While they were waiting impatiently word came to the Mission Board that a doctor was urgently needed at the Ganado Mission. Salsbury offered to fill the job but only on the condition that when his China orders came he would be free to go there. With this understanding the Salsburys set out for Tusayan. There they were to remain until his retirement in 1950.

Dr. Salsbury got off to a bad start at Ganado. His first surgical case was a young Navajo girl who had a badly broken leg. Without benefit of X-rays he set it as best he could, but the broken ends of the bone overlapped. To give the girl a straight leg he would have to operate. It took him three days to convince the parents and gain their permission. Unhappily, during the operation the girl died from an embolism.

When word of this spread through the small hospital, every patient, even those Navajo who were deathly ill, got up and bolted. To them the death of the girl was a bad omen indeed. Sick as they were, they would be better away from the hospital — a place where people were taken to die. It was quite some time before the dread of the hospital faded away and Navajo patients would entrust themselves to the care of the Salsburys.

There can be little question of the dedication of Clarence Salsbury and his small dynamo of a wife. They slowly gained the confidence of many of the Indians in the surrounding countryside, both Hopi and Navajo. The educational and religious work of the mission was also promoted to the fullest possible extent by their associates.

One of the most significant of Salsbury's projects was the establishment of a school for nursing. There Hopi, Navajo, and even girls from other tribes, received such training as to make it possible for them to pass the regular examinations of the State Board and become registered nurses.

Salsbury was a dynamic promoter who got national publicity through several national magazines and substantial contributions from his church and from private sources. In 1930 the Sage Memorial Hospital was dedicated, and Dr. Salsbury persuaded many a top specialist to pay his own transportation to Ganado and donate time to help keep the medical staff there up to date. A high school was established and by the time he retired Ganado Mission had become a fair sized town.

He never forgot, however, that conversion of the Indians to Christianity was basic to all of their endeavors. He was not a patient man and he showed little tolerance when Indian religious beliefs and customs hindered his work as a physician and a surgeon. Although not as fanatical as many of the Christian missionaries who came — and continue to come — to Tusayan, he made a decisive effort to convert away from his own religion every Indian the entire complex reached, whether it was a child in school or a patient in the hospital. This evangelical zeal naturally aroused considerable opposition, particularly among the religious leaders and healers among the Hopi and Navajo.

At one time Salsbury had long narrow billboards erected throughout Tusayan reading, "Tradition is the enemy of progress." The leaders of the Hopi particularly resented these, for the very roots of the Hopi lay in their adherence to the best of their traditional way of life. It is probable that by this excess of zeal Dr. Salsbury's billboards did much to militate against the work of the Ganado Mission.

In his final years at Ganado, Salsbury was in frequent conflict with representatives of the Bureau of Indian Affairs. He was very frank in voicing his opposition to Indian Bureau plans for schools, hospitals, and various other programs for the Hopi and the Navajo. Even the establishment of the Navajo Tribal Fair at Window Rock was deemed by Salsbury as an uncalled-for conflict with the mission's annual bazaar. Times were changing in Tusayan, and he found it difficult to adapt to them.

Following his retirement in 1950, he served the state of Arizona first as Chief of the Arizona Bureau of Preventive Medical Services and later as Director of the State Board of Health.

During his long term as head of the Ganado Mission Dr. Salsbury posted all over the mission compound this motto (from a statement by architect Daniel Burnham): "MAKE NO LITTLE PLANS. THEY HAVE NO MAGIC TO STIR MEN'S BLOOD AND PROBABLY THEMSELVES WILL NOT BE REALIZED. MAKE BIG PLANS, AIM HIGH, AND HOPE AND WORK, REMEMBERING THAT A NOBLE LOGICAL PROGRAM ONCE RECORDED WILL NEVER DIE, BUT LONG AFTER WE ARE GONE WILL BE A LIVING THING, ASSERTING ITSELF WITH INTENSITY."

Certainly, Dr. Clarence Salsbury never failed to live up to his own motto. The Presbyterian mission at Ganado, growing in tolerance of and adaptability to change, remains a significant institution and continues to influence the lives of many Hopi as well as those of the Navajo on whose reservation it was established.

The Era of Superintendents Lawshe and Crane

BY THE END of the first decade of the twentieth century, attitudes of official Washington toward the Hopi had changed little. There was objection to their marriage customs; when roads were built to the various villages, Hopi protests against destruction of their sacred shrines were ignored; school attendance continued to be ruthlessly enforced.

When Abraham L. Lawshe became school superintendent and agent at Keams Canyon on the first of November, 1910, he seems to have been favorably impressed with the Hopi but found the physical plant of the superintendency, as well as the schools below the mesas, in deplorable condition. He estimated that there were five hundred cases of trachoma on the reservation.

Hopi children had been herded into inadequate, unsanitary, and horribly overcrowded school facilities. The living conditions for the children at the Keams Canyon boarding school were vile. The result was the spread of many diseases for which the Hopi had developed no natural immunity.

Children who developed tuberculosis could not be adequately cared for and were simply sent home to die. Trachoma, that serious eye infection which so often results in blindness, became rampant. In those pre-sulfa and antibiotic days, the treatment available to the Hopi children and a few adults consisted of washing out the eyes with a copper sulfate (bluestone) solution. In severe cases doctors sometimes subjected the patient to a painful operation in which the granules inside the eyelid were broken out with metal rollers. When this operation was performed it was essential that the eyes be kept clean and the wounds sterile until healing was complete. Such postoperative care was difficult to secure in the boarding school and impossible in the villages. As a result, a tragic number of Hopi became blind.

Lawshe experienced no problem in maintaining law and order among the Hopi, and in his first report he proudly noted that not a single

Indian had been put in jail. Only one formal trial had been considered necessary. At one of the villages on Second Mesa during the annual Bean Dance one of the participating kachinas took offense at two white women spectators, one of whom, according to Superintendent Lawshe, was "a well known author." The kachina assaulted both women with a whip. When the culprit was hailed before the Indian judges, they decided that he would receive a treatment similar to that which he had meted out — a whipping. Superintendent Lawshe gave the man the option of being put in the guardhouse for fifteen days, but he chose the whipping.

It is significant that Lawshe, unlike most, if not all, of those early government officials, made no recommendation that the Hopi be forbidden to carry on their ceremonials. In fact, he concluded one section of his first report by commenting, "It would be as easy to stop the waters of Niagara as to stop these ceremonial dances."

In his 1911 report, Lawshe commented on the allotment idea, "Several futile attempts have been made to allot the lands on the Moqui Reservation. The latest attempt, begun some three years ago, was abandoned January 12 of this year. In the opinion of the writer, no greater injury could be done these Indians than to allot them the lands. The white man does not want, does not need, and would not use the surplus lands, if any."

It is interesting that Superintendent Lawshe should frankly mention the reason behind so many of the allotment schemes which so often were used to cheat the Indian of much of his reservation land.

The various schools being established in the Hopi country eventually were expected to follow the course of study adopted by Arizona public schools. However, the Hopi children had to wear uniforms which they found scratchy and uncomfortable. Only half the day was spent in school, the rest of the time was given over to such work as the school superintendent and the teachers should demand of them.

A very few pupils were selected to go on to such nonreservation schools as the government was bringing into operation in Riverside, California, in Phoenix, Arizona, and in Santa Fe, New Mexico. Lawshe and several other superintendents commented in their reports that Hopi students returning to their homes after attending these nonreservation schools were ill-equipped to find their proper places in their own Hopi village communities.

Early in 1911 Lawshe had thirty acres of ground at Keams Canyon set aside for experimental plantings of some seventy varieties of food plants not then grown in the Hopi country. This seems to have been the first attempt to try to find food plants that could eventually be grown by the Hopi as a valuable addition to their decidedly limited diet. The gardens at Keams Canyon were taken care of by the children of the school. It was hoped that the produce would provide an excellent supplement to the staff commissary and, possibly, even enough for that of the boarding school. The experiment was not much of a success. The plants that did best were those the Hopi already were growing.

Superintendent Lawshe also reported that early in February, 1911, Youkeoma, the village chief of Hotevila who had bitterly opposed the enforced education of the children of his village, had requested to be taken to Washington to meet the "Great Chief." Believing that such a trip might change Youkeoma's bitter attitude, Lawshe arranged to conduct him and an interpreter to the capital the following month. During his stay in Washington, Youkeoma visited both the Commissioner of Indian Affairs and President William Howard Taft. He pleaded with them, and even demanded of them, that he and his followers be let alone. He spoke eloquently of his opposition to the white man's way of life and against the force being exerted upon the children to attend school. From remarks upon his return to Hotevila, all that seems to have impressed Youkeoma about the President was his great girth.

It was during Lawshe's term of office that the suggestion was first made that Old Oraibi should be preserved as a national monument. No mention is made in the superintendent's report as to who initiated the idea.

A. L. Lawshe was succeeded as school superintendent and head of the Moqui Agency by Leo Crane, who held this position for eight years. That he held office for such a long period during a time of such historical importance, especially for the Hopi of Second and Third Mesas, makes it imperative that considerable space be allotted to his administration.

Crane had been an office employee, a copyist and stenographer, in the Bureau of Indian Affairs in Washington. He confesses to having written several stories and articles about the "wild west" he had never known. In 1910 illness prompted him to request transfer to an agency in the Far West. His request was granted, and in a short time he found himself chief clerk at Leupp, a subagency for the Navajo on the wide mud flats of the Little Colorado River north of Winslow.

The location was not quite what the writer of romantic tales of the great west had expected. Certainly the Leupp of those days was far from the sort of place that a conscientious doctor would recommend to an ailing patient. When Crane found the food far from his taste, he complained to his boss. Immediately he found himself appointed to administer the mess.

Despite this inauspicious introduction to the land of his imaginings, Crane, who had intelligence and was widely read, soon discovered that the dreary environment of Leupp was ringed by the spectacular wonders of the Painted Desert which he later so aptly dubbed the "Enchanted Desert."

In contrast to Superintendent Lawshe, Crane found great difficulty in maintaining law and order, as he understood law and order, on the reservation. In his first annual report, that of 1912, he wrote of the Navajo under his jurisdiction, "They are not disorderly but they simply cannot understand why the white man objects to so many things that they have for years considered as most commonplace, or which they may admit are only eccentricities." This first report demonstrated the stern disapproval, verging on outright hatred, that was to mark Crane's entire reign as representative of the United States government at Keams Canyon. "The Hopi," he wrote, "present so much immorality that an attempt to do more than protect children, keep returned students straight (which is not always possible), and round up the most scandalous of the older villagers, would project a moral war that would affect nearly every Hopi at some mesas . . . they begin as children to live on a moral plane little above their livestock."[39]

One cannot read far in Crane's reports to the Commissioner of Indian Affairs in Washington without concluding that Crane came to Keams Canyon with deep-seated prejudice against the Hopi. From reading his two books, *Indians of the Enchanted Desert* and *Desert Drums,* it is easy to conclude that Crane's admiration for the Franciscans was a basic factor in this prejudice. The fact that the Hopi had joined in the Pueblo Rebellion in which so many Franciscans were killed — and, unlike their friends the Pueblo Indians of New Mexico, had never allowed any Catholic priests, Franciscan or otherwise, to return to Tusayan — seems to have rankled constantly in Crane's mind while he served at Keams Canyon.

Also, like many another Indian agent, the virtually despotic powers inherent in that office at that time likely corrupted him to the point where he expected "Yes, sir" obedience from every Indian under his jurisdiction. When the Hopi stood firm in their Hopi way of life they antagonized him. When they followed his directives to live as second-class whites, he was pleased with them.

Shortly after Crane assumed the superintendency a severe epidemic of measles and dysentery broke out at the Keams Canyon boarding school and rapidly spread to all the villages. This caused thirty-eight deaths at First Mesa, and thirty-one at Mishongnovi; Shipolovi, Shongopovi, Oraibi, and Bacobi, each had similar fatalities. Crane made no attempt to ascertain the number of deaths at Hotevila, but he estimated that about half of the ninety to one hundred children of that village died.

Once more, like so many of his predecessors, Crane reported at length on the sad condition and inadequacy of the buildings and, indeed, on everything pertaining to the physical plant of the entire agency. However, unlike his predecessors, Crane seems to have had in Washington connections which made it possible for him to undertake an extensive program of building and repair. His list of, and comments upon, the improvements needed presents a shocking picture of the conditions under which Hopi youngsters lived at Keams Canyon boarding school and spent their long days at the various day schools. He even urged that a sanitary jail be built at Keams Canyon!

During his first months at Keams Canyon Crane seems to have made no attempt to meet with Youkeoma, and Hotevila's unwillingness to have the children there attend school continued. Early in his first year of office he sent for troops to collect the Hotevila children judged to be of school age and forcibly take them to the Keams Canyon boarding school.

In December, 1911, Colonel Hugh L. Scott with a detachment of black troops arrived at Keams Canyon. Colonel Scott explained that his instructions were to cooperate with Crane regarding the refusal of the Hotevila people to send their children to school and also to make a survey of conditions throughout the agency.

Colonel Scott went at once to Hotevila to interview Youkeoma. Crane gives a lengthy account of their meeting in his *Indians of the Enchanted Desert*. The "interview" lasted ten days and, according to Crane, Youkeoma did most of the talking. In the end, the troops were summoned to Hotevila to stand by as Crane and his assistants searched the village for the hidden children. Those that were judged in proper physical condition by three doctors Crane had with him were placed under guard in wagons for transportation to Keams Canyon. By noon they had captured fifty-one girls and eighteen boys, all that remained from the devastating measles epidemic.

That night Colonel Scott, Crane, the black troops, the sixty-nine terrified children, and the rest of the party camped below Oraibi. The following morning they continued up to Shongopovi, where Sackaletztewa also opposed sending the children of that village to school. Again, with the troops standing by to intimidate the people, Crane and his helpers searched the village for hidden children. Only three were found. One of the leaders of the village produced a small packet of letters written by various white Americans to Youkeoma and other Hopi leaders opposing the government policies — urging them to, as one letter put it, "Resist to the last gasp. Die rather than submit."

Crane was furious. He concluded that a particular letter had come "from some weak-minded woman," adding, "very likely she is now writing scenarios. . . . I have no sympathy with this type of sentimentalist. I deported some of them from the Hopi country when they appeared with their box of theoretical tricks."

Assisting Crane in collecting the children of Hotevila and Shongopovi was a husky Tewa policeman named Nelson. When Sackaletztewa protested the forcible taking of one of the children an argument broke out between him and the Tewa policeman. The policeman promptly stripped off his uniform, discarded his gun, and prepared to fight Sackaletztewa. The black soldiers were delighted at the prospect of a fight and formed a ring around the contestants. At this point Crane arrived on the scene and with acknowledged reluctance, stopped the fight.

When the seventy-two captured youngsters arrived at Keams Canyon they were enrolled in the boarding school where they spent four years virtually isolated from their families. During that time they were not allowed a single vacation.

The custom of young Hopi children going without clothes during the warm months struck Crane as being particularly uncivilized. One day a Hopi family drove up in their wagon to visit some of their older youngsters enrolled at the Keams Canyon school. When the day turned hot the young visiting children shed their clothes and placed them for safekeeping in the family wagon. They then proceeded to wander in the nude, here, there and everywhere around the agency grounds. This Crane found decidedly upsetting.

The incidents that have been related were typical of Crane's long term of office. On the credit side of his record he constantly urged, and usually secured, appropriations for improving the buildings and necessary facilities — not alone at Keams Canyon, but also at every government day school on the reservation. For some years the government had made wagons, tools, window frames, and a long list of other articles available to such Hopi as would pay for them by a stipulated schedule of work hours. Crane urged that the number of wagons, farm implements, tools, barbed wire, and similar articles be greatly increased. This should have been of benefit to the Hopi, but the fact that at that time nearly a million pounds of government freight were being hauled from Holbrook, seventy-eight miles away, would indicate that the additional wagons he requested were to benefit the agency as well as the Indians. To his credit, also, was his success in persuading the government to build a hospital at Keams Canyon.

Crane was a great tree planter at Keams Canyon. He reported that in the three years ending in 1914 he planted there five hundred cottonwood trees, one hundred Russian mulberry trees, and fifty black locust trees. Surely this was a good deed in that sun-drenched land!

He initiated stock improvement by upbreeding. Hereford bulls, Percheron stallions, Cotswold and Rambouillet rams were purchased and then resold to such Hopi as could afford them. The Percheron stallions were soon found to be decidedly unsuited to the Hopi country, as were the Cotswold rams. A plan was also worked out so that Hopi stockmen had help in gaining proper prices for such stock as they had available for sale. Crane also continued the program of well-drilling and spring improvement throughout the reservation. An attempt was even made to protect springs used for domestic purposes from contamination.

In July, 1915, the old boarding school at Keams Canyon was judged to be in such dangerous condition that it was closed. Provision was made to have the pupils then enrolled there taken care of at the several reservation day schools.

Again to Crane's credit is the firm stand he took in his report for 1918 against Navajo encroachments on Hopi lands. He also pleaded for all necessary support to end the growing list of crimes the Navajo were perpetrating against the Hopi.

Crane was the first superintendent who, by his skill with both typewriter and camera, could send reports to the Commissioner of Indian Affairs in Washington which gave vivid evidence of the problems besetting a superintendent at Keams Canyon. His ever-growing bitterness against those Hopi who held fast to their traditional way of life did not stop him from recommending developments on the reservations which he felt would be to their best interests. He had the intelligence to be objective at least to that extent.

Praise should also be accorded Crane for urging in his 1917 report that the name of the reservation be changed from Moqui to Hopi, with the explanation that the Moqui was a "misnomer and a term of opprobrium, one very offensive to the Hopi people."

The problem of getting and holding reservation doctors, field matrons, teachers, government farmers, and stockmen at the salaries then paid and with the existing living conditions plagued Crane as it had his predecessors. In his report for 1917 Crane stated that there had been 450 changes in employment for an average number of eighty-five jobs during a five-year period.

Realizing the economic value entailed, Crane encouraged the Hopi to hold to the highest possible standards in their manufacture of baskets, pottery, blankets, silver jewelry, kachina dolls, and all other articles suitable for sale to visitors either by the Hopi themselves or through the stores of the Indian traders and at such tourist spots as Grand Canyon.

It was in his report for 1916 that Crane mentioned for the first time certain special reports made personally by him to Commissioner

Cato Sells. These concerned Indian dances and ceremonials and in them he urged that a set policy should be adopted restricting or prohibiting them. Missionaries to the various tribes had been urging that "pagan" dance ceremonials should be prohibited. Several earlier superintendents to the Hopi had thought that by government prohibition of ceremonial religious observances, the Hopi way of life could be broken down. This controversy was to come to a crisis in a few short years.

From October, 1918, to January, 1919, the epidemic of Spanish influenza, which killed more than ten million people throughout the world, swept into Tusayan. Strange to say, the percentage of deaths among the Hopi during this epidemic was less than that in many white communities. The Navajo, however, were very susceptible, and the mortality rate among them was high.

With his final report of August 11, 1919, Leo Crane filed a memorandum history of the Moqui Indian Reservation from 1886 to 1903, inclusive, which still serves as a valuable annotated index for anyone wishing to delve into the detailed reports of the various superintendents during that period. This report gave Crane a good opportunity to sum up his own eight years as superintendent at Keams Canyon, to pay his respects to the Hopi leaders who did not agree with him, and to warn his successor that the only way to treat the Hopi was to rule with a steel hand.

Writing of the work of the superintendent, he stated that major portions of his time had been spent in supervising "Indian traders who are worse than the Indians, tourists who are worse than the Indian traders including interested but undisciplined 'friends,' curio hunters, actresses, authors, moving-picture fiends and just plain wandering openmouthed TOURISTS and last, but not least, THE SNAKE DANCE." This outburst was also evidently intended as a warning to his successor.

During his years with the Hopi, Crane developed a particular dislike for Tewaquaptewa. In his *Indians of the Enchanted Desert* he takes a parting shot at the once-friendly village chief of Oraibi: "Tewaquaptewa's portrait appears in that fine book of Indian chants, edited by Miss Natalie Curtis and published by the Harpers; and his singing countenance presents a rapt ecstatic expression as he yodels the Butterfly song. . . . As his Indian Agent, however, I tried for eight long years to make a sensible human being of him, and failed, for lack of material."

Despite Crane's unquestioned ability with words, they seem to have failed him when it came time for him in his final report to pay tribute to Youkeoma and the people of his village. All he could write was a reference to "Hotevila Hopi, like unto which there is nothing in the world, unless it be the Airedale dog."

Before leaving the Hopi country, Crane quoted Colonel Scott as advising him, "Young man! You have an empire to control. Either rule it, or pack your trunk." This was just the sort of advice that Leo Crane was pleased to receive as confirmation of his own concept of his responsibilities as superintendent. He happily passed it on to his successor!

Crane was transferred to the agency for the Pueblo Indians in New Mexico for four years. He then served terms as superintendent at the Crow Creek Agency in South Dakota, the Colorado River Agency in Arizona, and the Southern Navajo Agency in Arizona. From 1937 until 1947 he served as a guide and ranger for the Bureau of Reclamation at Boulder Canyon, Nevada.

Most of the Hopi hailed the news of Crane's transfer to New Mexico. They hoped against hope that whoever came to take his place would demonstrate more tolerance for those among them who wanted only to be let alone to live their lives according to their ancient traditions.

They were in for bitter disappointment.

President Theodore Roosevelt Visits the Hopi

Before ending the account of Leo Crane's years with the Indian Service we must turn back to the summer of 1913 when he was superintendent at Keams Canyon. Life for him was complicated at that time by the arrival in Tusayan of two visitors of such prestige in Washington that he could not possibly ignore, or be impolite to either of them — Theodore Roosevelt, whose term as president had ended only four years earlier, and Natalie Curtis.

Natalie Curtis (Mrs. Paul Burlin) had been working in the Hopi country collecting Indian songs and legends and in 1907 had published *The Indians' Book*. She had been enthusiastically encouraged in this task by the then President Roosevelt, and it was his personal interest that had made it possible for her to visit the various reservations and record Indian music — this at a time when such music was officially banned from Indian schools and held in high disfavor by Indian Bureau officialdom.

Theodore Roosevelt as a young man had had little or no particular interest in, or sympathy for, the Indian. His change in attitude in later life must be attributed in major degree to Charles F. Lummis. Lummis had kept urging Roosevelt to visit Tusayan to see for himself what the conditions in the Hopi country were. It was not until the summer of 1913 that Roosevelt found time to make the trip.

Crane had not made it easy for Miss Curtis to work at this particular time and had done everything within his power to throw her into contact only with such Hopi as he felt would give her a laudable account of his administration of the Hopi Reservation. She had decidedly annoyed him when she insisted upon making her own contacts, and talking again with such old Hopi friends as Lololomai, Tewaquaptewa, Lahpu, Koianimptiwa, Masahongva, Kavanghongevah, and many others who were certainly not on Crane's list of agency favorites. Crane knew only too well of her excellent connections with people in high position in official Washington. Even Francis Leupp, Commissioner of Indian Affairs, had enthusiastically endorsed her project. Now she was to join the party of the ex-president. Crane was not happy about any of it, but he and the members of his staff polished up everything so as to make as good an impression as possible upon the visitors.

The Roosevelt party crossed the Colorado River at Lee's Ferry and, after several days in the Navajo country, arrived at Walpi a day or two before that part of the Snake Ceremony which rises to such a dramatic climax as to lure spectators from near and far. Arrangements had been made for Miss Curtis to join the Roosevelt entourage there. (Later she wrote for *The Outlook* magazine an amusing account of her attempts to make herself presentable to meet the ex-president after her days of work in the Painted Desert.)

The Hopi at Walpi took a liking to Roosevelt, and he was invited into the kivas to see the preparations being made there for the final observances. With his zest and dynamic energy he keenly observed everything, from the dawn race of the final day to the night ceremonies in the kivas. The morning after the public ceremony Roosevelt read aloud a long article which, with his accustomed speed, he had dashed off in his tent the night before. This, with additional remarks, was later published in *The Outlook* of October 19, 1913.

In this article he set down not only vivid reporting of everything he saw during his stay at Walpi, but also his general observations regarding Indians, the Hopi in particular. The article is far too long to reprint in its entirety but the following are some significant excerpts:

> Several times we walked up the precipitous cliff trails to the mesa top, and visited the three villages thereon. We were received with friendly courtesy — perhaps partly because we endeavored to show good manners ourselves, which, I am sorry to say, is not invariably the case with tourists. The houses were colored red or white; and the houses individually, and the villages as villages, compared favorably with the average dwelling or village in many of the southern portions of Mediterranean Europe. . . . There were several rooms in each house; and the furniture included stoves, sewing-machines, chairs, window panes of glass, and sometimes window curtains. Most of the houses were scrupulously clean; although the condition of the streets — while not worse than in the Mediterranean villages above referred to — showed urgent need of a crusade for sanitation and elementary hygiene. The men and women were well dressed, in clothes quite as picturesque as,

and quite as near our own garb, as the dress of many European peasants of a good type; aside, of course, from the priests and young men who were preparing for the ceremonial dance, and who were clad or unclad, according to the ancient ritual. . . .

Many well-informed and well-meaning men are apt to protest against the effort to keep and develop what is best in the Indian's own historic life as incompatible with making him an American citizen, and speak of those of opposite views as wishing to preserve the Indians only as National bric-a-brac. This is not so. We believe in fitting him for citizenship as rapidly as possible. But where he cannot be pushed ahead rapidly we believe in making progress slowly, and in all cases where it is possible we hope to keep for him and for us what was best in his old culture. . . .

Of course all Indians should not be forced into the same mold. Some can be made farmers; others mechanics; yet others have the soul of the artist. Let us try to give each his chance to develop what is best in him. Moreover, let us be wary of interfering overmuch with either his work or his play. It is mere tyranny for instance, to stop all Indian dances. Some which are obscene, or which are dangerous on other grounds, must be prohibited. Others should be permitted, and many of them encouraged. Nothing that tells for the joy of life, in any community, should be lightly touched. . . .

Help them to make it in such fashion that when the change is accomplished we shall find that the original and valuable elements in the Indian culture have been retained, so that the new citizens come with full hands into the great field of American life, and contribute to that life something of marked value to all of us, something which it would be a misfortune to all of us to have destroyed.

As an example, take the case of these Hopi mesa towns, perched in such boldly picturesque fashion on high, sheer-walled rock ridges. Many good people wish to force the Hopis to desert these towns, and live in isolated families in nice tin-roofed houses on the plains below. I believe that this would be a mistake from the standpoint of the Indians — not to mention depriving our country of something as notable and as attractive as the castles that have helped make the Rhine beautiful and famous. . . . Moreover, the present Hopi house, with its thick roof, is cooler and pleasanter than a tin-roofed house. I believe it would be far wiser gradually to develop the Hopi house itself, making it more commodious and convenient, rather than to abandon it and plant the Indian in a brand-new Government-built house, precisely like some ten million other cheap houses. The Hopi architecture is a product of its own environment: it is as picturesque as anything of the kind which our art students travel to Spain in order to study. Therefore let us keep it. The Hopi architecture can be kept, adapted, and developed just as we have kept, adapted, and developed the Mission architecture of the Southwest — with the results seen in beautiful Leland Stanford University. The University of New Mexico is, most wisely, modeled on these pueblo buildings. . . .

I cannot so much as touch on the absorbingly interesting questions of the Hopis' spiritual and religious life, and of the amount of deference that can properly be paid to one side of this life. The snake dance and antelope dance, which we had come to see, are not only interesting as relics of an almost inconceivably remote and savage past — analogous to the past wherein our own ancestors once dwelt — but also represent a mystic symbolism which has in it elements that are ennobling and not debasing. These dances are prayers or invocations for rain, the crowning blessing in this dry land. The rain is adored and invoked both as male and female; the gentle steady downpour is the female, the storm with lightning the male. The lightning stick is "strong medicine," and is used in all these religious ceremonies. The snakes, the brothers of men, as are all living things in the Hopi's creed, are besought to tell the beings of the underworld man's need of water. . . .

It is to be hoped that the art, the music, the poetry of their elders will be preserved during the change coming over the younger generation.

Theodore Roosevelt's understanding interest in the Hopi had a slow but permanent influence on Washington officials, and he retained his personal interest in their welfare until his death in 1919.

Natalie Curtis had early developed a very high opinion not only of Hopi poetry and song, but also of the Hopi themselves. In *The Indians' Book* (pp. 473–74) she had written:

Song is the spontaneous expression of the people. It may be heard at all hours rising from the Hopi village or from the surrounding desert plains and cliffs. The shepherd driving his flock down the steep, rocky trail; the planter seeking his field at dawn; the woman at her task; the child at his play, all sing as naturally as the bird on the bough. Besides old traditional songs, the Hopis have countless songs of the moment, which are composed and sung for a few years and then forgotten.

To seize on paper the spirit of Hopi music is a task as impossible as to put on canvas the shimmer and glare of the desert. Hopi music is born of its environment. The wind sweeping among the crags and whirling down the trail has carved its strange melody upon the Indian's plastic mind, even as it has carved upon the rocks, in curious erosion, the record of its presence. Its echo is heard in the song of the Hopi, yodelling through the desert solitudes. There, in that wide land, under the blaze of the Arizona sun, amid the shifting color of the tinted sands and the purple-blue of the sharp-shadowed rocks must the songs be heard to be heard truly.

It is impossible to read far in Natalie Curtis's book without realizing that she possessed an amazing faculty for gaining the respect and cooperation of the Indians with whom she worked. This was certainly true of the Hopi who always spoke of her affectionately as "The Song Woman." Without this empathy it would have been absolutely impossible for her to record the songs she did. Among the singers and the songs they allowed her to write out in her notebook were the following:

Lololomai	— One of the songs of the *Wuwuchim*
Tewaquaptewa	— A Butterfly Dance song
Lahpu	— The *Anga* Kachina
Koianimptiwa	— A song of the *Korosta* Kachina
Masahongya	— A song of the *Heheya* Kachina, and one of the Owl Kachinas
Masaveimah and Kavanghongevah	— Joined in one of the Grey Flute ceremonial songs

Like all of us, the Hopi were astonished that the little black dots which she placed on the lines she drew across the pages of her notebook would indeed record for all time the music they were singing.

Natalie Curtis obviously took the time to explain to the people why she wanted to record their songs. Again from *The Indians' Book* (pp. 474–76):

> I sought Lololomai to tell him of my purpose with the Hopi songs. My interpreter was a Hopi lad, who, though blind, led with sure foot the way up the steep, rocky trail to the village. The chief was seated on his house-top, spinning, for in Hopi-land it is the men who spin and weave. He rose and met us at the head of the ladder that led to where he sat.
>
> "I have come to talk with you, friend, on something that concerns your people," I said.
>
> "Ancha-a ('Tis well)," he answered, solemnly, and motioned me to sit down with him.
>
> "Lololomai," I said, "the Hopi children are going to school; they are learning new ways and are singing new songs — American songs instead of Hopi. Some of the children are very young — so young that there have been, perhaps, but three corn-plantings since they came into the world. These little ones will never sing the songs of their fathers. They will not sing of the corn, the bean-blossoms, and the butterflies. They will know only American songs. Hopi songs are beautiful; it is sad that they should be forgotten."
>
> To all of this the old chief said, "Hao, hao (Even so, even so)," and nodded slowly.
>
> "But," I continued, "there is one thing in the school good for all to have and to know, and that is *books*. Books can be of many kinds, Hopi as well as English. As yet your people have no books nor do they read or write. That is why your songs will be forgotten, why even your language may some day pass away.
>
> "When you sing, your song is heard, then dies like the wind that sweeps the cornfields and is gone, none knows whither. But if you could write, you could put your song into a book, and your people, even to the children of their children, could know your song as if you yourself were singing. They could look upon the written page and say: 'Thus sang Lololomai, our chief, in the long ago. Thus sings Lololomai to-day.'"
>
> The head drooped lower and the aged face was grave.
>
> "But until the time shall come," I said, "when the Hopis shall themselves record their stories and their songs, someone must do this for them, else much will be lost — lost forever, like a windblown trail. So I have come from my far-distant home by the 'great waters' in the East to write the Hopi songs."
>
> There was a pause. Then the old chief turned to me pathetically. There was a wistful yearning in the aged eyes, a cloud of trouble on the wrinkled brow.
>
> "It is well," he said, "but will not the superintendent be angry if you do this thing? Are you sure that you will not bring trouble upon us? White people try to stop our songs and dances, so I am fearful of your talk."

"Be at rest, my friend," I said, "the great chief at Washington is father of all the people in this country, as you are father of all in this village. He has given his permission for the writing of the Hopi songs. He is glad to have them written, for he, too, knows that Hopi songs are beautiful."

"Then it is well," replied Lololomai — "then it is well, indeed. But will you, friend, explain to me that which I cannot understand? Why do the white people want to stop our dances and our songs? Why do they trouble us? Why do they interfere with what can harm them not? What ill do we do to any white man when we dance?"

"Lololomai, white men do not understand your dances or your songs. They do not even know one word of your language. When I have written your songs, I will write English words as well as Hopi, that white men may know of what you sing. When they understand, they will perhaps no longer want to stop your dances and your songs. To you, Lololomai, the Hopi chief, will I give the Hopi songs when they are written. You will keep them for your people with the other sacred things that are your trust. Then in the days to come the younger Hopis will read, and so the songs never will be forgotten."

Lololomai bowed his head. "Lolomai," he said, "pas lolomai (good, very good)."

After her final visit to the Hopi, Natalie Curtis planned to continue with her studies of Indian music, but during a visit to Paris in 1921 she was killed by an automobile while crossing a street.

Oppression by
Superintendent Daniel

ON THE FIRST PAGE of Superintendent Daniel's first annual report —
that of June 30, 1920 — he stated: "My predecessor, Leo Crane, in his
narrative statement for 1919, and the historical supplement thereto,
covered the conditions on this reservation so thoroughly that it would
be little more than repetition for me to undertake to cover much of the
same ground for the reason that many conditions are unchanged. . . ."

It is impossible to say whether Crane's hatred for the Hopi, so well
documented in the reports that Daniel mentioned, served to influence
Daniel's own attitude or whether he came to Keams Canyon already an
embittered man.

Although Leo Crane had given the Navajo under his jurisdiction
almost as bad a name as he had the Hopi, Daniel after his first confrontation with them seems to have decided that Crane may have been wrong
in doing so. This first meeting Daniel had with representatives of the
Diné — "the People," as the Navajo prefer to call themselves, was an
impressive occasion. A large delegation presented itself at his office and
every man of it was armed to the teeth. From that point on the Hopi came
to feel that Daniel showed definite favoritism to the larger and more
powerful tribe. Yet, in his report of 1920 he, as so many of his predecessors had done and others would continue to do long after him, urged
that the government take action against the Navajo to protect the Hopi.
He wrote:

"The Navajo population has encroached upon the Hopi Indians . . .
the Hopi is gradually being deprived of his water, land and pasturage.
Unless positive corrective measures are taken by the Government the
Hopi Indian will soon be a charge upon the Government, or objects of
charity for the public to consider."

Early in Daniel's first year as superintendent he followed Crane's
procedures to force enrollment of Hotevila children in school. He made
a brief mention of this in his first report, but is more explicit in his
second, having written, "A year ago it became necessary to surround

[176]

Hotevila — *this village of 400 degenerates* — with a dozen employees and police, at two o'clock A.M., and at daylight take their children and place them in school."

During this same year of Daniel's administration serious trouble developed between the Hopi of Moencopi who, for some reason known only to Washington, were under the jurisdiction of the Western Navajo Agency at Tuba City, and the people of Hotevila, who were answerable to Keams Canyon. Daniel stated that, although there had been no open break so far, "When it comes, if it ever does, I shall handle it without outside assistance." His actions in this matter aroused the ire of the superintendent at Tuba City who was beginning to feel that Daniel was overextending his authority.

When he wrote about problems pertaining to law and order on the Hopi Reservation his initial report reads like a bitter echo of something Leo Crane might have written: "The most pusilanimous nuisances we have to contend with are the pseudo archaeologists, anthropologists, ethnologists, artists, the little flickering tallow-dip literary lights, and the sudden rich misfits laboring under the delusion that law and order and Government officials in the field are evils to be put up with, if the cheap glare of wealth or political bluff doesn't work. The country gets its misinformation about Indians largely from this accumulation of intellectual discard."

There was at this time growing pressure upon the Bureau of Indian Affairs to prohibit all Indian "dances." Daniel, curiously enough, during his first year in Tusayan reported that, with the exception of the Snake Dance, he saw nothing very objectionable in them. "So far as I have been permitted to judge," he wrote, "they are mostly comic in nature." How little he understood what he was observing!

As for the Snake Ceremony, he offered a most astonishing and unique method of persuading the Hopi to abandon it. He suggested that the Smithsonian Institute make an authentic detailed photographic record of it and other Hopi ceremonies. Then reputable motion-picture companies should be allowed to film them under the supervision of the government "so that the general public could know all about them without affording the expense of a trip to the reservation."

Such commercialization of the ceremonies would certainly put an end to them, in Daniel's opinion.

By his second year at Keams Canyon, Daniel's policy for administrating the complex problems of the entire Moqui Reservation was well established. Foreseeing future needs, he renewed Crane's request for a new jail. Although Daniel did not suggest that it should be a sanitary one, he did specify that it should be large enough to take care of twenty prisoners.

At the urging of the reservation doctors he, to his lasting credit, urged a proper lighting plant for the hospital, detailing the danger to patients, doctors, and nurses while administering highly explosive anesthetics under open lights.

His growing regard for the Navajo, in contrast to his deepening dislike of the conservatives among the Hopi, was obvious in his report of July 25, 1921: "It is with unalloyed satisfaction that your attention is invited to the commendable conduct of the Navajo Indians in this jurisdiction." He then recounted at considerable length how he dealt with the conservative Hopi, who desired only to be let alone to live their own lives in their own way. He wrote almost eloquently of the contempt he felt for them.

Daniel was jubilant at being able to report on the numbers of Hopi who were deserting their homes on the mesa tops to live in new houses below the mesas. These movements, he wrote, "indicate advancement toward higher civilization," concluding, "they cannot take the Kiva with them and without it, Pagan ceremonies must sink into oblivion."

The Hopi were not the only residents to move down closer to their fields and more abundant water supplies. Daniel reported that a large group of the Tewa people of Hano laid out a new village for themselves adjacent to the excellent springs in the Wepo Wash, west of the Walpi mesa.

Agricultural experiments which had been undertaken by the University of Arizona's College of Agriculture in Tucson were now discontinued because, according to Daniel, the experts admitted that they could teach the Hopi nothing about growing food plants suited to the Hopi country.

The most dramatic event during Daniel's regime occurred at Hotevila on June 10, 1920. Like Superintendent Burton's ill-advised haircutting episode, it got unexpected publicity which resulted in widespread opposition throughout the country by organizations and individuals interested in the welfare of the Indian.

Daniel's own report of this incident is frank, although he quite understandably neglects to mention some of the more violent and inhumane incidents that took place. Again we quote him precisely:

On June 10, 1921, we went to Hotevilla village with eight employees and seven policemen, all well armed with revolvers, and requested the Indians to meet me in the plaza for conference. They refused to come out, as I expected from previous experience, but following my invariable rule to first explain my object before taking drastic action, I ordered our people to go and each bring a man into the plaza. After assembling about 25 by force, I explained clearly, the purpose and methods of delousing and told them I preferred that they come voluntarily and take the treatment, but if they did not, they would be taken by force. I also told them I had heard their threat against certain employes and I warned them if they attempted violence, I'd wipe up the face of the earth with them.

The next morning by seven o'clock, about seven or eight well meaning men and women presented themselves and were bathed and their clothing deloused. At eight o'clock, not another Indian appeared. I then issued hickory buggy spokes to my delousing party and police. Directing them not to use their revolvers, except as a last resort in self defense, we then went to the village, where all able-bodied men were stationed in and on top of certain houses (two or three) the women and children on other house tops. I again called upon them to come down peaceably, and gave them three minutes to comply. (May as well have given them a month.) Upon their failing to do so, I directed my force to bring them down. After about forty men had been forced to the street, they refused to budge, and suddenly turned in a threatening manner and show of resistance, when a policeman undertook to hand cuff a man. At this point the spokes came into play, and several heads were cracked. The ring leader was knocked down and received a scalp wound which bled freely; this lasted perhaps a minute or two, when I cautioned all my men to ease up on the use of the spokes. I then personally examined the man lying on the ground, and found he was not seriously hurt, but "playing possum" to excite others. I called the blacksmith to my side and directed him to get my car and bring the doctor to dress the fellow's head. The man was removed to a house a few feet away. We then commenced the task of dragging and shoving till we finally got them strung out toward the School, where the bathing equipment was, and where, in a short time they were deloused and their clothing boiled. We returned to the village for the next lot. At this time, the doctor arrived from Oraibi and was refused permission to see the man who was knocked down, until the house was cleared. The doctor pronounced the hurt superficial and of no consequence. I believe applied some simple remedy and left.

The second lot was not quite so hard to handle, and by noon, practically all able-bodied men were deloused. In the afternoon, the balance of the women were brought up on foot. Old men and women and cripples were brought by team, and handled with utmost care.

Only men were handled in one building; the women in another building two hundred yards away, by female employes and assistants, until they developed such offensive opposition that I detailed a squad of men to assist; then they were put into the bathing vats, without removing their clothing. I desire to state here that those women wear only a one piece garment, and putting them into the solution without disrobing was as effective as stripping them and boiling their clothing. Black leaf 40 (sheep dip) was used and it was as effective, and in many respects better than kerosene. It does not blister and is easier and quicker to handle.

There was no attempt by any employe to make an indecent exposure of any woman or child, and the only objectionable feature of the work was the obscene and revolting vituperation the Indian women hurled at the employes.

The language of the English speaking Indian man as applied to every one, Indians and Whites, assisting in the work, was too filthy to be recorded verbatim here.

A check of the Census, when the day's work was done, showed fifteen had escaped. The following Monday these were routed out of the rocks and other hiding places by the police, brought in and deloused.

We prepared their baths at the proper temperature, bathed them, and boiled and dried their clothes for them while they were being bathed. Yet they had to be driven or dragged to the tub, and forced into it like some wild beast, unblessed with human intelligence. Pure unadulterated fanatical perversity is the only explanation.[40]

Some months later this writer found himself personally involved in the web of events spun by Daniel's recent actions at Hotevila. As leader of a boys' outdoor organization I had been camping for a few days at Old Oraibi. A founder member of the Indian Welfare League and the National Association to Help the Indian, I had long been particularly interested in the plight of the Hopi. During this visit to Oraibi I had had several talks with Tewaquaptewa and other leaders at Old Oraibi, and had learned of the recent incident at Hotevila.

One morning, James Kewanytewa, who often acted as interpreter, brought Herman Mashaquaptewa, a young Hopi from Hotevila to see me. Mashaquaptewa spoke English well and gave me further particulars as to Daniel's treatment of his people.

The next day I visited Hotevila with Mashaquaptewa to ascertain first-hand what really had happened there. I was fortunate in contacting Violet Pooleyama, a young Hopi woman who had witnessed the whole affair. For some time she had been working for one of the leading families of Flagstaff and, as a result, spoke English fairly well. Her account of the affair differed very significantly from the one Daniel gave in his report. These excerpts from my interview with her, which were carefully noted at the time, contain many of the decidedly unpleasant incidents which were not reported by Superintendent Daniel:

Some weeks ago Agent Daniel from Keams Canyon came to Hotevilla with all the white men he could get and some Indians under his hire. He told us there was sickness everywhere in Arizona and that he had orders to spray our houses and to see that we all took a bath in disinfectant. These white men sprayed our houses, often spoiling great amounts of our corn and dried meat. Then they made a big bath like the one they dip the sheep in. They filled this with sheep-dip. They started putting our men and boys in it just as if they were sheep. They took the women and girls and put them in it, too. When the women fought with them they often threw them into the sheep-dip clothes and all. Sometimes they tore the clothes off the women and girls. It was not good for those men to look upon the bodies of our women and girls. They took old grandmothers and little girls — they took everybody — and threw them in the dirty sheep-dip. All the time the white men were laughing and making fun of them.

Our old chief, Youkeoma, and the few men who were in the village when this happened tried to stop the white men, but they were unable to stop them. The white men were armed with heavy sticks like baseball bats and they would hit our men over the head with them. One man, Tuvenqumbtewa, was hit over the head so hard that his head was split open and he was dead for nearly two hours. When he came alive again they put handcuffs on him and on another man and hung them to the horn of a saddle and sent them to the jail in Keams Canyon. Because they fought against the white men doing these things to us, ten of our men of our village were put in jail in Keams Canyon. They are still there. Besides the two men they hung from the saddle of the horse, they took to jail our chief, Youkeoma, and Henry Dalamanewa, Ralph Lomawyma, William Bahesie, Cochmasa, and Sacgyesva.

Do you wonder now that the people of Hotevilla tremble when they see white people coming to our village? Why don't they leave us to ourselves? We were so happy before the white man came, but if we must go to school, why don't they build us a school with all the grades somewhere near our villages so that we can see our children every day? If Washington must send a man to look after us, why cannot we have a good man, a kind man who understands the Hopi people?

The fact that the National Association to Help the Indian and the Indian Welfare League, which numbered among their members such well-known writers and scientists as Edward S. Curtis, Stewart Edward White, James Willard Schultz, Marah Ellis Ryan, Eugene Manlove Rhodes, the actor William S. Hart, Attorney Ida May Adams, and John Adams Comstock, Director of the Southwest Museum, became interested in the struggle between the conservative Hopi and the representatives of the United States Government infuriated Daniels. When these organizations gave considerable publicity to Violet Pooleyama's statement, using fictitious names to prevent retaliation against her and her family, he commented in his next yearly report:

Considerable unrest and trouble at Hotevilla and Oraibi has been created during the year by Harry C. James, an impostor operating under the cloak of the National Association to Help the North American Indian. It is believed his offense comes clearly under the intent of the United States Statutes, concerning offenses against the peace and tranquility of the United States. It is believed with the firm support of the Indian Office, the local reservation authorities will eliminate James' iniquitous work and its effect upon the Indians.

This statement is followed by the terse remark, "Emry Kopta, an itinerant artist, has been a disturbing element among the Hopis at Polacca. He has been eliminated, having left the reservation June 15, 1922."

These remarks were followed by the recommendation that "no permit should be issued to Artists and literary people for longer than ninety days, subject to renewal. This, of course, not to apply to representatives of the Smithsonian Institute and recognized scientific Institutes."

The publicity given the sheep-dip incident at Hotevila the year before resulted in so many protests to the Indian Bureau that in October, 1921, Youkeoma and his followers were released from the Keams Canyon jail. Daniel claimed that Youkeoma gave his word that he would never again disobey government regulations or the law. Supporters of the old chief denied this, claiming that Youkeoma did not understand enough English to knowingly make such an agreement.

In September, 1921, Hugh L. Scott revisited the Hopi country. A major general and a member of the Board of Indian Commissioners, Scott was but one of several government officials who descended upon Daniel during the months covered by his 1922 report. Among them were Charles H. Burke, Commissioner of Indian Affairs; Harvey B. Peairs, Chief Supervisor of Education; T. B. Roberts, Sr., Chief Inspector, and L. A. Dorrington, Inspector. Very evidently Washington was beginning to feel the pressure from growing public indignation over more than " a century of dishonor." Daniel closed his report with the declaration that the visits had lent him and his staff "new life and encouragement."

Shortly after General Scott left Tusayan, stories quickly circulated to the effect that he had recommended that the best way to settle the problems at Oraibi was to forcibly evacuate all the Hopi living in the old village and then destroy it — obliterate it from the mesa top, thus forcing its remaining inhabitants to scatter out to homes below the mesa. Such a course of action, it was presumed, would deal a death blow to religion-clan solidarity and so make easier the work of the missionaries and also would help to make the traditional Hopi more amenable to the demands of Washington.

If General Scott made such a suggestion it is not in the account of his visit contained in the published report of the Board of Indian Commissioners for the year ending June 30, 1922. It seems probable that Scott may well have made such a statement more or less off the top of his head, so to speak. Whatever the truth of the matter may be, the story soon reached various organizations which were by then waging a dynamic campaign for reform of United States Indian policies. It served them well as propaganda material.

Despite the reassurance voiced by Superintendent Daniel following the visits of Commissioner Burke, General Scott, and other officials of the Indian Bureau, he still seems to have been deeply concerned over Tewaquaptewa's growing contacts with people throughout the country interested in the Indian. Tewaquaptewa was arrested apparently on the complaint of a missionary that the chief had thrown him out of an Oraibi house. Frank Siemptiwa of Moencopi was also jailed with the chief at

Keams Canyon. While Tewaquaptewa and Siemptiwa were still in jail, Daniel, accompanied by the usual policemen, called a meeting of all Oraibi people at the schoolhouse below the mesa. Police were sent to round up any Hopi who were not there when the meeting was called to order. Through his interpreter Daniel asked why some of those present had been meeting and talking with me. Tewaquaptewa's deputy chief told him that they didn't want to discuss the matter unless I was present. Whereupon Daniel became very angry and hit the man and when he persisted, seized him by the hair and threw him out the door.

When order was restored, Daniel informed them that, as they all considered themselves loyal Americans, they could now prove it by signing a paper which he would send on to Washington. Despite very considerable reluctance on the part of many of the Hopi present, several were persuaded to sign this "pledge of loyalty." However, when Nasayungsi, Tewaquaptewa's wife, and his sister and mother-in-law came forward to sign they insisted on looking the paper over carefully. They spotted the name Harry C. James and realized that something was wrong and that the document was no mere pledge of their loyalty. They cried out their concern, and the meeting was interrupted by great disorder as the three women absolutely refused to sign.

Daniel threatened that all those who supported Tewaquaptewa would be arrested and that he intended to keep Tewaquaptewa in jail "until his hair was white." Finally Daniel and his staff supporters and policemen left for Keams Canyon.

Fearing that his action in jailing Tewaquaptewa and Siemptiwa, without even a nod in the direction of the Bill of Rights, and that other of his high-handed actions as superintendent might bring additional protests to Washington, Daniel attempted to use the "loyalty pledge," which several Oraibi people had signed, as a means of discrediting me, as well as the organizations I was connected with. Thanks to the usual efficiency of the Hopi "moccasin telegraph," word spread to all the villages as to what had really happened at the Oraibi meeting. As a result any possible value the document might have had for that purpose was negated.

According to several Hopi familiar with events of that time, Daniel then let it be known that he would like to be given a Hopi name obviously to demonstrate to his superiors the popularity he enjoyed among the Hopi. In a short time he did indeed become known to them by a nickname — "Cheevato," a Mexican term for billygoat. To the Hopi the word carried unflattering connotations as to body odor and unrestrained sex life.

Daniel began to realize that he was losing whatever respect the Hopi may have had for him. When visiting various villages he would see many of the people clasp their hands over their mouths to hide their laughter in the old Hopi and Oriental fashion.

He was embittered when Commissioner Burke bowed to mounting pressure and released Tewaquaptewa and Siemptiwa — action Daniel knew full well would be considered by the Hopi as a repudiation by Washington of his conduct. On his way back to Oraibi, Tewaquaptewa composed a song — "Midnight Journey" — telling of his arrest and his release, a song which several Hopi learned to sing in the days that followed.

Daniel seems to have become more and more irascible. He antagonized the well-known trader, C. N. Cotton of Gallup, who urged his dismissal. He quarreled with several of his top employes, as well as with Byron A. Sharp, Superintendent of the Western Navajo School at Tuba City, who had jurisdiction over the Hopi of Moencopi.

It is amusing to note that Daniel's low opinion of artists was no lower than that formed of Daniel by Charles M. Russell, famous western artist, who visited the Hopi country in 1921. A few weeks after meeting Daniel at the Snake Ceremony, Russell gave James Willard Schultz and me a colorful account of their encounter:

"Daniel was swellin' around in a Palm Beach suit and carryin' a cane. I heard him remark, 'Snake Dance! I'd snake dance 'em if I had my way about it. I'd bring a troop of soldiers and make them stop it or kill 'em all off.' "

This made Russell so mad, he said, that he confronted Daniel with, "You sure have a lot of sympathy for these Indians. They are only worshiping their gods as is their right. Seems to me you are not the right man to be in charge of them. You are nothing but a damned sissy dude."

When Daniel discovered who Russell was and that he was with the famous writer, Mary Roberts Rinehart and her party, he searched out Russell and tried to crawfish on what he had said, but Russell was not impressed.

Growing public concern over the plight of the American Indian finally made even the Bureau of Indian Affairs realize that a man like Daniel could no longer be tolerated as superintendent of an Indian reservation. In 1924 he was replaced by Edgar K. Miller. In that year too, at long last, the name of the agency was changed from Moqui to Hopi.

Opposition to
Hopi Religious Ceremonies

THE APPOINTMENT of Albert Bacon Fall as Secretary of the Interior by President Harding in 1921 gave grave concern to all friends of the Indian, as well as to such Indians in New Mexico as were familiar with Fall's reputation. Shortly after his appointment a series of moves made by Fall and his associates gave convincing proof that these fears were more than well justified. Few people realized that, along with various schemes to defraud the Indians of their land, oil, and mineral rights, would be injected a plan by Fall's Commissioner of Indian Affairs, Charles H. Burke, to deny to the Indian what freedom of religion he still enjoyed.

So coldly contrived and so widespread were Fall's schemes that all organizations working for the benefit of the Indian had little trouble in rousing the conscience of the white man as it had never been aroused before. Many new associations were formed, such as the Indian Defense Association, which played vital roles in the fight for Indian rights. Under prodding of the late Stella Atwood, the General Federation of Women's Clubs took a most important part in what was rapidly becoming a national crusade. The multiple problems of the Hopi became part of this intensive movement to gain a new deal for the Indian.

Freedom of religion, as provided for in the Bill of Rights, rarely, until recent times, was even considered as applying to religions of the Indians of the United States. In fact, as already has been stressed, it was government policy to aid missionaries in converting the Indians to one or another of the Christian denominations. Definite stipulations curtailing Indian freedom of religion were contained in the official Bureau of Indian Affairs regulations, often referred to as its "Religious Crimes Code."

The important Sun Dance ceremony of the Plains Indians was strongly opposed by missionaries and government officials who grossly misunderstood what it was all about. Their opposition led to the enactment of a regulation which, although aimed particularly at the Sun

Mixed Kachina Dance at Old Oraibi in the 1930s. This ceremony would have been banned, had Commissioner Burke and his cohorts had their way.

Dance, concluded that "all similar dances and so-called religious ceremonies, shall be considered 'Indian offences' " punishable by "incarceration in the agency prison for a period not exceeding thirty days."

With regulations of this kind, and with many precedents to justify their actions, it is not to be wondered at that such superintendents as Crane and Daniel felt quite within their authority in jailing Hopi leaders in the manner they did.

A serious and specific threat to the Hopi way of life came in the 1920s in a decidedly indirect manner.

In 1922 Secretary Fall and his associates succeeded in getting the Senate of the United States to pass the so-called Bursum bill which, if enacted into law, would have cheated the Pueblo Indians of New Mexico out of much of their most valuable agricultural land. In the estimation of many persons the sweeping provisions of this bill would have been a virtual death blow to many of the pueblos. For the first time since the famous Pueblo Rebellion in 1680 the people of the New Mexico Pueblos joined in a united front to meet the crisis. The Council of All the New Mexico Pueblos was formed.

The land-grab provisions of the Bursum bill were so contemptible that the various organizations interested in Indian affairs, along with the women's clubs and many influential church groups, raised such a hue and cry that Secretary Fall and Indian Bureau officials decided that they must take counteraction to discredit and undermine the high reputation enjoyed by the Pueblo Indians throughout the country. Realizing that their ceremonial religious life was the very foundation of Pueblo Indian security, an insidious plan was conceived to destroy it.

Commissioner Burke led off with a velvet-glove approach. Early in the spring of 1923 he issued a communication which read:

TO ALL INDIANS:

Not long ago I held a meeting of Superintendents, Missionaries and Indians, at which the feeling of those present was strong against Indian dances, as they are usually given, and against so much time as is often spent by the Indians in a display of their old customs at public gatherings held by the whites. From the views of this meeting and from other information I feel that something must be done to stop the neglect of stock, crops, gardens, and home interests caused by these dances or by celebrations, pow-wows, and gatherings of any kind that take the time of the Indians for many days.

Now, what I want you to think about very seriously is that you must first of all try to make your own living, which you cannot do unless you work faithfully and take care of what comes from your labor, and go to dances or other meetings only when your home work will not suffer by it. I do not want to deprive you of decent amusements or occasional feast days, but you should not do evil or foolish things or take so much time for these occasions. No good comes from your "giveaway" custom at dances and it

H. R. Voth photo; Field Museum of Natural History

Lancers of the Maru Ceremony at Old Oraibi, another of the ceremonies nominated for banning.

should be stopped. It is not right to torture your bodies or to handle poisonous snakes in your ceremonies. All such extreme things are wrong and should be put aside and forgotten. You do yourselves and your families great injustice when at dances you give away money and other property, perhaps clothing, a cow, a horse or a team and wagon, and then after an absence of several days go home to find everything going to waste and yourselves with less to work with than you had before.

I could issue an order against these useless and harmful performances, but I would much rather have you give them up of your own free will and, therefore, I ask you now in this letter to do so. I urge you to come to an understanding and an agreement with your Superintendent to hold no gatherings in the months when the seedtime, cultivation and the harvest need your attention, and at other times to meet for only a short period and to have no drugs, intoxicants, or gambling, and no dancing that the Superintendent does not approve.

If at the end of one year the reports which I receive show that you are doing as requested, I shall be very glad for I know that you are making progress in other and more important ways, but if the reports show that you reject this plea, then some other course will have to be taken.

With best wishes for your happiness and success, I am,

Sincerely yours,
CHARLES H. BURKE,
Commissioner.

To win public support for his decision to abolish the Indian's religion — that of the Pueblos particularly — the Indian Bureau sent out men to gather information designed to make out that Indian religious observances were pornographic in the extreme. The material they delivered was undoubtedly just what Commissioner Burke wanted. It was filthy — all 193 pages of it. Competent persons who read it considered it unprintable. None of this material was submitted to the objective scrutiny of a single ethnologist or Indian leader capable of passing judgment on its authenticity. Nevertheless, copies of it were widely circulated by the Indian Bureau to churchmen, editors, leaders among the women's clubs, and similar organizations.

Eventually the Indian Bureau forbade the excusing from school of the boys of Taos Pueblo to participate in their initiation ceremonies. But the ceremonies went on, and the entire governing council of the pueblo was thrown into jail.

The close ties that have always existed between the people of the New Mexican pueblos and the Hopi brought news of these happenings to Tusayan almost as soon as they occurred. The Hopi became apprehensive, knowing full well the attitude of missionaries and government officials toward their own religious observances.

Attempts were made by government officials to make it difficult for visitors to the Hopi villages to meet Hopi other than those who were Christian converts or of proven loyalty to Indian Bureau policies. Every effort was made to confuse and mislead leaders among the Hopi who had developed friendly and sympathetic contacts with off-reservation whites; in some cases this resulted in serious, but fortunately only temporary, misunderstandings.

Two of Tewaquaptewa's brothers, who used the names given them by white schoolteachers, Burt Fredericks and Monroe Fredericks, made trips away from the reservation on behalf of their brother who had also been given a white man's name — Wilson Fredericks. Burt Fredericks and Tewaquaptewa went to Santa Fe where they had many meetings with Margaret McKittrick and other members of the New Mexico Association for Indian Affairs. With his brother as interpreter, Tewaquaptewa made a long statement which Margaret McKittrick typed out. Copies of this statement were circulated among the various organizations to aid the Hopi, and this was of great help in clarifying the situation which Washington was doing everything in its power to obscure.

Tewaquaptewa and his supporters were particularly galled to learn that a third brother, Charles Fredericks, who had become a convert to Christianity, had joined with five other converted Hopi in a campaign to break down Hopi religious solidarity. To this end they went so far as to urge Daniel's successor, Superintendent Edgar J. Miller, to throw Tewaquaptewa into jail.

Franklin Nooma of Moencopi wrote to the Association on Indian Affairs in Phoenix stating that Charles Fredericks, upon returning to Oraibi from his meeting with Superintendent Miller, had informed Tewaquaptewa that there was a warrant out for his arrest as well as that of his brother, Burt, and of Harry C. James. Nooma asked the backing of the Phoenix Association in helping Tewaquaptewa "to retain his religion."

Monroe Fredericks came in California to visit and also to meet with members of the Indian Welfare League and the National Association to Help the Indian. Authors Edward S. Curtis, Marah Ellis Ryan, and James Willard Schultz, leading members of these organizations, were already deeply concerned over the government decision to stop Indian ceremonials. This fact assured Monroe Fredericks of an understanding and sympathetic hearing. Contacts were made by these southern California organizations with friends in the Indian Defense Association in northern California — influential people such as Maynard Dixon, Aurelia Reinhardt, James Swinnerton, and Walter V. Woehlke, who immediately threw their influence and help into the campaign.

More and more news came to the Hopi of the Indian Bureau's campaign to stamp out the religion of the Pueblo people. Bureau officials left no doubt in Hopi minds that a similar campaign would soon be waged against their religion also.

Concern among the Hopi reached a crisis in 1922 and an urgent plea was sent to us to meet immediately with several Hopi leaders at Winslow. It was feared that serious harassment and likely even arrest by Indian Bureau personnel would result if such a meeting were held on the reservation. The distinguished author and authority on Indian affairs, James Willard Schultz, went to Winslow as the representative of these various organizations. There he met with a dozen or so Hopi from different villages. Many statements were made to Schultz which indicated the widespread use of threats to persuade Hopi leaders to agree to Commissioner Burke's request that they give up their ceremonies.

A dramatic moment came after the meeting had gone on for an hour or two when one of the older Hopi jumped to his feet and declared fervently that he would rather be shot down by the white man while "doing his religion" than to try to live on without it. Unanimous approval was expressed by everyone present.

Schultz then assured the Hopi that they had many good white friends who would stand back of them in this decision. He also told them that Indian Bureau officials, by their vicious campaign against the Indian's right to worship his own gods in his own way, had gone to such violent extremes that they had aroused the antagonism of influential people all over the United States. He urged the Hopi leaders to continue with their religious ceremonies in spite of whatever harassment they might be subjected to by Indian Bureau personnel.

Immediately upon his return to Los Angeles a meeting was called of the members of the Indian Welfare League and its companion organization, the National Association to Help the Indian. W. V. Woehlke of the Indian Defense Association of Northern California attended as a representative of that organization, Schultz gave a detailed report of the Winslow meeting, and a decision was made by those present that the organizations they were associated with must back the Hopi to the limit in their determination to hold fast to their right to practice their own religion in their own way. Word of this action was sent to various leaders among the Hopi.

For some years Los Angeles attorney Ida May Adams, a member of the Indian Welfare League, had been determined that every Indian in the United States must have the rights and protections that full citizenship would automatically confer upon them. To this end she staged a one-woman fight with the result that on June 2, 1924, the Congress passed what must be one of the shortest pieces of legislation in its long-worded history — "That all non-citizen Indians born within the territorial limits of the United States be and they are hereby declared to be citizens of the United States."

Now that all Indians were full-fledged citizens it was hoped that the Indian Bureau would recognize their right to religious freedom under the Bill of Rights. However, that right was not to be so easily and quickly won. The granting of citizenship to Indians did serve to further awaken the American people to the un-American conditions under which the Indian had for so long been forced to live.

Word of the passage of the citizenship bill was greeted with mixed emotions by the Hopi. Concern was felt that it might be a trick of the Indian Bureau to thrust responsibilities upon them which they could not and should not carry. On the other hand, Hopi who had been to school and were familiar with the provisions of the Bill of Rights began to entertain hope that the attainment of full citizenship might indeed help them in the retention of their Hopi way of life which was so intimately bound up with their religious beliefs and practices.

Following the meeting with Schultz in Winslow and the assurances of support from individuals and associations from all over the United States, the Hopi stood firm and carried on their religious observances as before. Although outspoken and abusive disapproval was voiced by Indian Bureau officials and missionaries, seemingly no apparent moves were made to interfere. However, whenever an opportunity arose to harass the religious leaders in the performance of their duties it was taken advantage of. Often when information reached the agency that a certain village was preparing for a ceremony, one or more of the important religious leaders of that ceremony would be summoned to Keams Canyon for a meeting with the superintendent at the very time their presence in their kiva was of paramount importance, and thus that particular ceremony would have to be abandoned.

During these days of conflict between the entrenched bureaucracy of the Indian Bureau friendly to the rapacious Albert Fall administration and the forces among the whites determined to protect Indian rights and secure reform of the bureau, the Hopi too became torn with bitter dissent. It was the old story — hatred leading to hatred; violence, to violence. Passions were engendered that led to actions contrary to all Hopi philosophy. Many Christian converts became zealots and in fanatic zeal gathered up priceless ceremonial objects and burned them before the horrified eyes of fellow Hopi.

In 1923 Secretary Fall was forced to resign, but not until 1926 was the infamous Bursum bill defeated. It must be noted that in 1929 he was sent to prison for accepting a bribe while he had been Secretary of the Interior.

In 1927 Fall's successor, Hubert Work, under threat of a Senate investigation of Indian affairs, requested the reputable Brookings Institution of Washington to make an investigation of Indian affairs at a cost of $125,000 which was privately subscribed. When the Brookings report, *The Problems of Indian Administration,* was made public it supported the Indian demands for reform. Even before this, however, the Senate, in spite of stiff opposition by the Indian Bureau, adopted a resolution by Senator William King of Utah and Representative James A. Frear of Wisconsin calling for a Senate investigation of Indian affairs.

The Brookings report and the results of the Senate investigation led to the resignations of Commissioner Burke and Assistant Indian Commissioner Edgar B. Merritt, who had been a dominating influence in the Indian Bureau since 1921.

It can well be said that a "new deal" for the American Indian began after these reports became widely known and with the appointment by President Herbert Hoover of Ray Lyman Wilbur as Secretary of the Interior and Quaker Charles J. Rhodes as Commissioner of Indian Affairs.

Unfortunately, as far as the Hopi were concerned, it took a long time for the reforms which these two men of integrity initiated to filter down through the entrenched bureaucracy of the Indian Bureau of the agency at Keams Canyon.

Scientists in Tusayan

DURING THE YEARS when the Hopi of Third Mesa were having such constant trouble with the coterie of bureaucrats which represented the Bureau of Indian Affairs at Keams Canyon the annual reports of the superintendents contained little pertaining to the people of First and Second Mesa.

One reason for this was that the people of these villages had been most fortunate in that among their first contacts with white Americans had been men of the caliber of Alexander M. Stephen and Jesse Walter Fewkes.

The leaders of these villages were most helpful to Stephen and Fewkes in making possible their intensive studies of the Hopi way of life. In return, Stephen and Fewkes were always available for counsel to aid the Hopi in meeting the many problems that the rapidly changing times presented to them. The fact that Fewkes was a highly respected official of the Bureau of American Ethnology, with excellent connections in Washington, made superintendents like Crane and Daniel unwilling to engage in the ruthless treatment they felt safe in meting out to Hopi of the more distant villages.

Alexander M. Stephen was born in Scotland and graduated from the University of Edinburgh. In 1862 he was mustered into a New York infantry regiment as a private and served with it until his honorable discharge as a 1st lieutenant in 1866. He came to Tusayan about 1881. He and Thomas Keam, the trader, became friends. Stephen first became interested in the Navajo and learned their language. This served as his avenue of communication with the Hopi until he became fluent in their language.

When Victor Mindeleff came to Tusayan to carry on the fieldwork which resulted in his "A Study of Pueblo Architecture," Stephen was of invaluable assistance. Mindeleff wrote of him, "He has enjoyed unusual facilities for the work, having lived for a number of years in Tusayan and possessed the confidence of the principal priests."

Jesse Walter Fewkes, one of the most distinguished of American ethnologists, first visited the Hopi in 1890. He was then engaged in his first scientific fieldwork as Director of the Hemenway Expedition, going first to Zuñi and then to Tusayan. At Keams Canyon he met Stephen and they became close friends and collaborators.

In fact, School Superintendent Ralph P. Collins soon felt that Fewkes and Stephen were having a bad influence on the Hopi by becoming far too friendly with them and that their interest in the Hopi religious ceremonials would oppose "progress." Collins was particularly annoyed by the fact that Fewkes and Stephen were advising the Hopi not to desert their mesa-top homes.

Fewkes was born in Newton, Massachusetts, in 1850, graduated with honor from Harvard in 1875, and was elected to Phi Beta Kappa. While studying with Agassiz he determined to make his life work the study of marine biology. Postgraduate work earned him his Ph.D. He spent three years studying zoology at the University of Leipzig during which time he did considerable fieldwork along the Mediterranean coast. In 1888 while on a trip to California, he developed his first interest in ethnology which eventually led to his appointment as Director of the Hemenway Expedition and in turn to Tusayan.

Years later Dr. Fewkes recalled that first visit to the Hopi and it is interesting to compare conditions as he found them then with those of today. At that time virtually all the people of First Mesa still lived in their villages on the top of the mesa. They had no tables, chairs, iron stoves, or lamps. Many of the houses were still entered by ladders reaching through the roof. Very few persons spoke English and even they spoke it very poorly. The first trading post was kept by a man named Ramón and it was stocked only with the simplest of staple commodities such as calico, sugar, salt, tobacco and coffee. These goods were purchased in Santa Fe and were freighted across the desert in wagons, the wheels of which were solid disks of wood. This trading post was located near Coyote Spring.

At that time the spring, which is now named after Tom Polacca of Hano, was known as *Tawapa,* Sun Spring, and Fewkes was informed that at the time of the Pueblo Rebellion in 1680 the *santos* belonging to the mission were buried near it.

On that first visit Dr. Fewkes was shown a row of marks on a cliff above the north trail to the top of First Mesa. These marks indicated, he was told, the number of Utes killed in their last war with the Hopi. Pointed out to him also were the deep niches in the edge of the mesa through which Hopi warriors shot their arrows at the Utes below.

At the first Snake Ceremony observed by Fewkes there were only about a dozen white visitors and these were chiefly cowboys from ranches near Flagstaff, Winslow, and Holbrook.

Fewkes also stated that Keams Canyon was named after William and not Thomas — as is so generally believed — and in this he was correct, but he was in error in thinking these two men were brothers. Copies of their birth registrations obtained from England by Don Perceval show that they were cousins.

Although drawings in Fewkes's sketchbook awakened some concern among the Hopi during his first visit, he soon won the confidence of the people of First Mesa and became known among them as Nakwipi (Boiled Medicine).

Although Fewkes was not allowed to accompany the men and boys on their hunts for snakes for the Snake Ceremony, he was allowed to witness those parts of the ceremonial that took place in the kiva. In fact, he and Stephen by this time were so familiar with the details of the kiva altars that one night in the Antelope kiva he noted an error being made by Wiki in making the sand picture for the altar, an error which Wiki corrected as soon as it was pointed out to him. Fewkes even made a prayer-stick which was added to those later placed at Sheep Spring.

These incidents show clearly that Fewkes had been accepted with unusual trust and confidence by the ceremonial leaders of First Mesa. Kopeli and Supela of the Snake Society and Wiki and Kakapti of the Antelope Society were his particularly close friends.

Fewkes later did extensive and important work at Mesa Verde, Casa Grande, along the Gulf Coast of Mexico, and in the West Indies, but his interest in the Hopi remained constant. In 1918 he became chief of the Bureau of American Ethnology, but his administrative duties did not deter him from spending considerable time in the field.

His last fieldwork was the excavation and partial restoration of Elden Pueblo near Flagstaff, Arizona. On January 15, 1928, he retired because of physical disability, and on May 31, 1930, he died.

Following Fewkes's death his fellow ethnologist, Dr. Walter Hough, paid tribute to him as a truly outstanding scientist who was eminently fitted to do the important basic work he had accomplished during his lengthy career. Hough pointed out that his training as a zoologist had contributed significantly to his successful work as an anthropologist and, because his work was so largely based on personal observation, it would prove more and more valuable as time passed.

One could not meet Fewkes, either at his office in Washington or in the field, without being impressed by the richness and scope of his general culture. His horizons were not those of a man limited in any way by specialization, but swept wide as those of the Painted Desert country which he loved so well.

During his long life Fewkes received many honors — Knight of the Royal Order of Isabella the Catholic, a gold medal from King Oscar of Sweden, and membership in the National Academy of Science. He also was a fellow of the American Academy of Arts and Sciences and received the honorary degree of LL.D. from the University of Arizona. These were indeed high honors, but to Fewkes himself his most treasured distinction was his initiation into the Antelope and Flute religious societies of Walpi.

It seems likely that it was at Fewkes's suggestion that Stephen began his systematic recording of the daily life and ceremonies of the people of First Mesa. These notebooks, with their innumerable sketches, were edited and indexed by the indomitable Elsie Clews Parsons and published as *Hopi Journal* by Columbia University Press in 1936. These two volumes form one of the great treasure houses of Hopi lore. Unfortunately Stephen lived but a few years after his first meeting with Fewkes. He died at Keams Canyon in April, 1894.

It is a matter of considerable controversy even today as to the judgment of the Hopi ceremonial leaders in allowing Stephen and Fewkes — and even Fewkes's assistant, John G. Owens — to witness, record, and participate in the kiva preparations and ceremonials, as well as in the public performances of so many of the most important of the Hopi religious observances.

With the publication of their reports many of the leaders who had done so much to help Stephen and Fewkes gain the information contained therein began to have grave misgivings, especially when some of the missionaries excerpted certain passages which they used, out of context, for purposes of ridicule.

Fewkes published more than twenty-four books and articles about the Hopi. These, like Stephen's *Hopi Journal,* will remain as long as libraries exist — invaluable sources of reference for Hopi ceremonial leaders and for all students of the Hopi way of life.

In 1895 Fewkes began the excavation of the Sikyatki ruin, which is located about three miles northeast of Walpi. Among the workmen he engaged was a Tewa from Hano named Lesou. The hiring of Lesou, by one of those strange quirks of fate, had a significant and lasting effect on Hopi history.

Lesou's wife was Nampeyo, who was born in Hano in 1859 or 1860. Her father was very proud of his attractive baby daughter and often took her to Walpi to visit his mother, who was one of the pottery makers of that Hopi village. As the child grew older she became fascin-

Nampeyo, the most famous of Hopi pottery makers.

ated with watching the old Hopi woman at work and soon she was fashioning tiny pots of her own. By the time Nampeyo was a young woman she was considered one of the best of all the women on First Mesa who were making Hopi-type pottery. She was particularly skillful in design, and as her grandmother's eyesight began to fail she not only painted the designs on her own pots but on those of the old woman as well.

Long before he went to work with Fewkes, Lesou had become interested in the unusual designs found on pottery sherds at Sikyatki and other ancient ruins. He brought some of these fragments home with him to show Nampeyo. She was impressed with them and went with Lesou several times to Sikyatki to search for sherds bearing attractive bits of design. Fewkes became interested in her work and encouraged her to include some of the Sikyatki designs on her own work. Soon Nampeyo became so familiar with the Sikyatki style that she could use it freely in making her own pottery designs.

At first she was the only potter at Hano who was making true Hopi-type pottery, but as her work began to command good prices from the traders many followed her lead until there were several Tewa women making Hopi pottery. So successful was Nampeyo that Lesou visited other ancient ruins, such as Awatobi, to gather sherds bearing interesting designs which his wife could use in an attempt to make every vessel as unique as possible.

In 1875, when Nampeyo was a young woman of fifteen or sixteen, William H. Jackson, one of the earliest photographers to visit the western states, had come to Tusayan as a member of a United States Geological Survey party. Lugging his gigantic camera, which took 20 x 24-inch glass plates, to the top of First Mesa, he made a charming picture of Nampeyo.

With Jackson was E. A. Barber, a naturalist and special correspondent to *The New York Times*. The October 1, 1875, issue of the *Times* contained a letter from Barber describing their meeting with Nampeyo:

> As we dismounted from our animals at the entrance of the town, two men advanced to meet us — one, the foremost, a bright fine-looking young fellow . . . who took off his hat, shook hands, and in broken English, interspersed with Spanish, bade us welcome. . . . After we had shaken hands with several more of the prominent men, our mules were taken from us and lavishly fed with corn, and our host invited us to enter his house. Following up a ladder to the roof of the second story, and thence to a third by a series of stone steps, we passed through a low aperture into a room on this floor. Here we were bidden to be seated on a raised platform at one side of the room, on which had previously been placed robes made or woven from rabbit skins. Behind us a maiden was grinding corn in the primitive manner of the Moquis. Scarcely had we become seated when a beautiful girl approached and placed before us a large mat heaped with pee-kee, or bread. . . .
>
> The pretty Moqui princess who had waited upon us sat down in another part of the room and resumed her occupation of shelling corn from the cob into a dish. From where we were seated we could gaze upon her unobserved, and many an admiring glance was sent in that direction. She was of short stature and plump, but not unbecomingly so. Her eyes were almond shape, coal black, and possessed a voluptuous expression, which made them extremely fascinating. Her hair was arranged in that characteristic Oriental manner, peculiar to her tribe, which denoted her a maid [maiden]. It was parted in the center, from the front all the way down behind, and put up at the sides in two large puffs, which, although odd to us, nevertheless seemed to enhance her beauty. Her complexion was much lighter than that of her family, and every movement of her head or exquisitely molded hands and arms or bare little feet was one of faultless grace.
>
> All the surroundings of the place, our reception, and the presence of this damsel, so unexpected and novel to us, overwhelmed us for a while with mute surprise, and we could only eat and look about us, almost believing we were acting in a dream. We had entered abruptly and awkwardly enough, with our hats unremoved and our garments ragged, travel-stained, and dusty; but on the approach of the modest and beautiful Num-pa-yu — signifying in the Moqui tongue a snake that will not bite — every head was uncovered in a moment, and each of us felt clumsy, dirty, and ashamed of our torn garments and unshaven faces.

In 1898 the Santa Fe Railroad arranged with G. A. Dorsey, then Curator of Anthropology at the Field Museum in Chicago, and the Mennonite missionary H. R. Voth to bring Nampeyo and Lesou to Chicago where they made pottery at an exhibition held at the Coliseum. In 1904 and again in 1907 Nampeyo made pottery for the Fred Harvey people at the south rim of Grand Canyon, and in 1910 she and some members of her family visited Chicago once again to give exhibitions of Hopi pottery making. By this time Nampeyo had an international reputation and her work brought excellent prices and was in great demand.

Nampeyo began to have trouble with her eyes, but her excellent sense of touch made it possible for her to continue molding pottery which Lesou could decorate with a skill equal to that of his wife.

When Lesou died in 1932 Nampeyo continued to mold pottery which her daughters — already skilled pottery makers on their own — decorated for her so that, although having grown old and feeble with the passing years, Nampeyo remained active almost to the day of her death on July 20, 1942.

In assessing Nampeyo's contribution to the potter's art the Coltons wrote:

Nampeyo in her early days, may have made replicas of Sikyatki pottery, though this is extremely doubtful as the Indian artist rarely makes an exact copy. However, it is certain that the vessels that came on the market were not mere copies but had a living quality of their own. She caught the spirit of the old Sikyatki potters and used her own rare good taste in making compositional arrangement.

Her work was distinguished from that of Hopi potters by a sense of freedom and a fluid flowing quality of design, together with an appreciation of space as a background for her bold rhythmic forms. Nampeyo's interest did not confine itself to design and its application, but also included the basic forms of her pottery; she introduced the beautiful low wide shouldered jars characteristic of Sikyatki and other fine forms not heretofore in use.

Before Nampeyo's time, the Hopi potters' art was slowly fading. With the coming of the trader the use of china ware and cook pots, purchased at the store, were hastening the process. Decorated ware had already ceased being made at Second and Third Mesa, and Walpi and Sichomovi were keeping the art alive by supplying the other Hopi towns with mutton stew and corn meal mush bowls, just as they do today. There was then no outside market for Hopi pottery.

The financial success of Nampeyo stimulated a host of other women, including her own daughters, to use prehistoric motifs. This type of Hopi pottery soon was manufactured in great volume and was traded to the outside world.[41]

Nampeyo won a place in the history of the Hopi not alone because she revived an interest in the making of traditional Hopi-type pottery of high quality, but also because her success was responsible, to a

Fred Kabotie (left) and Paul Saufkie pointing out a Hopi
textile design to a class in silversmithing.

significant degree, for stimulating among the Hopi an interest in various
other Hopi arts and crafts.

Indian traders found a ready market for baskets, pottery, fabrics,
kachina dolls, and other crafts known to the Hopi for generations. During
the 1960s even the making of kachina dolls reached a high point in artistic
development, both in carving and decoration.

Fred Kabotie of Shongopovi began to show how Hopi pottery and
basket designs could be adapted to the manufacture of quite distinctive
silver work. This led to the formation of a Hopi Silvercraft Co-operative
Guild to encourage the maintenance of standards and aid in the development of adequate marketing. This guild was reorganized as the Hopi Arts
and Crafts and Silvercraft Cooperative Guild and has done much to
elevate Hopi arts and crafts to an enviable position.

The organization in 1973 of an artists' guild termed *Artist Hopid*
was a significant page in the history of Hopi art. The objectives were "to
experiment and test new ideas and techniques in art by using traditional
Hopi designs and concepts as well as their own concepts of the inner Hopi.
Eventually *Artist Hopid* hopes to document Hopi history and events
through visual art." Guild plans included exhibits to be held at the Hopi
Cultural Center and elsewhere.

The international success achieved by Fred Kabotie as a painter
stimulated an interest in painting among the Hopi. Otis Polelonema,
Delbridge Honanie, Bevins Yuyaheova, and Michael Kabotie (Fred
Kabotie's son) at Shongopovi, Raymond Naha at Polacca, Homer
Cooyama of New Oraibi, and others have made names for themselves in
the art world. Their paintings have been reproduced in magazines and
are found in galleries in many countries as well as in private collections.

Indian Reorganization
and the Hopi

THE MILLS OF THE GODS may grind slowly, but they are as speedy as computer-directed machines compared with the Congress of the United States when it comes to enacting legislation pertaining to the welfare of the American Indian.

The publicity that attended the notorious Albert Fall affair and his eventual arrest and imprisonment had at long last awakened the American conscience. The various organizations formed by whites to work specifically to gain Congressional action on behalf of the Indian were now joined by the Quakers and other religious groups. Mrs. Stella Atwood and her loyal supporters in the General Federation of Women's Clubs threw their very considerable persuasive power behind the crusade.

In Congress the Indian finally had gained the support of several influential members, among them Senator William A. King of Utah and Representative James A. Frear of Wisconsin. In 1934 the Wheeler-Howard Act, sponsored by Senator Burton K. Wheeler of Montana and Representative Edgar Howard of Nebraska, was presented to the Congress for its consideration.

The measure was at first subjected to a certain amount of ridicule because of its length of fifty-two printed pages. Those responsible for drawing up the measure had labored manfully to present in it a viable substitute for the more than one thousand pages of Indian law which had been accumulating in the law books down through the years. Considering this fact, the Wheeler-Howard Act must be considered something of a model for terseness in legal literature.

After debate which lasted several months, the bill was finally passed with certain amendments. This measure, now generally referred to as the Indian Reorganization Act, has often been spoken of, with some justice, as the Magna Carta of the Indians of the United States.

By this act the allotment system was abolished and Indian lands were to be protected from further loss. Also, Indian lands ruled to be surplus by the Indian Bureau and thrown open to white homesteaders, but not acquired by them, might be restored to the original Indian owners. Furthermore, lands needed by the Indians might be bought for them.

Tribes or portions of tribes might organize themselves for their mutual benefit and, when organized, enjoy self-government under federal guardianship. Tribes might incorporate for business purposes, and a revolving fund was made available to incorporated Indian communities to aid them in establishing themselves on a self-supporting basis.

A fund was established to provide scholarship loans to enable gifted Indians to secure advanced education.

The Secretary of the Interior could establish rules to make it easier for Indians to gain Civil Service protection.

Immediately upon passage of the Indian Reorganization Act officials and interpreters made extensive visits to the various reservations urging the tribes to take advantage of the provisions of the bill.

One section of the original bill as presented to the Congress provided for the consolidation of fractionally allotted lands and for the return of previously allotted lands to tribal ownership under a system which provided safeguards for individual property rights. Unfortunately, this section did not gain Congressional approval and was omitted from the final version of the bill. From the standpoint of the Hopi this was unfortunate as this provision might well have given security to them. The years that followed have demonstrated all too well that Hopi lands were, and still are, tragically in need of protection.

Most of the representatives of the government under Commissioner of Indian Affairs John Collier came to Tusayan ill-prepared for the job ahead of them. The great majority of them seemed to feel assured that — as the objectives of the administration, in their opinion, were all for the good of the Indian — the Hopi would welcome them and every suggestion they made with the utmost friendliness and with instant agreement. They had no understanding of the deep, long-lasting, and fundamental erosion of confidence in everything stemming from "Washington" which had existed since the Stars and Stripes first flew over Keams Canyon.

Many holdover government employees throughout the reservation were decidedly opposed to the policies and plans of the Collier administration and they worked full time to sow doubts and misgivings regarding it among the Hopi people. Some business interests in northern Arizona which had financial interests in trading posts on the reservation also did their full share in working up antagonism to that same end. So far as the Hopi were concerned, various programs devised for their supposed benefit by "Washington" under the provisions of the Indian Reorganization Act awakened their instant distrust.

In the years following passage of the act during which its various programs were being implemented, the three which distressed the Hopi gravely were: (1) the pressure to establish a Hopi Tribal Council, (2) a drastic program for livestock reduction, and (3) the establishment in 1943 of Land Management District Number Six, which gave the Hopi exclusive use of only about one-fourth of what they had been led to believe was their reservation. All three of these programs were enforced upon the Hopi with decidedly inadequate explanations.

Tribal Council Plan

The program that gave the gravest concern to a very large number of Hopi was that which provided for the establishment of legally constituted tribal councils. The Hopi had never had such a tribal organization. Each village had its own traditional government that was closely integrated with its complex clan organization. The Hopi feared that the establishment of such a tribal council as suggested in the Reorganization Act would jeopardize much, if not all, of the traditional secular-religious life of the villages.

Many whites advised against the council's establishment simply because they enjoyed economic benefits from the reservation and feared that a tribal council would lead to such Hopi independence as to curtail their profits.

As the months passed, the issues became more and more confused and the arguments for and against the establishment of a tribal council became acrimonious. In 1936 Collier requested Oliver LaFarge to undertake the task of trying to convince the Hopi of the desirability of such a council.

LaFarge took the job with grave misgivings, as he clearly evinced in his letter to Collier in April, 1936: "I do not wish to assume the task of pushing the Hopis toward an organization which does not interest them. . . . I warn you that my early progress will be very slow."

Despite his misgiving, he accepted the assignment, but he left the reservation before the vote was taken. During this period he kept his family posted as to his progress, or lack of it. Upon completion of his work and just before he left Tusayan, he wrote them:

The Hopis are going to organize, first, because John Collier and a number of other people decided to put through a new law, the Reorganization Act. The Indians didn't think this up. We did. . . . We came among these people, they didn't ask us, and as a result, they are our wards. It's not any inherent lack of capacity, it's the cold fact of cultural adjustment. . . . I said all the right things — "this is your decision, it is up to you" — but my manner was paternal and authoritarian. . . . We bring to these Indians a question which their experience cannot comprehend, a question which includes a world view and a grasp of that utterly alien, mind-wracking concept, Anglo-Saxon rule by majority vote, with everything that follows in the train of that. . . . I knew I was robbing these people of their alibi, of their grievance, and I knew the hell that will be to pay when they realize that they have accepted responsibility as well as power. . . .

Superintendent Alexander G. Hutton did all in his power to convince the Hopi that they should adopt the tribal-council plan. Hopi employees of the Indian Bureau and Hopi converts to Christianity, generally speaking, were in favor of it, and they managed to convince some of their relatives and friends to vote for its adoption when the time came to do so.

When the final vote was taken, the Hopi who opposed the establishment of a tribal council were true to their traditional procedure in such matters and simply abstained from voting either for or against it.

The commissioner's office in Washington had been given to understand that the majority of the Hopi approved the plan. As a result, on December 14, 1936, Commissioner Collier signed his approval. Whereupon, whether the majority of the Hopi wished it or not, the Hopi "Tribe" — so far as the government of the United States was concerned — was officially established with a constitution and by-laws written for the most part by the distinguished author and anthropologist Oliver LaFarge.

During the early summer of 1937 I arrived at Old Oraibi to find that Tewaquaptewa, the village chief, and several of the leading men of Old Oraibi and Moencopi were down in the chief's kiva with the late Byron Cummings, well-known Southwestern archaeologist. On inquiry we found that they were talking over the "Constitution and By-Laws of the Hopi Tribe," prepared copies of this document having been sent to them for their reconsideration and hoped-for approval. Late that afternoon Cummings emerged from the kiva apparently shaken by his experience there.

Upon being invited to do so, we descended into the kiva and learned that Cummings and one of the younger Hopi who read English had been reading aloud the proposal section by section. Following the translation of each section into Hopi there would be a lengthy discussion. From time to time we took a hand at the reading and in the discussion to point out some of the advantages the Hopi might gain by the establishment of such a council.

We could well understand and sympathize with the position being taken by Tewaquaptewa and the other traditional leaders from both Old Oraibi and Moencopi who were assembled in the kiva. We could also appreciate that the absence of any overall tribal solidarity was, and would continue to be, a handicap in meeting many of the major problems of the day. Political, cultural, economic, developmental, and even psychological problems certainly were, and would continue to be, beyond the scope of the village governments to meet "on their own."

We tried to express these ideas and they were given courteous consideration and some signs of approval. But after long discussion one of the men from Moencopi pointed out that the tribal-council plan had come from "Washington." That ended it! The memories of the leaders of Old Oraibi and Moencopi were too long, their distrust of anything from "Washington" too deep.

The Hopi Tribal Council and its assumption of overall authority is still a matter of great controversy among the Hopi. At one time the controversy developed to such a point that the Tribal Council was disbanded for a time. It was reorganized in 1951 and although it still does not meet with the complete approval of all Hopi it is functioning about as well as could be expected. In view of the important part it now plays in Hopi affairs its provisions must be given consideration [see Appendix].

Many years later when we were discussing Hopi affairs with Walter Woehlke, who had been Assistant Commissioner of Indian Affairs with John Collier, he was surprised to learn that very many Hopi had been, and still were, opposed to the formation of the Tribal Council. So far as he had been aware, the Hopi had been decidedly in favor of the plan.

The Collier administration made a grave error in not recognizing the fact that every Hopi village had its traditional governing "council" which in a majority of cases could have been used as a "tribal council." If these traditional governing bodies had been so recognized it undoubtedly would have been possible at some later date to have joint meetings of these village leaders, or their representatives, to deal with problems beyond the jurisdiction of any individual village.

The white officials were in too much of a hurry to see their cherished reforms put into effect. Whites do not live as part of time itself, as do the Hopi. For the Council's constitution and by-laws, see Appendix.

Stock-Reduction Program

For several years before the Indian Reorganization Act became law there was little question in the minds of all who had known the Tusayan country that as range land it was becoming sadly depleted. The ecology of the entire region was adversely affected and there was controversy as to whether this was being brought about by drought, by overgrazing, or by a combination of the two.

To rectify the situation the Collier administration decided upon a far-reaching program of stock reduction, not only on the Hopi and Navajo reservations but also on the range lands of all Southwestern tribes that were in similar condition.

It was decided by Indian Bureau officials that Hopi stock — cattle, sheep, goats, and horses — must be drastically reduced in numbers. The 31,189 sheep owned by the Hopi in 1942 were to be cut down to 23,627 by the following year. The sheepmen of First Mesa were to cut their flocks by 20 percent; those of Second Mesa, by 22 percent; but Third Mesa sheepmen had to reduce their flocks by 44 percent. The government contended that this high percentage of reduction of the Third Mesa flocks was demanded in view of its contention that these range lands were the most seriously depleted of all Hopi lands.

The sheepmen of Third Mesa contested this explanation as to why they were expected to kill double the number of their sheep as their fellows of the other Hopi mesas. They felt that they were being discriminated against because of long opposition by the traditional leaders of their villages and their supporters to so many of the directives imposed upon them by "Washington."

At that time 34 percent of Hopi income came from livestock. Such a serious cut in their sheep flocks was a cruel blow, especially since, according to Laura Thompson's *Culture in Crisis,* the mean income per Hopi family in 1942 was $439.82. But even that figure, "mean" as it is indeed, is misleading — for more than half of all Hopi families then had an income of less than $300.00 a year, and the loss of a single sheep can be of major concern to a family under such circumstances.

Considering the ruthless way in which the stock-reduction program was impressed upon the Hopi, it is interesting to compare how it was put into effect at the Pueblo of Acoma in New Mexico.

When it was decreed that the Acoma flock was to be reduced, Collier himself went to Acoma to meet with the governor and his leading councillors. Sophie Aberle, superintendent of the United Pueblo Agency which includes Acoma, and her range management men and others familiar with the range depletion problem at Acoma, took time to explain the need for the sheep reduction program. According to Collier in his *The Indians of the Americas,* they told the Acoma people that this was no command from the government, this was no fiat, and there would be none. Acoma was merely being furnished the facts and it would also be furnished technical assistance if desired. The whole reduction program was gone into thoroughly. Explained in detail were the need for range rest, reseeding, water-spreading projects, healing of gullies, and, very important, the upgrading of the flocks themselves by modern breeding techniques.

Granted that the people of Acoma may have been an easier people to convince than the Hopi, the significant fact is that Commissioner Collier himself visited Acoma and took time to counsel with the governor and his staff. Also the superintendent and her staff took time to demonstrate in detail the need of stock reduction. No similar effort was made to convince the Hopi. Even more important, the Hopi were certainly given the impression that they had no choice in the matter. Their flocks and herds had to be reduced whether they liked it or not.

In this, as in many other matters pertaining to the Hopi, Collier and Woehlke only too often were very badly served by representatives of their administration in the field. This clearly was evident from our many talks with Woehlke following his resignation from the Indian Service.

When the stock-reduction program was put into effect a few Hopi sheepmen agreed to the plan, feeling that it was hopeless to resist. Many, if not most of them, refused to accept the regulation of their flocks and herds as provided for in "temporary stock-reduction permits" served them by officials from the Keams Canyon Agency. That this was not to be considered an official *command* to comply certainly was not made clear to Hopi sheepmen.

Land Management District Six

Hopi roots have penetrated deeply into what they consider *their* lands. There is not a mesa, a butte, a spring, a wash, a field, or even a rock outcropping which is not significant in their traditions. Reverence for his land permeates the Hopi soul. Therefore, they suffered a bitter awakening when in 1943 they were advised that the Bureau of Indian Affairs, without making even an attempt to consult them, to all intents and purposes had cut to one-fourth the Hopi Reservation which Chester A. Arthur established in 1882 by presidential decree.

It was in 1943 that in "Land Management District Six" the Bureau of Indian Affairs circumscribed a Hopi Reservation of 631,194 acres as opposed to the 2,499,558 acres in the Hopi Reservation decreed by President Arthur. Even the area granted them under that decree was very decidedly smaller than the territory they traditionally considered to be theirs and theirs alone.

As has been stressed earlier in these pages, for many years the Navajo had been moving into various parts of the Hopi country to secure grazing land. They had squatted in very considerable numbers in and around Moencopi Wash, one of the best pieces of agricultural land in the entire area. Since the days of their captivity at the Bosque Redondo the Navajo have been more malleable in their dealings with

Washington than have the traditional Hopi, and for this reason the former have enjoyed preferential treatment by Indian Bureau officials. Navajo encroachments on Hopi lands were given scant attention in Washington. It was, therefore, natural for the Hopi to consider that the bureau's action in restricting them to "Land Management District Number Six" was a measure to favor permanent occupancy by the Navajo of three-fourths of the reservation to which they felt they should have exclusive ownership.

On August 1, 1958, Willard Sakiestewa, then Chairman of the Hopi Tribal Council, initiated legal action to regain ownership of lands which had been taken from them by the encroaching Navajo as well as by the Bureau of Indian Affairs by its establishment of "Land Management District Number Six." The Navajo entered a counter suit. The suit of the two plaintiffs, named as the Hopi Tribe and the Navajo Tribe, eventually were merged in a joint action against the United States of America as defendant and placed before the Indian Claims Commission.

Preliminary to making any decision, the commission reviewed in detail the extensive area of the Hopi Tusqua and the history of the Hopi, especially as it related to their early contacts with the whites in relationship to land use. The Navajo presented archaeological data comprising twenty-three volumes of site-sheet reports in an attempt to prove the antiquity of Navajo occupation of much of the land in controversy.

As to the Navajo contention that tree-ring and other archaeological data proved their long-time occupancy, the commission "found after careful consideration of all such evidence that the identity as well as the date of construction and date of actual use of many of the abandoned Indian sites within the subject tract was still a matter of conjecture" and "concluded that the weight of this archaeological evidence failed to overcome the many historical accounts written during this early American period which do not show any substantial Navajo tribal movement into the overlap area prior to the establishment of the 1868 Navajo Treaty Reservation."

On June 29, 1970, the Indian Claims Commission signed the following "Interlocutory Order" in Washington, D.C.:

Based upon the Findings of Fact and Opinion this day entered herein, which Findings of Fact and Opinion are hereby made a part of this order, the Commission concludes as a matter of law that,

1. The Hopi Tribe and the Navajo Tribe of Indians have the right and capacity to bring and maintain the respective claims herein.

2. As of December 16, 1882, the Hopi Tribe had Indian title to that tract of land described in the Commission's finding of Fact 20.

3. On December 16, 1882, the United States without the payment of any compensation, extinguished the Hopi Indian title to all lands within

the aforesaid tract lying outside the boundaries of the 1882 Executive Order Reservation.

4. On June 2, 1937, the United States extinguished the Hopi Indian title to some 1,868,364 acres of land within the 1882 Executive Order Reservation, said acreage being the balance of the land in the 1882 Reservation lying outside of that part of the reservation known as "land management district 6."

The evidence of record does not support Hopi aboriginal title claims to the balance of the land in suit.

IT IS ORDERED, that this case shall proceed to a determination of the acreage and December 16, 1882 fair market value of the lands described in the Commission's Finding of Fact 20 lying outside of the boundaries of the 1882 Executive Order Reservation, the June 2, 1937 fair market value of the 1,868,364 acres within the 1882 Executive Order Reservation lying outside the boundaries of "land management district 6," and all other issues bearing upon the question of the defendant's liability to the Hopi Tribe.

The Hopi rather generally hailed the commission's "Interlocutory Order" as a decided victory for them. They look forward to the day when, represented by the Hopi Tribal Council, they will receive "fair market value" for their lost lands. The more traditional among them wonder how the Tribal Council will use the money that may eventually come to it and sadly doubt that there can ever be adequate recompense for the loss of traditional lands.

When it was considering the Hopi claim to the Moencopi region, the commission seems to have given scant attention to the fact that back in 1778 Escalante reported with some amazement on the large herds of Hopi cattle feeding near Moencopi.

Following the "Interlocutory Order" of the Indian Claims Commission, the Hopi Tribal Council filed a motion for rehearing of the title issues. The Navajo Tribal Council took similar action.

In 1972 Congressman Sam Steiger of Arizona introduced legislation in Congress in the hope of eliminating the necessity for further action by the courts. However, three other bills pertaining to the Hopi-Navajo land controversy were introduced in the House.

In February 1974, the House Committee on Interior and Insular Affairs approved H. R. 10337, which had been introduced by Representative Wayne Owens of Utah. Unlike Steiger's bill, which provided for the division of the disputed lands by Congress, Owen's bill stipulated that these lands be apportioned by the Federal Courts.

The steady growth of the Hopi in recent years makes it imperative that for their economic security they, as well as the Navajo, have every possible acre of land that can be granted them. In this situation the fact that Hopi roots in these lands are old indeed compared with those of the Navajo warrants much more consideration than bureaucratic Washington has seen fit to accord it in the past.

Hearings on Reservation

Many problems which the Hopi faced in their transition from a subsistence to a dollar economy were brought to the fore during the final weeks of July 1955 when a team headed by Thomas A. Reid, Assistant to the then Commissioner of Indian Affairs Glenn L. Emmons, held a series of hearings at the various Hopi villages.

These hearings were the result of continued opposition by large numbers, if not by the majority, of Hopi to a variety of conditions then existing on the reservation which were inimical to the Hopi way of life. Foremost among the matters brought before the officials conducting the hearings were the widespread Hopi opposition to (1) the curtailment of their reservation by "Land Management District Six," sometimes referred to as the "Hopi Jurisdiction"; to (2) the Hopi Tribal Council idea; and to (3) the stock-reduction program.

More than four hundred pages of single-spaced typewritten testimony were given by Hopi at these hearings. They show all too clearly how bureaucratic impositions, no matter how well-intentioned, serve to confuse, divide, and to push the Hopi toward what may prove in the end to be destruction of the village communities which are so vital to the continuance of their way of life.

The record of these hearings which was published in mimeographed form by the Bureau of Indian Affairs, comprises one of the important documents in the library of Hopi historical material. A few excerpts from the recorded testimony will serve to illustrate the tenor of Hopi thought and life at that time.

During the hearing at Hotevila on July 15, George Nasewiseoma stated that agency policemen came to Oraibi and Hotevila and demanded that various sheepmen there agree to the reduction of their herds. He, Chester Motah, Rubin Cheykaychi, and Paul Siwinyouma all refused to accept the proffered reduction permits.

George Nasewiseoma is quoted in the record of the hearings as follows:

The policemen after several attempts to force these permits upon us when we did not accept it, they put us in a car and drove us over to Keams Canyon to be placed in prison again. We were in prison because we refused to go along with these programs under grazing rules and regulations. The Judge gave us 90 days on top of all the sheep that were taken away. There were 266 head that were actually taken away from me. Two hundred of them actually belonged to me, and 66 belonged to my wife. There were three horses and all of these were taken away. . . . So I spent 90 days in jail and lost all my sheep and horses because I want to live my own way of life and adhere to my own Hopi religious teachings.

At Shongopovi on July 18, Andrew Hermequaptewa gave an account of the traditional history of the Hopi as background for his position on the stock-reduction plan. He finished by saying: "This program practically took everything — it took our stock away from us. We cannot make much of a livelihood out of fifteen head of sheep. It seems that the government wants us to be poor so that we will only have to depend on the government to feed us. . . . This hurts me very much as I do not want to go under these new policies."

At Polacca a few days later Roscoe Navasie pleaded that the Hopi claim to lands beyond the limits of the "Hopi Jurisdiction" be given proper consideration by government authorities:

Because of the acreage of our land being diminished down to its [present] size, I have no place to go but to the very end, to the fence that is closing us in. Instead of going about and making use of what rightfully belongs to me, I am fenced in. . . . Instead of roaming in a large area with my sheep I roam in a radius of one mile. Consider our plight. If you can make it possible, give us back what rightfully belongs to us so that we can have enough land to take care of ourselves.

Logan Koopee pointed out that the "majority of our Hopi people have never given one traditional village authority to speak for all the villages, because we know that each village has its own form of government, and the authority covers only that particular village." He added:

We think that our differences and conflict between the traditional group and the progressive people has been described not accurately, and misinterpreted, because many traditional people actually support the Hopi Council. Many of them have encouraged the Council to continue to work, but many of these people will not speak out in public meeting out of respect for their village leaders, who have different views.

Livestock grazing outside village holdings, the building of good roads beyond the village limits, oil and gas and mineral development of the tribal land, cannot be settled on a village basis. The gradual transition from the old to the new which has taken place, has been indeed painful and undesirable to the traditional group. Fear is evident that their own power and authority would be hurt by another group who has something to say about the management of tribal land.

After castigating those Hopi who did not favor such government policies as the Hopi Tribal Council, the stock-reduction program, and the establishment of the Hopi Jurisdiction, Koopee spoke in angry contempt of off-reservation Hopi and of white friends of the Hopi who were counseling the traditional Hopi to stand their ground.

In closing, he even spoke against any move to relocate those Navajo who live and graze their stock on Hopi lands: "I think we have now realized the people before us had made a grave error and mistake in the motive of their desire to get the Navajo entirely off the 1882 reservation. Another attempt by us would be a great mistake for us."

However, after a careful reading of statements made by the dozens of Hopi and the few Tewa of Hano who testified, one cannot help but conclude that Koopee's statement of support for Bureau of Indian Affairs programs was contrary to the opinions expressed by the great majority.

Personnel of the Bureau of Indian Affairs who drafted the programs for stock reduction and for the establishment of "Land Management District Six" may have thought that they were in accord with the provision of the Indian Reorganization Act. But how far, far afield these enforced programs are from the spirit and intent of that act is all too tragically shown in the remarks made by a Hopi woman on the final day of the hearings, July 30.

This educated, articulate woman had approved the idea of a Hopi Tribal Council and had urged its acceptance when it was first suggested. At the hearings, however, she presented a dignified and eloquent account of the schisms and tragic events which had resulted within the scope of her connections with three different villages.

When recognized by acting Chairman Graham Holmes, Mrs. Daisy Albert of Upper Moencopi turned to the Hopi people in the audience and asked them for their permission to speak. When their permission was assured, after a few introductory remarks she continued:

In 1934 is what I am talking about — That was the Hopi Tribal Council. In the Upper Moencopi Village I remember clearly on that day in 1934 there was much confusion among the people in Moencopi. We had been approached by different men who were working this Wheeler-Howard Bill through. They were our own people, our very own Hopi men. I do not know exactly what explanation they gave to each home but when I was approached in my home by a man . . . we were told by this man that if we voted we would get a piece of land when it was allotted to the Hopi tribe to each individual family when the right time came; that we would get cattle and we would get sheep, and when trouble came to my family the Government was supposed to protect us from all these troubles; if anyone slandered against us we would be protected by the Government. He said the Government would be obligated to us, if we would go his way. I thought that was a very good thing because I had returned from Riverside about three years before this came through. Because I was taught in school to read and write and to speak English, to understand English, to be a good worker, to be polite, to be a Christian, and above all to be patriotic, I went along with this group who voted for the council that day, but it was a sad day. The Lower Village did not want to go and vote because they did not want to go the white man's way and we who voted for the council were mad at them. We were unreasonable with them. On that very day, as you people in Lower Moencopi know, the word "Aih-yeh-vi" became known. "Aih-yeh-vi" to a Progressive means hostile, a man who does not want to go the white man's way, a person who always wants to go the other way. I helped throw those words at these people down here and I remember so clearly where the voting took place and what men sat at the table trying to encourage the people to vote for the council. Then it came about that the council was voted for. We do not know how many had voted for it that day but weeks went by then we found that it had passed, much to the surprise of the lower group people, but I was not surprised it had passed. From then on I felt so secure that I would be free to do the things that I wanted to and to look forward to the things I would get through this council and through the Government.

Things went on in a way that is sad to remember. We became split, Hopis against Hopis, grandmothers against their children, and parents against their children. It was sad, and I helped break up that unison in the village, but since I had become a part of that Progressive group I had to stick along or else. . . . We never knew what fear was until I had joined that council. We had meetings where women were invited. Sometimes they were good meetings we would plan for our future but it always ended up with a quarrel. . . . As time went along we felt free to persecute the lower group. . . . We all remember that. There is not one Hopi in this room that can deny that. We, the group who called ourselves the Progressive group, who were the white people, who wanted the white man's way, were there to destroy our own people.   ·

·   ·   ·   ·   ·   ·   ·   ·   ·   ·   ·   ·   ·   ·

Now when the tribal council was formed, we were to be taught democracy in the white man's way, but this is the democracy we hold. My people, a long time ago, had good lives; they loved one another; they were united, and they had a good life but this democracy the Hopi Tribal Council has taught us is not the way we want to take it. Now problems are being forced upon the Hopi people. . . . My people have opposed a lot of these problems but no heed was given to them ever, so they had to go to Washington to have you people come out here so that they could tell you about these things.

My people have their own way of life. They have their own religious life and their own traditional life, and they have a right to carry on that life. Now, why couldn't they be permitted to live their own life without this council coming in and trying to force them . . . to unite with them in their council ways? They have a right to reject those things. . . . our good father the white man in Washington . . . denied these rights all along because the tribal council wants their own way of forcing things and getting the power over my people. In order to get this power over my people they have lied, cheated and plotted behind my peoples' back. You have heard these stories in other villages, I am sure. You have heard many of the troubles with our traditional people. Now, are you going to go back to Washington and give this kind of council the power to hold over our heads? I don't know how long it will take you to go over these notes and put out the minutes to decide if you are going to give the council power or not, but I want to say that if you, the people from the Indian Bureau, are the right minded people you will look into both sides to see which is right before you decide. . . .

Whether I have been a Progressive woman before or not, I had a right to change my ways. You people may think that I am discarding my education which I received in the Indian School when I talk this way. My husband, as I said, is a Hotevilla. He will always be a Hotevilla. He will die a Hotevilla.

He is nothing else but a Hotevilla Hopi. His life is a good life. People think of him as a good man although the council has dragged his name through the mud and it took him a long time for him to hold up his head again. Now I ask you if you are going to use this kind of a tool against my people in order to get anything out from under them. We will not stop fighting because we have our own life to live.

Viets Lomaheftewa also spoke, and some of his words follow:

I have a grandfather whose name is Honanie. He was at one time the head leader in this village and is well known to many white leaders in Washington. He and many other leaders were sent to Washington to work on this land problem of the Hopis. Loloma from Oraibi, and Semo from Walpi, and Anaweto from Walpi, and Polaccaco from Walpi who belongs to Tewa people and who was interpreter at that time because he knew how to speak the Spanish language. These men went into Washington to present the land claim of the Hopi people, and when they returned they told us that they had presented their case, and that the government officials have agreed that whatever land they have presented will be respected and that they will have that land to use as they have in the past. All people were told of this, and were glad that we will have our land and work it the way we have done in accordance with our teachings.

The interest, real or assumed, demonstrated by Assistant Commissioner Reid and the members of his official group during these 1955 hearings gave many of the village leaders who testified, as well as other Hopi, a feeling of certainty that official administration of the Hopi Reservation would be modified to complement the Hopi traditional system and that their suggestions for the improvement of their way of life would be given prompt attention. How justified they were in this feeling only the future can tell.

The Late
Twentieth Century Hopi

ANYONE WHO THOUGHT that the Hopi could escape involvement with the complex environmental problems of the late twentieth century suffered a rude awakening when the plans of the Western Energy Supply and Transmission Association became public. To meet the stated 1985 demand for electric power, the United States Reclamation Service, the Bureau of Indian Affairs, the Nevada Power Company, the Los Angeles Department of Water and Power, and the Arizona Public Service Company, among other agencies, have pooled their various resources in the colossal association known as WEST.

A significant feature of WEST is the construction of a series of mammoth steam-powered generating plants to be fired from the coal deposits existing in and around the "Four Corners" junction of Utah, Colorado, Arizona, and New Mexico. One of these coal deposits underlies Black Mesa in Arizona, just north of the Hopi villages, and thus within the boundaries of the extensive area claimed by the Hopi.

In 1969 the Hopi Tribal Council signed a contract with the Peabody Coal Company for the strip mining of coal on Black Mesa. Conservationists familiar with the devastation brought about in Pennsylvania by strip mining — before state regulations were enacted — were particularly concerned.

For a time it was difficult to find out what, if any, safeguards to protect the environment of Black Mesa had been written into the Peabody contract. One answer came from Hopi Agency Superintendent Homer M. Gilliland in a letter dated June 5, 1970, stating that no air or water pollution was anticipated. The Peabody Coal Company agreed to regulations requiring prior approval of reclamation plans. The main effect would be on the vegetation. Grass would be reseeded; trees would take longer to replace.

Many disagreed with Gilliland's optimism, arguing that arid lands devastated by strip mining take centuries to make a comeback. As for

Gilliland's statement that no air pollution was anticipated, this is not given much credence by conservationists alarmed over the multiple generating plants to be powered not only by Black Mesa but by other Southwestern coal deposits.

Some Hopi approved the stand taken by the Tribal Council because they felt the developments it sanctioned would prove economically feasible to all the Hopi people. The Hopi opposed to it were chiefly concerned lest the operation on Black Mesa endangered the limited water supplies.

For a long time it had been believed that Black Mesa was the water source for the ancient springs adjacent to the Hopi villages and for the wells developed later in nearby washes. The Hopi opposing the Council's action were particularly concerned over the Peabody contract's permission to drill several deep wells for operation of the 275-mile-long slurry line carrying coal to power one of five planned generating plants for WEST.

On February 6, 1970, Acting Associate Commissioner of Indian Affairs William J. Benham, wrote that the Hopi springs and wells would not be affected by mining developments on Black Mesa. This would appear to be justified by two reports: *Regional Hydrogeology of the Navajo and Hopi Indian Reservations, Arizona, New Mexico, and Utah,* by M. E. Cooley, J. W. Harshbarger, J. P. Akers, and W. F. Hardt and *The Changing Physical Environment of the Hopi Indians of Arizona* by John T. Hack.

In his letter of April 24, 1970, Edwin D. McKee of the United States Geological Survey (a man who is familiar with the geology of the Hopi country and concerned with any threat to its water supply) said that judgment concerning the water problem in Hopi country should be made by monitoring the water from the wells in the area. The groundwater in the area is located in separate aquifers. They are independent. Thus taking water from one does not necessarily mean it will affect another. But, he added, there always is some danger in depleting any water table. Therefore he urged that data be obtained on the rate of depletion and recharge.

That such action was being taken was indicated in a letter dated Flagstaff, Arizona, September 19, 1972, by E. H. McGavock, Subdistrict Chief, Water Resources Division, United States Geological Survey.

Controversy over air pollution in the area continued to rage in the 1970s. It was reported in the May 1, 1971 issue of *Conservation News* that the only object visible in a photograph made by Gemini 12 at an altitude of 170 miles was a plume of smoke from the coal-fueled Four

Corners Generating Plant near Farmington, New Mexico. According to this report the smoke covered about 10,000 square miles of the earth's surface even though at that time the Four Corners Plant was not running at full capacity. When this photograph was made public, the news media, the bulletins of the conservation organizations, and the mail of representatives in Washington were flooded with protest. Conservationists expressed the gravest fears as to the inevitable consequences when the whole complex of coal-burning generating plants was in operation.

In a 1972 press release by the Arizona Public Service Company, Dr. Paul Lowman, geologist of the Goddard Space Flight Center of NASA and principal synoptic terrain investigator for the Gemini 12 photographs, stated that in his opinion it was not a plume of smoke from the generating plant at all, but nothing more than a long cirrus cloud. Lowman's interpretation, however, was promptly challenged by scientists competent in the field of geology and planetary research and the pressure of conservationists continued.

Evidence was produced that the smoke-haze from the plant so obscures the silhouette of the eastern skyline at dawn that the Sun Watcher of Shongopovi has difficulty in observing the exact moment of sunrise by which he sets the dates for important religious ceremonies. Furthermore the spectacular view from the Hopi mesas far across the Painted Desert to the Mountains of the Kachinas, the San Francisco Peaks north of Flagstaff, has been described as "entirely smudged out."

This "scenic pollution" has been attacked by such organizations as Black Mesa Defense, Friends of the Earth, Sierra Club, Desert Protective Council and ecology action groups in various schools and universities, who are also voicing concern over the mining of Black Mesa and the pollution of the air by the coal-burning generating plants. They have expressed concern, too, over extensive use of Colorado River water by some of the components of the WEST project, claiming that water heated and consumed in such quantities will increase the river's salinity with resulting harmful effects on domestic, agricultural, and industrial water users in Arizona, California, Nevada, and Mexico.

Some of the crusades in opposition to the strip mining operation on Black Mesa and the air pollution resulting from the coal-burning generator plants have served to awaken both public and governmental interests in the threats posed by such mammoth industrial undertakings as WEST to the environment not only of the Hopi country and the Southwest but also to wide areas of the country as a whole. That the conservation crusades have served to waken both public and private interests to environmental threats was demonstrated in the April 1972 draft of the report by a study management team for a Federal Task Force titled "Southwest Energy Study — An Evaluation of Coal-Fired Electric Generation in the Southwest."

This report deals in considerable detail, not only with the threats to ecology by the operations on Black Mesa and the electric generating plants, but also with the effects of similar projected plants in Utah, Colorado, and Wyoming.

Important, in the view of many of the Hopi who are familiar with it, is their feeling that the report offers guidelines for ameliorating whatever deficiencies may remain in the environmental protection program operations now functioning in the area.

Meantime, pending before the Ninth Circuit Court of Appeals, as of mid-1974, is case number 73–2132 brought by Starlie Lomayaktewa *et al* against Rogers C. Morton, Secretary of the Interior, and the Peabody Coal Company. Lomayaktewa and his associates charge, among other things, that the Hopi Tribal Council and the Secretary of the Interior acted unlawfully in approving the Peabody Coal Company's contract for the mining of Black Mesa.

Problems With Visitors

Although the Hopi appreciate the varied gains that have been made in their way of life since the mid–1900s, at the same time they are concerned about certain troublesome factors that have become evident during the same period. For example, during the middle 1950s the villages of Third Mesa became the mecca for a curious procession of whites, young for the most part, and uninvited; a few coming individually, but many in groups.

Given a romantic concept of Hopi life by the "underground press" of Los Angeles, San Francisco, and other cities, the visitors descended upon the Hopi villages in the belief that they would find a permissive society and one in which they would be made welcome. The fact that some Hopi had opposed military service also served to convince these visitors that they shared common values. Having little real knowledge of the Hopi, the newcomers had no conception of the complex system of traditional checks and balances that govern the life of the individual in a viable Hopi community. They were slow to learn that in such villages their own concept of freedom was greatly at odds with the Hopi way of life and that therefore they were far from welcome. Eventually they were to find themselves more at home in Hotevila and Old Oraibi where traditional village systems of government had broken down.

By the late 1960s many of those visitors who had come to the Hopi country in the 1950s had drifted away. However, at that time there came to the fore a small but vocal and aggressive group of what the late Harold Colton of The Museum of Northern Arizona referred to as "atypical whites and atypical Hopi." The nucleus of this group presumed to speak for all the "traditional Hopi," and its leader termed himself "Spokesman for the traditional Hopi." This clique achieved an astonishingly large but uncritical following. It gained an unfortunate entry to the news media and appeared at various hearings in Washington and elsewhere. Taking full advantage of the current interest in the American Indian and the preservation of man's environment, the group was particularly prominent in the councils and publications of the *Black Mesa Defense* of Santa Fe.

In the 1970s this group of crusaders established something it called "Traditional Indian Unity Caravan." This seemed to widen their audience among that segment of the public which has little knowledge of the intricate web of Hopi life. They have been able to voice their arguments in the established news media without protest by the majority of the Hopi people, and unfortunately, in the view of many, they have been accepted as the authoritative voice of the traditional Hopi by many reputable conservation groups.

In this manner, during a most critical transition period in Hopi history, these Hopi visitors have become a divisive force among the very people they claim to serve.

In earlier times most visitors, both white and Indian from other tribes who went to the Hopi villages to observe the various ceremonies, have behaved with the decorum and reverence suited to such observances. But in the last two decades, some of the villages have had bitter experiences with groups of young rowdies. There are Hopi reports of extensive stealing, including robbery at some of the ancient shrines and desecration of Hopi graves. Their cultural role as peaceful people who deplore aggression has made it difficult for the Hopi to know exactly how to meet such problems.

In the summer of 1971 the Snake and Antelope priests of Mishongnovi concluded, as a result of misbehavior during earlier ceremonies, that no visitors would be allowed to witness their Snake Ceremony. This move by Mishongnovi aroused considerable turbulence among the other villages many of which had had unfortunate experiences with young non-Indian visitors.

At the Niman and Shalako Ceremonies at Shongopovi in 1972 also, the behavior of dozens of young hippies led to much discussion among the villages and their leaders. Should they follow the lead of Mishongnovi and ban white visitors from watching the Snake Ceremony which would be performed there late in the summer?

After careful consideration the leaders of the Snake and Antelope Societies, who were in charge of that ceremony and who were in control of the village at this time (with an authority that superseded that of the *kikmongwi* or Village Chief) ruled that *all* visitors were to be permitted.

The *kikmongwi* disagreed with the decision of the Snake and Antelope priests, and a week or so before the Shongopovi Snake Ceremony there arrived on the reservation a group consisting of members of the American Indian Movement and the Traditional Indian Unity Caravan, led by Thomas Banyacya of New Oraibi. According to Abbott Sekaquaptewa in *Hopi Action News* (August 31, 1972), this group was invited by Mina Lansa, self-appointed village chief of Old Oraibi, to camp and hold meeting there. Terrance Talaswaima of Shipolovi stated in the same issue of *Hopi Action News* that this assembly consisted of young people from various tribes in the East and California and Oregon. Many witnessing Hopi, however, stated that included were several white hippies dressed Indian style.

On August 29, 1972, the dissenters attempted to expel all white visitors from the village. After Fred Kabotie and other Shongopovi leaders tried to explain to them the decision of the Snake and Antelope Society priests, the crowd mobbed the demonstrators, spitting on them and roughing them up violently — an event unique in Hopi history.

In spite of the marked lack of support by the great majority of the Shongopovi people, the demonstrators continued their harassment. Two Snake priests were dispatched from their kiva to the scene where they apprehended a demonstrator and follower of Banyacya, Earl Pela, on the basis that he was a Snake priest of Shongopovi and had no right to go against the orders of the leaders of the Snake Society. They fashioned a snake kilt around Pela and carried him to the kiva.

Bob Wolfe, American Indian Movement spokesman and a demonstrator, informed Nathan Begay, Tribal Operations Officer of the Agency at Keams Canyon, that the demonstrators had come to the reservation at the invitation of Banyacya to meet with all the villagers; not to create dissension among them. Wolfe charged that they had been misled by Banyacya and intended to leave the reservation which they did. Banyacya and the remaining demonstrators, finding themselves under heated attack by Shongopovi people and reservation police, also left threatening, however, to return later to break up the coming Butterfly Dance if white visitors were allowed to witness it. This they failed to do.

Banyacya and the remaining demonstrators went to Hotevila where they had been invited by David Monongye, a supporter of Banyacya. There they met with little support and the group dispersed.

Hope for the Hopi

Traveling the road into the twenty-first century, the Hopi face many detours, chuckholes, and roadblocks, although as a people their fortunes have shown a decided improvement in recent years.

The passage and implementation of the Indian Reorganization Act of 1934 did not establish a Utopia for the Hopi in what was left of that extensive area of Tusayan traditionally considered theirs. Still, even the most traditional-minded Hopi agree that living conditions in their villages have improved since the mid-1900s to the point where there is no longer the feeling of hopelessness so prevalent among them in the decades just preceding the implementation of the Act.

Certainly superintendents, teachers, and other officials have begun coming to Tusayan with a friendly attitude toward the Hopi and an appreciation of their way of life. There is no longer, for example, talk of putting an end to their colorful religious ceremonies. In administrative procedures, too, there has been considerable change.

The Hopi, as well as other Indians of the United States benefited greatly when in 1955 the United States Public Health Service took over full responsibility from the Bureau of Indian Affairs for all health services on the reservations. On the Hopi Reservation this changeover has brought about a decisive upgrading of medical personnel, facilities, and services.

The substandard Hopi economy has been given a significant lift by Social Security provisions and by the development and marketing of Hopi arts and crafts. Light industry has been encouraged to locate in the area, thus affording employment opportunities to the villagers.

In 1966 the Hopi Tribal Council entered into a leasing agreement with the BVD garment company to expend $1,600,00 in tribal funds to construct and equip a factory at Winslow, Arizona. Hopi were to be given preference in employment. The city of Winslow had deeded 220 acres to the Hopi Tribe for an industrial park, forty acres of which were occupied by the BVD plant. In a dedication ceremony attended by more than 2,000 people the plant was accepted by the BVD company and approximately one hundred Hopi began employment there.

The Tribal Council has sponsored bus service from the reservation to the plant for the benefit of Hopi wishing to commute the eighty miles to work. The plant has been in full operation, and plans were under way in 1972 to expand the work force to five hundred, with continuing priority for the Hopi.

As a result of the plant, certain thrifty Hopi women have converted waste fabric from the manufacturing process into attractive Hopi rag dolls and have found a market for them.

Throughout Tusayan there have developed many of the organizations and activities found in the typical Anglo community — Boy Scouts, American Legion, Future Farmers of America, Parent-Teacher Associations. By the 1970s elementary schools were even introducing their students to the novel ceremonies of the white man's Halloween. Through the Arizona Library Extension Service bookmobile service is now available to all Hopi. There was at least one women's bridge club, and even the potluck dinner had come to Tusayan. A few homes boasted television sets. Motels were being built, and a supermarket had replaced the old trading post at Oraibi. According to Mischa Titiev some villages now have a sanitary inspector who is jokingly referred to as "outhouse chief."

Today water is being piped to the villages and plans for modern sewage disposal are under way. There are electric lights and refrigerators in many homes. Some Hopi pottery is being baked in an electric kiln rather than in a fire of dried sheep dung.

Also on the side of progress must be mentioned roads, better school facilities, improved economic conditions brought about by projects fostered by the Tribal Council, the building of community centers and a tribal administration headquarters. Law enforcement is now largely in the hands of the Hopi themselves.

Some question the judgment of federal officials in meeting the Hopi demand for better housing with boxlike, prefabricated houses below the mesas rather than modified Hopi-style houses on the mesa tops fashioned of the native rock that is so available. The critics argue that the latter structures, with doors and windows on both sides to form a breezeway, are ideally suited to the environment.

One of the most significant acts of the Tribal Council was the development on Second Mesa of The Hopi Cultural Center with its exceptional museum, comfortable motel, and attractive restaurant, all near the Hopi Arts and Crafts-Silvercraft headquarters.

Obstacles notwithstanding, the Hopi seem on the way to establishing a stable society in which the traditional ceremonial community life can merge successfully with valuable aspects of the white American way of life. Their history indicates not only an exceptional ability to change but also a willingness to take time to discriminate and reflect before abandoning the old for the new. Even today the Hopi are much more likely to reckon time by the stately march of the sun across the far reaches of the desert sky than by the quick second tick of a clock. Possibly this is why they can take the long view of events tending to shape their lives.

Appendix

CONSTITUTION AND BY-LAWS OF THE HOPI TRIBE

Preamble

This Constitution, to be known as the Constitution and By-Laws of the Hopi Tribe, is adopted by the self-governing Hopi and Tewa villages of Arizona to provide a way of working together for peace and agreement between the villages, and of preserving the good things of Hopi life, and to provide a way of organizing to deal with modern problems, with the United States Government and with the outside world generally.

Article I — Jurisdiction

The authority of the Tribe under this Constitution shall cover the Hopi villages and such land as shall be determined by the Hopi Tribal Council in agreement with the United States Government and the Navajo Tribe, and such lands as may be added thereto in future. The Hopi Tribal Council is hereby authorized to negotiate with the proper officials to reach such agreement, and to accept it by a majority vote.

Article II — Membership

Section 1. Membership in the Hopi Tribe shall be as follows: (a) All persons whose names appear on the census roll of the Hopi Tribe as of January 1st, 1936, but within one year from the time that this Constitution takes effect corrections may be made in the roll by the Hopi Tribal Council with the approval of the Secretary of the Interior.

(b) All children born after January 1, 1936, whose father and mother are both members of the Hopi Tribe.

(c) All children born after January 1, 1936, whose mother is a member of the Hopi Tribe, and whose father is a member of some other tribe.

(d) All persons adopted into the Tribe as provided in Section 2.

Sec. 2. Non-members of one-fourth degree of Indian blood or more, who are married to members of the Hopi Tribe, and adult persons of one-fourth degree of Indian blood or more whose fathers are members of the Hopi Tribe, may be adopted in the following manner: Such person may apply to the Kikmongwi of the village to which he is to belong, for acceptance. According to the way of doing established in that village, the Kikmongwi may accept him, and shall tell the Tribal Council. The Council may then by a majority vote have that person's name put on the roll of the Tribe, but before he is enrolled he must officially give up membership in any other tribe.

Sec. 3. Resident members shall be those who actually live in the Hopi jurisdiction and who have been living therein for not less than six months. Only resident members of twenty-one years of age or over shall be qualified to vote in any election or referendum. Any adult member who is away from the jurisdiction for six months continuously, shall cease to be a resident member until he has again lived in the jurisdiction for the necessary time.

Article III — Organization

Section 1. The Hopi Tribe is a union of self-governing villages sharing common interests and working for the common welfare of all. It consists of the following recognized villages:

First Mesa (consolidated villages of Walpi, Shitchumovi and Tewa).
Mishongnovi.
Sipaulavi.
Shungopavi.
Oraibi.
Kyakotsmovi.
Bakabi.
Hotevilla.
Moenkopi.

Sec. 2. The following powers which the Tribe now has under existing law or which have been given by the Act of June 18, 1934 (48 Stat. 984), and acts amendatory thereof or supplemental thereto, are reserved to the individual villages:

(a) To appoint guardians for orphan children and incompetent members.

(b) To adjust family disputes and regulate family relations of members of the villages.

(c) To regulate the inheritance of property of the members of the villages.

(d) To assign farming land, subject to the provisions of Article VII.

Sec. 3. Each village shall decide for itself how it shall be organized. Until a village shall decide to organize in another manner, it shall be considered as being under the traditional Hopi organization, and the Kikmongwi of such village shall be recognized as its leader.

Sec. 4. Any village which does not possess the traditional Hopi self-government, or which wishes to make a change in that government or add something to it, may adopt a village Constitution in the following manner: A Constitution, consistent with this Constitution and By-Laws, shall be drawn up, and made known to all the voting members of such village, and a copy shall be given to the Superintendent of the Hopi jurisdiction. Upon the request of the Kikmongwi of such village, or of 25% of the voting members thereof, for an election on such Constitution, the Superintendent shall make sure that all members have had ample opportunity to study the proposed Constitution. He shall then call a special meeting of the voting members of such village, for the purpose of voting on the adoption of the proposed Constitution, and shall see that there is a fair vote. If at such referendum, not less than half of the voting members of the village cast their votes, and if a majority of those voting accepts the proposed Constitution, it shall then become the Constitution of that village, and only officials chosen according to its provisions shall be recognized.

The village Constitution shall clearly say how the Council representatives and other village officials shall be chosen, as well as the official who shall perform the duties placed upon the Kikmongwi in this Constitution. Such village Constitution may be amended or abolished in the same manner as provided for its adoption.

Article IV — The Tribal Council

Section 1. The Hopi Tribal Council shall consist of representatives from the various villages. The number of representatives from each village shall be determined according to its population, as follows: villages of 50 to 250 population, one representative; villages of 251 to 500 population, two representatives; villages of 501 to 750 population, three representatives; villages of over 750 population, four representatives.

The representation in the first Tribal Council shall be as follows:

First Mesa	4
Mishongnovi	2
Sipaulavi	1
Shungopavi	2
Oraibi	1
Kyakotsmovi	2
Bakabi	1
Hotevilla	2
Moenkopi	2

Sec. 2. Representatives shall serve for a term of one year, and may serve any number of terms in succession.

Sec. 3. Each representative must be a member of the village which he represents. He must be twenty-five years or more of age, and must have lived in the Hopi jurisdiction for not less than two years, before taking office, and must be able to speak the Hopi language fluently.

Sec. 4. Each village shall decide for itself how it shall choose its representatives, subject to the provisions of section 5. Representatives shall be recognized by the Council only if they are certified by the Kikmongwi of their respective villages. Certifications may be made in writing or in person.

Sec. 5. One representative of the village of Moenkopi shall be selected from the Lower District, and certified by the Kikmongwi of Moenkopi, and one representative shall be selected by the Upper District, and certified by the official whom that District may appoint, or who may be specified in a village Constitution adopted under the provisions of Article III, section 4. This section may be repealed, with the consent of the Tribal Council, by vote of a two-thirds majority at a meeting of the voting members of Moenkopi village called and held subject to the provisions of Article III, section 4.

Sec. 6. No business shall be done unless at least a majority of the members are present.

Sec. 7. The Tribal Council shall choose from its own members a Chairman and Vice-Chairman, and from the Council or from other members of the Tribe, a Secretary, Treasurer, Sergeant-at-Arms, and interpreters, and such other officers and committees as it may think necessary, subject to the provisions of the By-Laws, Article I.

Article V — Vacancies & Removal From Office

Section 1. Any representative or other officer found guilty in a tribal or other court of a misdemeanor involving dishonesty, of a felony, or of drunkenness, shall be automatically removed from office, and the Council shall refuse to recognize him.

Sec. 2. Any officer or representative may be removed from office for serious neglect of duty, by a vote of not less than two-thirds of the Council, after the officer to be so removed has been given full opportunity to hear the charges against him and to defend himself before the Council.

Sec. 3. Vacancies occurring for any reason among the representatives shall be filled for the rest of the term by the village concerned, in the same manner as a representative from that village is ordinarily chosen.

Vacancies occurring for any reason among the officers appointed by the Council shall be filled by the Council.

Article VI — Powers of the Tribal Council

Section 1. The Hopi Tribal Council shall have the following powers which the Tribe now has under existing law or which have been given to the Tribe by the Act of June 18, 1934. The Tribal Council shall exercise these powers subject to the terms of this Constitution and to the Constitution and Statutes of the United States.

(a) To represent and speak for the Hopi Tribe in all matters for the welfare of the Tribe, and to negotiate with the Federal, State, and local governments, and with the councils or governments of other tribes.

(b) To employ lawyers, the choice of lawyers and fixing of fees to be subject to the approval of the Secretary of the Interior.

(c) To prevent the sale, disposition, lease or encumbrance of tribal lands, or other tribal property.

(d) To advise with the Secretary of the Interior and other governmental agencies upon all appropriation estimates or Federal projects for the benefit of the Tribe, before the submission of such estimates to the Bureau of the Budget or to Congress.

(e) To raise and take care of a tribal council fund by accepting grants or gifts from any person, State, or the United States Government, or by charging persons doing business within the Reservation reasonable license fees, subject to the approval of the Secretary of the Interior.

(f) To use such tribal council fund for the welfare of the Tribe, and for salaries or authorized expenses of tribal officers. All payments from the tribal council fund shall be a matter of public record at all times.

(g) To make ordinances, subject to the approval of the Secretary of the Interior, to protect the peace and welfare of the Tribe, and to set up courts for the settlement of claims and disputes, and for the trial and punishment of Indians within the jurisdiction charged with offenses against such ordinances.

(h) To act as a court to hear and settle claims or disputes between villages in the manner provided in Article VIII.

(i) To provide by ordinance, subject to the approval of the Secretary of the Interior, for removal or exclusion from the jurisdiction of any non-members whose presence may be harmful to the members of the Tribe.

(j) To regulate the activities of voluntary cooperative associations of members of the Tribe for business purposes.

(k) To protect the arts, crafts, traditions, and ceremonies of the Hopi Indians.

(1) To delegate any of the powers of the council to committees or officers, keeping the right to review any action taken.

(m) To request a charter of incorporation to be issued as provided in the Act of June 18, 1934.

(n) To adopt resolutions providing the way in which the Tribal Council itself shall do its business.

Sec. 2. Any resolution or ordinance which, by the terms of this Constitution, is subject to review by the Secretary of the Interior, shall be given to the Superintendent of the jurisdiction, who shall, within ten days thereafter, approve or disapprove the same.

If the Superintendent shall approve any ordinance or resolution, it shall thereupon become effective, but the Superintendent shall send a copy of the same, bearing his endorsement, to the Secretary of the Interior, who may, within ninety days from the date of enactment, veto said ordinance or resolution for any reason by notifying the Tribal Council of his decision.

If the Superintendent shall refuse to approve any ordinance or resolution submitted to him, within ten days after enactment, he shall report his reasons to the Tribal Council. If the Tribal Council thinks these reasons are not sufficient, it may, by a majority vote, refer the ordinance or resolution to the Secretary of the Interior, who may, within ninety days from the date of its enactment, approve the same in writing, whereupon the said ordinance or resolution shall become effective.

Sec. 3. The Hopi Tribal Council may exercise such further powers as may in the future be delegated to it by the members of the Tribe or by the Secretary of the Interior, or any other duly authorized official or agency of the State or Federal Government.

Sec. 4. Any rights and powers which the Hopi Tribe of Indians now has, but which are not expressly mentioned in this Constitution, shall not be lost or limited by this article, but may be exercised by the members of the Hopi Tribe of Indians through the adoption of appropriate by-laws and constitutional amendments.

Article VII — Land

Section 1. Assignment of use of farming land within the traditional clan holdings of the villages of First Mesa, Mishongnovi, Sipaulavi, and Shungopavi, and within the established village holdings of the villages of Kyakotsmovi, Bakabí, Oraibi, Hotevilla, and Moenkopi, as in effect at the time of approval of this Constitution, shall be made by each village according to its established custom, or such rules as it may lay down under a village Constitution adopted according to the provisions of Article III, section 4. Unoccupied land beyond the clan and village holdings mentioned shall be open to the use of any member of the

Tribe, under the supervision of the Tribal Council. Nothing in this article shall permit depriving a member of the Tribe of farming land actually occupied and beneficially used by him at the time of approval of this Constitution, but where an individual is occupying or using land which belongs to another by agreement with the owner, that land shall continue to belong to that owner.

Sec. 2. In order to improve and preserve the range, range land shall be supervised by the Tribal Council in cooperation with the various United States Government agencies.

Sec. 3. All springs shall be considered the property of the Tribe, and no individual or group of individuals shall be allowed to prevent the reasonable use of any spring by members of the Tribe generally, but the individual who develops a spring, or on whose land it is, shall have the first use of it.

Sec. 4. The administration of this article shall be subject to the provisions of section 6 of the Act of June 18, 1934.

Article VIII — Disputes Between Villages

Section 1. When a dispute arises between villages over any matter, the Kikmongwi of any village party to the dispute may inform the Chairman of the Tribal Council of the nature of the dispute, and ask him to call a special meeting of the Council to settle the matter.

The Chairman shall thereupon call a special meeting of the Council, to be held on the eighth day from the day of such request, at which meeting he, and the Council representatives or other persons chosen by each village party to the dispute to speak for it before the Council, may summon all witnesses having evidence to give in the matter, and may examine them.

When the Council has heard all the evidence and examined the witnesses to its satisfaction, it shall hold a secret meeting which shall not be attended by the representatives of the villages party to the dispute, and after full and careful consideration and discussion, shall vote on a decision. Such decision shall become effective when it is carried by a majority of the Council members present. The Council shall keep a record of the evidence and the reasons for its decision.

Sec. 2. If both the Chairman and the Vice-Chairman are representatives of villages party to the dispute, the Council shall elect a temporary Chairman to serve for the duration of the trial.

Sec. 3. If any village party to the dispute feels that the decision of the Council in such case is unjust, the Kikmongwi of that village may notify the Superintendent within ten days, and the decision of the Council shall then be subject to review by the Secretary of the Interior, within ninety days thereafter, in the manner provided in Article VI, section 2.

Article IX — Bill of Rights

Section 1. All resident members of the Tribe shall be given equal opportunities to share in the economic resources and activities of the jurisdiction.

Sec. 2. All members of the Tribe shall be free to worship in their own way, to speak and write their opinion, and to meet together.

Article X — Amendment

Any representative may propose an amendment to this Constitution and By-Laws at any meeting of the Council. Such proposed amendment may be discussed at that meeting, but no vote shall be taken on it until the next following meeting of the Council. If the Council shall then approve such proposed amendment by a majority vote, it shall request the Secretary of the Interior to call a referendum for accepting or rejecting such amendment. It shall then be the duty of the Secretary of the Interior to call such referendum, at which the proposed amendment may be adopted subject to the Secretary's approval, in the same manner as provided for the adoption and approval of this Constitution and By-Laws.

BY-LAWS OF THE HOPI TRIBE

Article I — Duties and Qualifications of Officers

Section 1. The Chairman shall preside over all meetings of the Tribal Council. He shall perform all duties of a Chairman fairly and impartially, and exercise any authority delegated to him by the Council. He shall vote only in case of a tie.

Sec. 2. The Vice-Chairman shall help the Chairman in his duties when called upon to do so, and in the absence of the Chairman shall act as Chairman with all the attendant powers and duties.

Sec. 3. The representatives shall perform the duties of the Council, set forth in this Constitution and By-Laws. They shall inform the people of their villages of the matters discussed and the actions taken, and they shall fairly and truly represent the people of their village.

Sec. 4. The Secretary shall write all tribal correspondence, as authorized by the Council, and shall keep an accurate record of all action of regular and special meetings of the Council. He shall keep a copy of such records in good order and available to the general public and shall send another copy of them, following each meeting of the Council, to the Superintendent of the jurisdiction. He shall have a vote in the Council only if he is a regular representative.

The Secretary must be a resident member of the Hopi Tribe, and must be able to speak the Hopi language fluently, and to read and write English well.

Sec. 5. The Treasurer shall receive, receipt for, and take care of all funds in the custody of the Council, and deposit them in a bank or elsewhere as directed by the Council. He shall make payments therefrom only when authorized by a resolution of the Council, and in the manner authorized. He shall keep a faithful record of such funds, and shall report fully on receipts, payments, and amounts in hand at all regular meetings of the Council and whenever requested to do so by the Council. His accounts shall be open to public inspection.

He shall have a vote in the Council only if he is a regular representative.

The Treasurer may be required by the Council to give a bond satisfactory to the Council and to the Commissioner of Indian Affairs.

The Treasurer must be a resident member of the Hopi Tribe, and must be able to speak the Hopi language fluently and to read and write English well.

Sec. 6. The interpreter or interpreters shall be resident members of the Hopi Tribe, and shall be able to interpret fluently and accurately in the Hopi, English, and Navajo languages, and shall do so whenever requested by the Council. Interpreters shall have a vote in the Council only when they are regular representatives.

Sec. 7. The Sergeant-at-Arms, at the orders of the Chairman, shall enforce order in the Council, and shall summon all persons required to appear before the Council, and deliver notices of special meetings, and perform such other duties as may be required of him by the Council.

The Sergeant-at-Arms shall be a resident member of the Hopi Tribe, and must be able to speak Hopi fluently, and to speak English.

Sec. 8. The qualifications and duties of all committees and officers appointed by the Council shall be clearly defined by resolution of the Tribal Council at the time the positions are created. Such committees or officers shall report to the Council whenever required.

Article II — Meetings of the Council

Section 1. Regular meetings of the Tribal Council shall be held on the first day of December, March, June, and September, at such place as shall be determined by the Council.

Sec. 2. Within sixteen days after this Constitution goes into effect, the villages shall choose their representatives for the first term of one year, and on the sixteenth day the first meeting of the Council shall be held at Oraibi Day School.

Sec. 3. Special meetings of the Council shall be called by the

Chairman in his discretion or at the request of four representatives, or in the case of a dispute between villages, as provided in Article VIII of the Constitution. Notice of special meeting shall be delivered to each representative not less than eight days before such meeting, together with a statement of the business to be discussed thereat.

Sec. 4. All members of the Hopi Tribe may attend any meeting of the Council, but they may not speak, except by invitation of the Council. Non-members may be invited by the Council to attend any meeting and to address it.

Sec. 5. The Council may employ, or may request the Superintendent of the jurisdiction to furnish, a clerk trained in shorthand, to take down verbatim minutes of any meeting.

Sec. 6. When the Council desires advice of, or consultation with, any officer of the Federal Government, it may invite him to attend any meeting and may give him the privilege of the floor.

Article III — Ordinances and Resolutions

All ordinances and resolutions shall be recorded and available at all times for the information and education of the Tribe. Copies of all ordinances shall be posted from time to time in a public place in each village.

Article IV — Eagle Hunting Territories and Shrines

The Tribal Council shall negotiate with the United States Government agencies concerned, and with other tribes and other persons concerned, in order to secure protection of the right of the Hopi Tribe to hunt for eagles in its traditional territories, and to secure adequate protection for its outlying, established shrines.

Article V — All-Pueblo Council

The Tribal Council may appoint delegates to speak for the Tribe at the All-Pueblo Council, and to report to the Council and the Tribe on all proceedings thereof.

Article VI — Adoption of Constitution and By-Laws

This Constitution and By-laws, when ratified by a majority vote of the adult members of the Hopi Tribe voting at a referendum called for the purpose by the Secretary of the Interior, provided that at least thirty percent of those entitled to vote shall vote at such referendum, shall be submitted to the Secretary of the Interior, and if approved, shall take effect from the date of approval.

Certification of Adoption

Pursuant to an order, approved September 30, 1936, by the Secretary of the Interior, the attached Constitution and By-laws was submitted for ratification to the Hopi Tribe residing on the Hopi Reservation, and was on October 24, 1936, duly adopted by a vote of 651 for, and 104 against, in an election in which over 30 percent of those entitled to vote cast their ballots, in accordance with section 16 of the Indian Reorganization Act of June 18, 1934 (48 Stat. 984), as amended by the Act of June 15, 1935 (49 Stat. 378).

GEORGE COOCHISE,
Chairman of Election Board.
ALBERT YAVA,
Secretary of Election Board.

A. G. Hutton, Superintendent.

Approved by Harold L. Ickes, Secretary of the Interior on December 19, 1936.

The following amendments were adopted by elected qualified voters of the Hopi Tribe on June 24, 1969, and approved by Harrison Loesch, Assistant Secretary of the Interior, on August 1, 1969.

AMENDMENT I

Section 3 of Article II, Membership, shall be deleted in its entirety.
The first sentence of Article IV, The Tribal Council, shall be amended to read:

Section 1. The Hopi Tribal Council shall consist of a chairman, vice chairman and representatives from the various villages.

Section 2 of Article IV, The Tribal Council, shall be amended in its entirety to read as follows:

Sec. 2. The term of office of the representatives shall be two years, except that at the first election or choosing of representatives following the adoption of this section, approximately one-half of the representatives shall serve for a term of one year. The determination as to which representative shall serve for one year shall be made by the tribal council and announced to each village Kickmongvi or Governor on or before the first day of October 1969. Representatives may serve any number of terms in succession or otherwise.

Section 7 of Article IV, the Tribal Council, shall be amended to read as follows:

> *Sec. 7.* The chairman and vice-chairman shall be elected by secret ballot by all members of the Hopi Tribe. The tribal council shall choose from its own members or from other members of the tribe, a secretary, treasurer, sergeant-at-arms and interpreters and such other officers and committees as it may determine necessary, subject to the provisions of the By-laws, Article 1.

Article IV, The Tribal Council, shall be amended by adding to it Sections 8, 9, 10, 11, 12 and 13 as follows:

> *Sec. 8.* All members of the Hopi Tribe twenty-one years of age or over shall be qualified to vote in any election or referendum, other than village elections and referendums under such rules and regulations as may be prescribed by the Hopi Tribal Council and approved by the Secretary of the Interior.

> *Sec. 9.* The chairman and vice-chairman shall each serve for a term of four years. Candidates for the offices of chairman and vice-chairman shall be members of the Hopi Tribe, twenty-five years of age or older and must be able to speak the Hopi language fluently. Each candidate for either of said offices must also have lived on the Hopi Reservation for not less than two years immediately preceding his announcement of such candidacy.

> *Sec. 10.* Candidates for the offices of chairman and vice-chairman may declare their candidacy by filing with the tribal secretary or tribal chairman or vice-chairman a petition signed by at least ten adult members of the tribe at least 15 days before the date set for the election. It shall be the duty of the secretary to post the names of the qualified candidates for both the primary and final elections in a public place in each village at least ten days prior to the election.

> *Sec. 11.* A primary election shall be held on the first Wednesday in November in 1969 and on the first Wednesday in November in every fourth year thereafter, provided that, no primary election shall be held in the years when there shall be no more than two candidates for either of the offices of chairman and vice-chairman.

The two candidates in a primary election receiving the highest number of votes for each of said offices of chairman and vice-chairman shall have their names entered in the final election. In the event there are not more than two candidates for either of such offices these candidates with no more than one competing candidate shall have their names entered in the final election without the necessity of a primary election.

Sec. 12. The general election shall be held on the third Wednesday in November 1969 and on the third Wednesday in November in every fourth year thereafter.

Sec. 13. Inauguration of the chairman and vice-chairman shall take place at the first regular tribal council meeting following their election.

AMENDMENT II

Article V, Vacancies and Removal from Office, shall be amended as follows:

Section 1. Any chairman, vice-chairman, representative or other officer found guilty in a tribal or other court of a misdemeanor involving dishonesty, of a felony, or of drunkenness, shall be automatically removed from office, and the council shall refuse to recognize him.

Section 3, paragraph 3 shall be added as follows:

Vacancies occurring for any reason in the offices of chairman and vice-chairman or in the office of any other officer shall be filled for the rest of the term in the same manner as those officers are ordinarily chosen.

Notes

1. George Parker Winship, trans., "The Narrative of the Expedition of Coronado by Castañeda," Bureau of American Ethnology *Annual Report* 14 (Washington, D.C.: 1896), pp. 488–89.
2. *Ibid.*, pp. 489–90.
3. *Ibid.*, p. 490.
4. *Ibid.*
5. Herbert E. Bolton, "The Espejo Expedition," in Bolton, ed. and trans., *Spanish Exploration in the Southwest, 1542–1706* (New York: Charles Scribner's Sons, 1916), pp. 185–86.
6. Bolton, "The Oñate Expeditions...." in *ibid.*, pp. 235–36.
7. *Ibid.*, pp. 236–37
8. F. W. Hodge, George P. Hammond, and Agapito Rey, trans. and eds., *Fray Alonso de Benavides' Revised Memorial of 1634* (Albuquerque: University of New Mexico Press, 1945), pp. 76–77.
9. Charles Wilson Hackett, *Historical Documents Relating to New Mexico, Nueva Vizcaya, and Approaches Thereto, to 1773.* Carnegie Publication No. 330. (Washington, D.C.: Carnegie Institution, 1937), Vol. 3, pp. 359–60.
10. France V. Scholes, *Troublous Times in New Mexico, 1659–1670* (Historical Society of New Mexico, 1942), pp. 13–14.
11. Hackett, Vol. 3, p. 141.
12. *Ibid.*
13. *Ibid.*
14. Hubert Howe Bancroft, *History of Arizona and New Mexico, 1530–1888* (San Francisco: The History Co., 1889), p. 185 note.
15. Herbert S. Auerbach, trans. and ed., "Father Escalante's Journal, 1776–77," *Utah State Historical Quarterly*, Vol. 11 (1943).
16. Sigüenza y Góngora, Carlos de, *The Mercurio Volante....* Irving Albert Leonard, trans. Quivira Society Publications No. 3. (Los Angeles: The Quivira Society, 1932), pp. 80–88.
17. *Ibid.*
18. Hackett, Vol. 3, pp. 385–87.
19. Herbert E. Bolton, *Pageant in the Wilderness* (Salt Lake City: Utah Historical Society, 1950), pp. 2–3.
20. *Ibid.*, p. 235.
21. *Ibid.*, p. 237.
22. *Ibid.*, p. 246.
23. James S. Calhoun, *The Official Correspondence of...* Annie Heloise Abel, ed. (Washington, D.C.: Government Printing Office, 1915), p. 45.
24. *Ibid.*, p. 172.
25. *Ibid.*, pp. 264–65.
26. *Ibid.*, p. 415.

27. Edwin L. Sabin, *Kit Carson Days, 1809–1868* (New York: Press of the Pioneers, 1935), p. 875.

28. *Ibid.,* p. 874.

29. *Ibid.,* pp. 874–75.

30. James A. Little, *Jacòb Hamblin, a Narrative of His Personal Experiences as a Frontiersman, Missionary to the Indians and Explorer* (Salt Lake City: Juvenile Instructor Office, 1881), pp. 61–62.

31. Juanita Brooks, ed., "Journal of Thales Haskell," *Utah Historical Quarterly,* Vol. 12, Nos. 1–2 (1944), p. 75.

32. *Ibid.,* p. 88.

33. *Ibid.,* p. 94.

34. John Wesley Powell, *Canyons of the Colorado* (Meadville, Pa.: Flood and Vincent, 1895), pp. 335–45.

35. Wallace Stegner, *Beyond the Hundredth Meridian* (New York: Houghton Mifflin, 1954), p. 131.

36. Powell, pp. 351–52.

37. Thomas Donaldson, *Moqui Pueblo Indians of Arizona.* Extra Census Bulletin 11 (Washington, D.C.: U.S. Census Printing Office, 1893), p. 38.

38. *Ibid.,* p. 39.

39. Leo Crane, ed., "History of the Moqui Indian Reservation, Compiled from Annual Reports of Indian Agents at Keams Canyon and Fort Defiance." Manuscript at Museum of Northern Arizona, Flagstaff. MS 135-2-3.

40. *Ibid.*

41. Mary-Russell F. and Harold S. Colton, "An Appreciation of the Art of Nampeyo and Her Influence on Hopi Pottery," *Plateau* (Museum of Northern Arizona), Jan. 1943, pp. 44–45.

Bibliography

It has been impossible to limit this bibliography to publications of a purely historical nature. Interesting historical facts have often been found in books and papers dealing with seemingly totally unrelated subjects. The literature pertaining to the Hopi is vast and varied. I have listed those books, papers, and reports that have been of significant value to me.

Ambler, J. Richard, Alexander J. Lindsay, Jr., and Mary Anne Stein. *Survey and Excavations on Cummings Mesa, Arizona and Utah, 1960–61.* Museum of Northern Arizona Bulletin no. 39, Glen Canyon Series no. 5. Flagstaff: Northern Arizona Society of Science and Art, 1964.

Amsden, Charles Avery. *Prehistoric Southwesterners From Basketmaker to Pueblo.* Los Angeles: Southwest Museum, 1949.

Auerbach, Herbert S., trans. and ed. "Father Escalante's Journal, 1776–77," *Utah State Historical Quarterly,* Vol. 11 (1943).

Bailey, Lynn R. *Indian Slave Trade in the Southwest.* Los Angeles: Western- lore Press, 1966.

Bailey, Paul D. *Jacob Hamblin, Buckskin Apostle.* Los Angeles: Westernlore Press, 1948.

Bancroft, Hubert Howe. *History of Arizona and New Mexico, 1530–1888.* San Francisco: The History Co., 1889.

Bartlett, Katharine. "The Navajo Wars," *Museum Notes* (Museum of Northern Arizona), Vol. 6, 1934.

———. "Spanish Contacts With the Hopi," *Museum Notes* (Museum of Northern Arizona), Vol. 6, 1934.

Beaglehole, Ernest and Pearl. *Hopi of Second Mesa.* American Anthropologi- cal Ass'n., Memoir no. 44. Menasha, Wis., 1935.

Bloom, Lansing B. "A Campaign Against the Moqui Pueblos," *New Mexico Historical Review,* Vol. 6, no. 2, 1931.

Bolton, Herbert E. *Coronado, Knight of Pueblos and Plains.* New York and Albuquerque: Whittlesey House and University of New Mexico Press, 1949.

———. *Pageant in the Wilderness.* Salt Lake City: Utah State Historical Society, 1950.

———, ed. *Spanish Exploration in the Southwest, 1542–1706.* New York: Charles Scribner's Sons, 1916.

Bourke, John Gregory. *On the Border with Crook*. Glorieta, N.M.: Rio Grande Press, 1969. Reprinted edition with index.

————. *The Snake Dance of the Moquis of Arizona*. Chicago: Rio Grande Press, 1962. Reprinted from original 1884 edition.

Brandon, William, ed. *The American Heritage Book of Indians*. New York: American Heritage Publishing Co., 1961.

Brooks, Juanita, ed. "Journal of Thales Haskell," *Utah State Historical Quarterly*, Vol. 12, nos. 1–2 (Jan.–April), 1944.

Brophy, William A. and Sophie D. Aberle, comps. *The Indian: America's Unfinished Business*. Norman: University of Oklahoma Press, 1966.

Burland, C. A. *The Gods of Mexico*. New York: G. P. Putnam's Sons, 1967.

Calhoun, James S. *The Official Correspondence of . . .* Annie Heloise Abel, ed. Washington, D.C.: Government Printing Office, 1915.

Carson, Christopher. *Kit Carson's Own Story*. Blanche C. Grant, ed. Taos, N.M., 1926.

Carter, Kate B., comp. *Indian Slavery in the West*. Salt Lake City: Daughters of Utah Pioneers, 1938.

Caso, Alfonso. *The Aztecs, People of the Sun*. Norman: University of Oklahoma Press, 1958.

Cohen, Felix S. "Americanizing the White Man," *American Scholar*, Vol. 21, no. 2, 1952.

————. *Handbook of Federal Indian Law*. Washington, D.C.: Department of the Interior, 1945.

Collier, John. *From Every Zenith: A Memoir*. Denver: Sage Books, 1963.

————. *The Indians of the Americas*. New York: W. W. Norton & Co., 1947.

Colton, Harold S. *Black Sand: Prehistory in Northern Arizona*. Albuquerque: University of New Mexico Press, 1960.

————. *Hopi Kachina Dolls, With a Key to Their Identification*. Rev. ed. Albuquerque: University of New Mexico Press, 1950.

———— and Frank C. Baxter. *Days in the Painted Desert and the San Francisco Mountains; a Guide*. 2d ed. Flagstaff: Museum of Northern Arizona, 1932.

Colton, Mary-Russell F. and Harold S. Colton. "An Appreciation of the Art of Nampeyo and Her Influence on Hopi Pottery," *Plateau* (Museum of Northern Arizona), Jan. 1943.

Cooley, M. E., J. W. Harshbarger, J. P. Akers, and W. F. Hardt. *Regional Hydrogeology of the Navajo and Hopi Indian Reservations, Arizona, New Mexico, and Utah*. Washington, D.C.: Government Printing Office, 1969.

Covarrubias, Miguel. *Mexico South*. London: Cassell and Co., 1947.

Crane, Leo. *Indians of the Enchanted Desert*. Boston: Little, Brown and Co., 1925.

————, comp. "History of the Moqui Indian Reservation, Compiled from Annual Reports of Indian Agents at Keams Canyon and Fort Defiance." Manuscript at Museum of Northern Arizona, Flagstaff. MS 135-2-3.

Cummings, Byron. *First Inhabitants of Arizona and the Southwest*. Tucson: Cummings Publications Council, 1953.

Curtis, Natalie. *The Indians' Book*. New York: Dover Publications, 1968. Reprint edition.

————. "Theodore Roosevelt in Hopiland," *The Outlook*, Sept. 17, 1914.

Cushing, Frank Hamilton. "Contributions to Hopi History, I: Oraibi in 1883," *American Anthropologist* (n.s.), Vol. 24, no. 3, 1922.

de Terra, Helmut. *Man and Mammoth in Mexico.* London: Hutchinson, 1957.

Díaz del Castillo, Bernal. *The True History of the Conquest of Mexico.* 2 vols. New York: Robert M. McBride & Co., 1927.

Di Peso, Charles C. "Casas Grandes and the Gran Chichimeca," *El Palacio* (Santa Fe, N.M.), Winter 1968.

Dockstader, Frederick J. *The Kachina and the White Man.* Bloomfield Hills, Mich.: Cranbrook Institute of Science, 1954.

"Don Santiago Kirker" (Reprinted, with notes by Arthur Woodward, from the *Santa Fe Republican,* Nov. 20, 1847). Los Angeles: Muir Dawson, 1948.

Donaldson, Thomas. *Moqui Pueblo Indians of Arizona.* Extra Census Bulletin 11. Washington, D.C.: U.S. Census Printing Office, 1893.

Dorsey, George A. and H. R. Voth. *The Oraibi Soyal Ceremony.* Field Museum of Natural History, Anthropological Series no. 55. Chicago, 1901.

Dunn, Dorothy. *American Indian Painting of the Southwest and Plains Areas.* Albuquerque: University of New Mexico Press, 1968.

Durán, Diego. *The Aztecs: The History of the Indies of New Spain.* New York: Orion Press, 1964.

Estergreen, M. M. *Kit Carson, a Portrait in Courage.* Norman: University of Oklahoma Press, 1962.

Euler, Robert C. and Henry F. Dobyns. *The Hopi People.* Indian Tribal Series, Phoenix, 1971.

Favour, Alpheus. *Old Bill Williams, Mountain Man.* Norman: University of Oklahoma Press, 1962.

Fewkes, Jesse Walter. "Awatobi, an Archaeological Verification of a Tusayan Legend," *American Anthropologist* (o.s.), Vol. 6, no. 4, 1893.

———. "Contributions to Hopi History, II: Oraibi, 1890," *American Anthropologist* (n.s.), Vol. 24, no. 3, 1922.

———. "Designs on Prehistoric Hopi Pottery," Bureau of American Ethnology, *Annual Report* 33. Washington, D.C., 1919.

———. "The Kinship of the Tusayan Villages," *American Anthropologist* (o.s.), Vol. 7, no. 4, 1894.

———. "Tusayan Kachinas," Bureau of American Ethnology, *Annual Report* 15. Washington, D.C., 1897.

———. "Tusayan Migration Traditions," Bureau of American Ethnology, *Annual Report* 19. Washington, D.C., 1900.

——— and A. M. Stephen. "The Na-ac-nai-ya, a Tusayan Initiation Ceremony," *Journal of American Folklore,* Vol. 5, pp. 189–221, 1892.

Glen Canyon Series, *Anthropological Papers.* Department of Anthropology, University of Utah, by various authors.

Glen Canyon Series, *Bulletins* of the Museum of Northern Arizona by various authors.

Goldfrank, Esther S. "The Impact of Situation and Personality on Four Hopi Emergence Myths," *Southwestern Journal of Anthropology,* Vol. 4, no. 3, 1948.

Gumerman, George J. *Black Mesa: Survey and Excavation in Northeastern Arizona, 1968.* Prescott, Ariz.: Prescott College Press, 1970.

Hack, John T. *The Changing Physical Environment of the Hopi Indians of Arizona*. Papers of the Peabody Museum, Vol. 35, no. 1. Cambridge, Mass., 1942.

Hackett, Charles Wilson. *Historical Documents Relating to New Mexico, Nueva Vizcaya, and Approaches Thereto, to 1773*. Carnegie Publication no. 330. 3 vols. Washington, D.C.: Carnegie Institution, 1923–37.

―――. *The Revolt of the Pueblo Indians of New Mexico and Otermín's Attempted Reconquest, 1680–1682*. 2 vols. Albuquerque: University of New Mexico Press, 1942.

Haldeman, E. M. *Historical Sketch of Ganado Mission*. Board of National Missions, United Presbyterian Church, U.S.A., 1967.

Hammond, George P. and Agapito Rey. *The Rediscovery of New Mexico, 1580–1594*. Albuquerque: University of New Mexico Press, 1966.

Hanke, Lewis. *Aristotle and the American Indians*. London: Hollis and Carter, 1959.

Hargrave, Lyndon L. "First Mesa," *Museum Notes* (Museum of Northern Arizona), Vol. 3, 1931.

―――. "The Jeddito Valley and the First Pueblo Towns in Arizona," *Museum Notes* (Museum of Northern Arizona), Vol. 8, no. 4, 1935.

―――. "Oraibi," *Museum Notes* (Museum of Northern Arizona), Vol. 4, 1932.

―――. "Shungopovi," *Museum Notes* (Museum of Northern Arizona), Vol. 2, 1930.

Haury, Emil W., ed. "Southwest Issue," *American Anthropologist*, Vol. 56, no. 4, part 1, 1954.

Helm, June, ed. *Pioneers of American Anthropology*. American Ethnological Society Monograph 43. Seattle: University of Washington Press, 1966.

Hewett, Edgar Lee. *Ancient Life in the American Southwest*. Indianapolis, Ind.: Bobbs-Merrill Co., 1930.

Hodge, Frederick Webb. *Handbook of American Indians North of Mexico*. Bureau of American Ethnology Bulletin 30. Washington, D.C., 1901.

―――. *History of Hawikuh, New Mexico, One of the So-called Cities of Cibola*. Los Angeles: Southwest Museum, 1937.

―――, ed. *Spanish Explorers in the Southern United States, 1528–1543*. New York: Charles Scribner's Sons, 1907.

―――, trans. *Espejo's Journey to New Mexico in 1583*. London: Thomas Cadman, 1928.

―――, George P. Hammond, and Agapito Rey, trans. and eds. *Fray Alonso de Benavides' Revised Memorial of 1634*. Albuquerque: University of New Mexico Press, 1945.

Hough, Walter. *The Hopi Indians*. Cedar Rapids, Iowa: The Torch Press, 1915.

―――. "Jesse Walter Fewkes," *American Anthropologist*, Vol. 33, no. 1, 1931.

Kelly, William H. "Applied Anthropology in the Southwest," *American Anthropologist*, Vol. 56, no. 4, 1954.

―――. *Indians of the Southwest, a Survey of Indian Tribes and Indian Administration in Arizona*. University of Arizona Bureau of Ethnic Research, First Annual Report. Tucson, 1953.

Kennard, Edward A. and Edwin Earle. *Hopi Kachinas*. New York: J. J. Augustin, 1938.

Klauber, L. M. *A Herpetological Review of the Hopi Snake Dance*. Zoological Society of San Diego, Bulletin no. 9. 1932.

LaFarge, Oliver. *A Pictorial History of the American Indian*. New York: Crown Publishers, 1950.

————. *Santa Fe: The Autobiography of a Southwestern Town*. Norman: University of Oklahoma Press, 1959.

Las Casas, Bartolomé de. *The Tears of the Indian*. Stanford, Calif.: Academic Reprints, n.d.

Lindgren, Raymond E., ed. "A Diary of Kit Carson's Navaho Campaign, 1863–64," *New Mexico Historical Review*, Vol. 21.

Lipe, William D. and others. *1959 Excavations, Glen Canyon Area*. Glen Canyon Series no. 13. Salt Lake City: University of Utah Press, 1960.

Little, James A. *Jacob Hamblin, a Narrative of His Personal Experiences as a Frontiersman, Missionary to the Indians and Explorer*. Salt Lake City: Juvenile Instructor Office, 1881.

Lockett, Hattie Greene. *The Unwritten Literature of the Hopi*. University of Arizona Social Science Bulletin no. 3. Tucson, 1933.

Lowie, Robert H. "Notes on Hopi Clans," *Anthropological Papers*, Vol. XXX, part 5, American Museum of Natural History, 1929. New York.

Lumholtz, Carl. *Unknown Mexico*. Explorations and Adventures Among the Tarahumare, Tepehuane, Cora, Huichol, Tarasco, and Aztec Indians. Originally published 1902. Reprint by the Rio Grande Press (Glorieta, N. M.) 1973.

Lummis, Charles Fletcher. "Bullying the Quaker Indians," *Out West*, Vols. 18 and 19 (April–Sept.), 1903.

McClintock, James H. *Mormon Settlement in Arizona*. Phoenix, Ariz.: The author, 1921.

McGregor, John C. *Southwestern Archaeology*. 2d ed. Urbana: University of Illinois Press, 1965.

McNickle, D'Arcy. *Indian Man: A Life of Oliver La Farge*. Bloomington: Indiana University Press, 1971.

Mindeleff, Victor. "A Study of Pueblo Architecture: Tusayan and Cibola," Bureau of American Ethnology *Annual Report* 8. Washington, D.C.: 1891.

Montgomery, Ross G., Watson Smith, and J. O. Brew. *Franciscan Awatovi*. Peabody Museum Papers, Vol. 36. Cambridge, Mass., 1949.

Nagata, Shuichi. *Modern Transformations of Moenkopi Pueblo*. Urbana: University of Illinois Press, 1970.

Nequatewa, Edmund. "Mexican Raid on Oraibi," *Plateau* (Museum of Northern Arizona), Vol. 16, no. 3, 1944.

————. *Truth of a Hopi*. Museum of Northern Arizona Bulletin no. 8. Flagstaff, 1936.

Page, Gordon B. "Hopi Land Patterns," *Plateau* (Museum of Northern Arizona), Vol. 13, no. 2, 1940.

Parsons, Elsie Clews. "Contributions to Hopi History, III: Oraibi," *American Anthropologist* (n.s.), Vol. 24, no. 3, 1920.

————. "Contributions to Hopi History, IV: Shohmopavi," *American Anthropologist* (n.s.), Vol. 24, no. 4, 1920.

————. *Pueblo Indian Religion*. 2 vols. Chicago: University of Chicago Press, 1939.

Powell, John Wesley. *Canyons of the Colorado.* Meadville, Pa.: Flood and Vincent, 1895.

Powell, W. C. "An Account of the Hopi Towns," *Utah State Historical Quarterly,* Vols. 16–17, 1948–49.

Prescott, W. H. *The Conquest of Mexico.* London: Chatto and Windus, 1922.

Prucha, Francis P. *American Indian Policy in the Formative Years.* Cambridge, Mass.: Harvard University Press, 1962.

Qoyawayma, Polingaysi (Elizabeth White). *No Turning Back.* Albuquerque: University of New Mexico Press, 1964.

Sabin, Edwin L. *Kit Carson Days, 1809–1868.* New York: Press of the Pioneers, 1935.

Schmidt, J. F. "Voth, Heinrich R., 1855–1931." Reprinted from *The Mennonite Quarterly Review* in July 1966.

Scholes, France V. *Troublous Times in New Mexico, 1659–1670.* Historical Society of New Mexico, 1942.

Sigüenza y Góngora, Carlos de. *The Mercurio Volante.* . . . Irving Albert Leonard, trans. Quivira Society Publications no. 3. Los Angeles: The Quivira Society, 1932.

Simpson, Lesley Byrd. *The Encomienda in New Spain.* Berkeley: University of California Press, 1929.

Smith, Ralph. "Mexican and Anglo-Saxon Traffic in Scalps, Slaves and Livestock," *Year Book* 1960, West Texas Historical Association.

Smith, Watson. *Kiva Mural Decorations at Awatovi and Kawaika-a.* Peabody Museum Papers, Vol. 37. Cambridge, Mass., 1952.

Snyder, Don. *Beyond Reason — A Portfolio of Photographs.* New York: Horizon-American Heritage Publishing Co., 1970.

Spicer, Edward H. *Cycles of Conquest: The Impact of Spain, Mexico, and the United States on the Indians of the Southwest, 1533–1960.* Tucson: University of Arizona Press, 1962.

Stegner, Wallace. *Beyond the Hundredth Meridian: John Wesley Powell and the Second Opening of the West.* Boston: Houghton Mifflin, 1954.

Stephen, Alexander M. *Hopi Journal of* . . . Elsie Clews Parsons, ed. Columbia University Contributions to Anthropology, Vol. XXIII, 2 parts. New York: Columbia University Press, 1936.

Sykes, Godfrey. *A Westerly Trend.* Tucson: Arizona Pioneers' Historical Society, 1944. (Has an interesting sketch of Thomas Keam.)

Talayesva, Don C. *Sun Chief: The Autobiography of a Hopi Indian.* Leo W. Simmons, ed. New Haven, Conn.: Yale University Press, 1963.

Taylor, Walter W. "Southwestern Anthropology, Its History and Theory," *American Anthropologist,* Vol. 56, no. 4, 1954.

Ten Kate, H. F. C. "Ten Kate's Account of the Walpi Snake Dance: 1883," *Plateau* (Museum of Northern Arizona), Vol. 41, no. 1, 1968.

Thompson, Laura. *Culture in Crisis: A Study of the Hopi Indians.* New York: Harper and Brothers, 1950.

———— and Alice Joseph. *The Hopi Way.* Chicago: University of Chicago Press, 1944.

Titiev, Mischa. *The Hopi Indians of Old Oraibi, Change and Continuity.* Ann Arbor: The University of Michigan Press, 1972.

————. *Old Oraibi.* Peabody Museum Papers, Vol. 23, no. 1. Cambridge, Mass., 1944. (One of the most significant books on the Hopi.)

Tolman, Newton F. *The Search for General Miles.* New York: G. P. Putnam's Sons, 1968.

Turner, Christy G., II, and Nancy T. Morris, "A Massacre at Hopi," *American Antiquity,* Vol. 35, no. 3, pp. 320–31, 1970.

Twitchell, Ralph E. "Colonel Juan Bautista de Anza, Diary of His Expedition to the Moquis in 1780." Paper read at the annual meeting of the New Mexico Historical Society, 1918.

Udall, Louise, *Me and Mine: The Life Story of Helen Sekaquaptewa as told to.* . . . Tucson: University of Arizona Press, 1969.

Underhill, Ruth M. *The Navajos.* Norman: University of Oklahoma Press, 1956.

————. *Red Man's America.* Chicago: University of Chicago Press, 1953.

U.S., Indian Commissioners, Board of. Fifty-third *Annual Report* for the Fiscal Year Ending June 30, 1922. Washington, D.C.

————, Dept. of the Interior, Office of Indian Affairs. *Annual Reports* 1880–.

————, ————, Bureau of Indian Affairs, Phoenix Area Office. *Hopi Hearings, July 15–30, 1955.*

————, ————, *Constitution and By-laws of the Hopi Tribe.* Washington, D.C.: Government Printing Office, 1937.

Voth, Heinrich R. *Brief Miscellaneous Hopi Papers.* Field Museum of Natural History, Anthropological Series no. 157. Chicago, 1912.

————. *The Mishongnovi Ceremonies of the Snake and Flute Fraternities.* Field Museum of Natural History, Anthropological Series no. 66. Chicago, 1901.

————. "Notes of the First Decade of the Mennonite Mission Work Among the Hopi of Arizona, 1893–1902." A manuscript written in January, 1923, at Goltry, Oklahoma.

————. *The Oraibi Oaqol Ceremony.* Field Museum of Natural History, Anthropological Series no. 84. Chicago, 1903.

————. *The Oraibi Powamu Ceremony.* Field Museum of Natural History, Anthropological Series no. 61. Chicago, 1901.

————. *The Oraibi Summer Snake Ceremony.* Field Museum of Natural History, Anthropological Series no. 83. Chicago, 1903.

————. *The Traditions of the Hopi.* Field Museum of Natural History, Anthropological Series no. 96. Chicago, 1905.

Wallis, Wilson D. "Folk Tales from Shumopovi, Second Mesa," *Journal of American Folk-lore,* Vol. 49, nos. 191–92, 1936.

Whiting, Alfred F. *Ethnobotany of the Hopi.* Museum of Northern Arizona Bulletin no. 15. Flagstaff, 1939.

Whorf, Benjamin Lee. *Language, Thought, and Reality.* Cambridge, Mass.: The MIT Press, 1956.

Willey, Gordon R. *An Introduction to American Archaeology.* Vol. 1: *North and Middle America.* Englewood Cliffs, N.J.: Prentice Hall, 1966.

Winship, George Parker, trans. "The Narrative of the Expedition of Coronado by Castañeda," *Bureau of American Ethnology Annual Report* 14, part 1. Washington, D.C., 1896.

Wormington, H. M. *Prehistoric Indians of the Southwest.* Rev. ed. Denver, Colo.: Denver Museum of Natural History, 1964.

Wright, Barton. *Kachinas,* A Hopi Artist's Documentary. Flagstaff: Northland Press, 1973.

Wright, Margaret Nickelson. *Hopi Silver.* Flagstaff: Northland Press, 1972.

Index